Hard Times in the Heartland

Hard Times in the Heartland

To Freda Thomason — God bless — Sally Jadlow

By Sally Jadlow

ISBN:13: 978-1537083179
ISBN:10: 1537083171

Cover by Warren Ludwig

Visit the author's website: http://www.sallyjadlow.com
Blog: https://hardtimesintheheartland.wordpress.com
Amazon Author Page: https://www.amazon.com/Sally-Jadlow/e/B007F5H0H4

From the Author

Mother kept everything—including Daddy's letters. While reading them, I was struck with the similarities of pre-WW II to our present day. His off-the-cuff insights added fresh understanding not normally found in history books. The lines of his letters are his own words.

This is the third book in a trilogy of family history spanning the years 1886 before Oklahoma's first land run to 1945.

To create this work, I drew on my mother's written recollections, my father's booklet of memories, and his letters written to Mother and me. I also consulted the book *Trailblazers—The Story of the 70th Infantry Division* by Edmund C. Arnold and various online references.

The historical facts are true, but a few of the characters are fictional. I have changed a name or two of other characters.

The Odd Fellows Home mentioned in this book still stands today in Liberty, Missouri. It has been repurposed into a venue site for weddings and receptions and also serves as an outlet for the Belvoir Winery.

I believe history is best learned when it is surrounded by story rather than memorizing dates. Perhaps if we learn history well enough, we won't have to repeat it.

Chapter 1

"Ma, wake up! It's past eight! I'm late for school!" Eleven-year-old David jumped from their shared bed and thrust his skinny legs into his overalls.

In the kitchen, he threw a couple of pieces of wood into the stove and stirred the almost-dead fire with the poker. The firewood crackled as it caught. "I'll put the oatmeal on to boil."

His words echoed off the kitchen walls. He ran back to their bedroom. "Mother! It's late." He reached out to touch her. No response. A tightness grabbed his stomach.

Sprinting to their neighbor's house, he banged on the back door. "Mrs. Hammond. Help."

She opened the door and wiped her hands on her apron. "What's the trouble, sonny?"

"Can't wake Mother. Come quick."

Mrs. Hammond bustled behind David into the small bedroom. She touched Nora's pale arm. "Oh! Sonny, get Doc Liston. Quick."

Mr. Pickerell's rusty 1923 Ford pickup bounced over the rough furrows kicking up more Kansas dirt than yesterday's dust storm. He waved a piece of paper out the window.

Henry turned from picking corn and pulled up the strap on his overalls. "Wonder what all the fuss is about."

His brother, Homer scowled. "Don't know. Somethin' sure got a knot in his tail. Wonder if we did somethin' wrong."

Their employer pulled the pickup to a halt, set the hand brake, and jumped out. “Got a telegram for ya’. Don’t think it’s good news, from the look on the delivery boy’s face.”

Henry tore open the envelope, read it, and ran a hand through his mop of black hair. He handed the telegram to Homer and whispered, “Mother’s dead.”

Chapter 2

Henry and Homer caught the next train from Iola, Kansas for a seventy-five-mile ride to their home town of Walker, Missouri.

Homer gazed out the train window as the cool October breeze blew in. "Got any ideas what we're going to do with David?"

"Nope. He's too young to come back to Mr. Pickerell's with us. Do you?"

"Any chance he could live with Uncle Al in Ottawa?"

Henry shifted in his seat. "Nope. Last I heard, they were about to go belly up. Don't want to add to their burden."

As they rode along, Henry mulled over the past twelve years. Their brother, David Elijah was born a year after their two youngest brothers died within three days of one another. Before David's seventh birthday, their dad passed away months before the stock market crash. This left their mother, Nora, to support her boys. Now, four years later, she was gone. Henry, the eldest at twenty-three, felt the heavy burden of headship of the four remaining Freeman boys.

He cried out, "Lord help me. Help us. How am I supposed to figure all this out?" Glessner Edmiston came to mind. She had been his mother's best friend. Perhaps she would have some answers. He'd go see her as soon as they got to Walker.

Henry's heart was heavy as he trudged along the dirt road outside Walker, ten miles east of Nevada, Missouri. He pulled his light jacket closed against the cool wind. How life could change in a moment.

A prosperous-looking man in a new, 1933 Model T Ford passed Henry, leaving him in a dust cloud. Must be a banker—they were the only ones with enough money for a new car since the stock market crash in '29.

Henry spit to rid himself of the dry grit sticking to his teeth. Oh for a dipper of water to relieve his mouth of the red Missouri dust. He flicked the tear that dared roll out the corner of his eye.

Turning into the lane at the Edmiston farmhouse, memories flooded his thoughts of the many times he'd been at this place. Mounting the steps, a fresh gust of wind and dirt swirled crisp red and yellow maple leaves around his feet. He knocked on the front screen door.

A beautiful young woman answered. Henry caught his breath at the sight of her. She was stunning, even with a tea towel thrown over one shoulder.

"H-Harriet? Er, Miss Edmiston?"

"Oh, Henry. Come in. So sorry to hear of your mother's passing."

Henry followed her into the kitchen. The wonderful aroma of a chicken boiling in a big pot on the kerosene stove filled the room. His stomach growled. He hadn't seen Harriet since he graduated high school five years before. He struggled to picture the scrawny redhead with freckles he'd known from church. This worm, three years his junior, had certainly turned into a gorgeous butterfly.

Glessner Edmiston turned her slender frame from her dishwater, dried her hands on a tea towel, and gave him a long hug. "Oh, Henry, I'm so sorry about your mother. Sit. I'll get you a cup of coffee. Can't believe Nora's gone. She—she was such a good friend. Never dreamed her time would come so soon. What was she, about forty-six?"

"Yes. In August. Doc said it was a heart attack. Sure surprised us all."

"You poor boys—especially David. Can't imagine being an orphan at his age." Glessner pulled the coffee pot off the stove.

He watched Harriet ladle cream into a small pitcher and set it on the table. "No. No thanks. I drink it black."

Glessner set the steaming cup in front of him, poured two more for herself and Harriet, and slid into a chair across the table. He cupped his hands around the warm liquid and waited for the grounds to sink to the bottom before he took a sip of the bitter brew of depression coffee—peas mixed with coffee beans.

"What can we do to help y'all, Henry?"

He cleared his throat and forced his attention on his intended mission. “Well, ma’am, I’m in need of some wisdom. Mother always said you had plenty of it.”

“The feeling was mutual.” Glessner shook her head as she removed the lid on the sugar bowl and put a spoonful into her cup.

Henry noticed the thin coating of fine dust covering the sugar in the bowl from the latest dust storm.

“How Nora managed all you boys was a wonderment to me. Especially after your papa died.”

“She had a struggle, for sure.

“Indeed. What wisdom do you seek?”

He paused and took a deep breath. Words stuck behind his Adam’s apple. “I—I don’t know what to do with David. An eleven-year-old can’t stay by himself. Homer and I can’t take him with us. We’re working on farms, sleeping in barns, and following the harvests. That’s no life for him. He’s gotta get his education.”

“What about sending him to stay with your brother Oscar over at Mr. Brown’s?”

Henry sighed. “I’m afraid things aren’t too good over there either. My brother sleeps in the barn. Mr. Brown can hardly afford to feed him, let alone another.”

Glessner stood, and peered out the window at their few lean cattle on the dry landscape. “These are indeed desperate times.” She turned to him and hesitated. “We’ll just have to ask God to make a way—some way, somehow.”

Henry lowered his eyes to his rough hands. “Yes, ma’am, we will.” He hoped God would answer soon.

Harriet watched Henry from the front door until he rounded the corner to head back the four miles to Walker.

She took up her dish drying again and put a stack of plates in the cabinet. “Mother, what do you think will happen to David?”

Her mother carried the dishpan to the front porch. Harriet followed. Mrs. Edmiston threw the dishwater on the half-dead mums beside the steps. "Don't really know. Have to pray on it a while."

"Could you and Pops take him?"

Glessner straightened and propped the dishpan on her hip. "I seriously doubt that, Sis. Don't think Pops would agree to it. I'll tell you something, but you must keep it quiet."

Back in the kitchen, she checked on the chicken and poured them another cup of coffee before she spoke.

"Pops wouldn't like it if I told you this, but I think you need to know. When he shipped his cattle to market last month he heard they were paying better prices in Chicago than Kansas City, so he shipped them there. By the time he paid the freight bill clear up there, he lost money. Lots of it."

Harriet lowered her eyes and slid her spoon over the gingham tablecloth. "What's he going to do?"

Her mother continued in a raspy whisper. "He went to Nevada and applied for a loan so he could buy some young steers to feed out for next year. The banker turned him down. He's gone to the Harwood bank this afternoon. If he doesn't get the money there, we'll lose the farm."

She sat in stunned silence. He'd been a successful cattle rancher for almost twenty-five years. He was a pillar in the community. Where could her parents go—what would they do? Ranching had been Pops whole life.

The last few years had been a struggle for Harriet. She received a scholarship to Parkville, Missouri her first year of college in '31. The second year there was no money for scholarships. She moved to her grandparent's home in Nevada, Missouri to work at the dime store on Saturdays and attended the local women's junior college.

At graduation time she was denied a diploma because one teacher lacked state credentials to teach college level classes. Without those credits, Harriet didn't meet the requirements for graduation. Because of the hard times, she took a full-time position in the dime store and gave up her dream of completing a college education.

A year later she accepted a position in her Uncle Vernon's newly-opened clothing store in Nevada. But her salary wouldn't be enough to support her parents, her fifteen-year-old brother, and twelve-year-old Janie. Oh, God, please help Pops and help Henry find a spot for David!

Chapter 3

Henry squinted against the weak afternoon sun as he returned to Walker along the dirt road. Ezra Palmer, one of the old timers of the town, waved Henry over to Ezra's usual perch on the park bench in front of the general store.

"Shore sorry to hear of your mother's passin'. A fine woman, she was. I especially liked how she played them hymns in church."

"Thank you, Ezra."

"Here. Sit a spell. You look like you got the weight of the world on your shoulders. Anythin' I can do to help?"

Henry sat. "I doubt it, but thanks for the concern."

Ezra pushed his felt hat back and scratched his head. "It's a sad day when you lose a parent, fer shore."

"I agree. But that's not the half of it. I've got to figure out someplace for David."

Leaning forward, his elbows on his knees, he said, "Well, now, that is a problem. Got any relatives you could send him to?"

"All our grandfolks are dead. Got an uncle up by Ottawa, Kansas, but I don't think they could take on another mouth to feed. Besides, I'd hate to send him out of Walker."

"Well, I'll put my thinkin' cap on. Let ya know if I come up with anythin'. Hang in there, young fella. Somethin' will work out, one way or the other."

Henry stood and shook Ezra's extended hand, hoping the old man was right. He'd have to come up with something quick. "Thanks for the thoughts, sir."

He crossed the street to the funeral home to make arrangements for his mother's service and then on to Brother Frazier's house to discuss the funeral.

When Henry got home, Mrs. Hammond, his mother's next-door neighbor, came out the back door of the Freeman house.

"Oh, Henry, I left a pot roast on the stove. You boys heat it up for supper. I'll bring some fresh bread over when it's out of the oven."

His throat tightened. He'd never again taste the wonderful bread his mother made almost every day. He was sure Mrs. Hammond's bread was tasty, but nothing could compare to hers. He managed a weak, "Thank you, ma'am," and turned quickly into the house.

He found David laying across the bed. He appeared to be asleep until Henry heard a muffled sob. The springs squeaked as he eased down on the edge of the bed. The same bed his mother had occupied the day before.

"You OK, buddy?"

He shook his head.

"Want to talk about it?"

After a long pause, David whispered, "Why'd she have to die? What's going to happen to us? Will we still be a family?"

Henry placed his hand on his brother's back. What could he say to ease the pain? Finally, he answered. "I don't know why she died so soon, but there's one thing I do know. We'll get through this somehow. We'll always be family, no matter what, little brother."

The day of the funeral, Henry made sure David wore a clean pair of overalls and had washed behind his ears. The four boys, Henry, Homer, Oscar, and David sat on the front pew as Mrs. Edmiston played the piano.

Nora's funeral was a simple one, held in the same little one-room wood frame church where she played the piano for years. The fall wind moaned through the windows. Brother Frasier had to pause several times during the service while he delivered his short eulogy. This woman had served as one of two main hymn-players for over twenty years.

While the townsfolk gathered at the Walker cemetery after the service, Henry shivered in the cool wind. His mind wandered to the week twelve years earlier when they buried his young brothers, Albert and Charles. One died of pneumonia, the other of burns within three days of one another.

It seemed like a lifetime ago since he sat on the front porch and visited with his papa—and yet it had only been four years. He so missed Papa's wisdom and the laughter of his little brothers.

Henry felt a tug on his sleeve, bringing him back to the present. Brother Frasier motioned the four boys to come close to their mother's simple pine box. If only this was merely a bad dream. He hardly heard Brother Frasier's words meant for comfort and breathed a sigh of relief when the graveside service was over.

As they walked on the dirt road toward home, Henry heard someone call his name. It was Harriet. Had she been at the funeral?

"Wait up. I'll walk with you."

He felt the same attraction to her as when he saw her at her parents' house the day before. "Did you get off work to come to the service?"

"Yes. I'm going back now but Mother wanted me to tell you she was going to drop off some vegetable soup at your mother's place tomorrow after she finished playing for church."

"That's very kind of her."

Harriet smiled and drew her coat snug to her body against the wind. "Mom always said it was your mother who taught her to cook when she and Pops were first married. It's the least she can do."

Henry took a quick glance to check David's whereabouts and spotted him up the road a bit. "Has she come up with any solutions for David?"

She hesitated, then shook her head. "No. Not that I know of." She didn't dare betray her mother's confidence about their financial situation. Besides, the banker hadn't given Pops a firm answer yet. "Do you know how long you'll stick around Walker?"

"Well, Mr. Pickerell won't be too happy if Homer and I don't show up soon. Homer will probably catch the train this afternoon. I'll have to stay a while longer until I can figure out—you know—the other situation."

She turned to make her way toward home and smiled, "Maybe I'll see you in church tomorrow."

Her scent lingered a few seconds as he watched her leave. What a beauty.

In the afternoon, Henry and David went to the general store for a few things. Ezra flagged them down from the park bench before they entered.

"Hey, Henry. I've got an idea. Come sit a spell."

Henry handed his grocery list and some coins to David. "Why don't you go in and gather these things while I talk with Ezra?" He seated himself on the park bench.

"Your dad was an Odd Fellow, wasn't he?"

"Odd Fellow?"

"You know, the lodge that meets here above the general store. Well, I was sittin' here yesterday thinkin' on your plight when I looked up and saw the Odd Fellows sign hangin' off the buildin' there. I said to myself, 'Odd Fellows. That's the ticket.'"

Henry turned to look up at the Odd Fellows insignia. "I don't understand. What do you mean?"

"That lodge runs an orphanage up in Liberty, Missouri. You know. Up by Kansas City? You ought'a join the Odd Fellows Lodge, and then you could send David there."

Henry scowled. "To Liberty? That's awful far away. I was kind of hoping we could find someplace for him around here."

"Well, you may not have a choice. May be your only solution. Me and the fellas sure will miss your younger brother. When he was just a little shaver we always pitched him pennies so he'd sing us a song."

Henry smiled. So that's where he got the money for the penny candy he came home with so often.

Ezra continued. "I heard good things about that orphanage. It beats leavin' him here by hisself."

"Thank you, Ezra. I'll give it some thought." Henry stood to head into the general store. When he turned, David stood directly in his path, eyes wide. Henry opened his mouth but before he could utter a word, David dropped the package and headed home as if chased by a herd of wild buffalo.

Henry gathered the groceries and turned in the same direction, at a slower pace. Surely, this wasn't God's solution. Liberty was a long way away. Besides, he had promised David they would always be family. An orphanage wasn't family.

Chapter 4

By the time Henry got home, David had a tea towel laid out on the bed his spare pair of overalls and a worn plaid shirt thrown in the middle.

Henry took one look at the bed and then at his brother. "What do you think you're doing?"

With a tear-stained face, David put his mother's Bible on the top of the clothes and began to tie the edges into a lumpy bundle. "I'm going with Homer back to Mr. Pickerell's. You're not shipping me off to an orphanage."

"Now simmer down. Nobody said you were going to an orphanage."

David picked up the bundle and clutched it to his chest. "Old man Palmer said I was."

"Mr. Palmer only suggested that's where you *could* go. I don't like the idea anymore than you do. We've got to find a better way. Now unpack those things and let's put together some food for Homer to carry on the train."

At six Henry and David went with Homer to catch the express train for Nevada. From there, he would transfer to the one going to Iola, Kansas, a full seventy-five miles west of Walker. At bedtime, Henry noticed the tea towel bundle tucked under the bedside table. He started to say something but thought better of it. No use stirring up more trouble.

The next morning, Henry rose early. He had wrestled all night with his dilemma and didn't seem to be any closer to a solution. He woke David in time to get ready for church. Henry knew Mrs. Edmiston would be there to play the piano for the service. Maybe she had thought of a solution.

Before the service, he approached Mrs. Edmiston and asked if he could meet with her afterward. She agreed.

During the sermon, Henry had a hard time keeping his eyes on Brother Frasier and off Harriet who sat two rows in front of him. He wanted to ask Brother Frasier if he had any ideas of what to do but decided against it. He didn't need more opinions to deal with—especially if they were along the lines of Ezra's suggestion.

After the benediction, Henry watched the congregation file out. Now he could talk to Mrs. Edmiston in private. Maybe she and her husband would be open to taking David.

As Harriet left she flashed Henry a quick smile. His heart gave a little flip. She was a beauty, for sure.

Mrs. Edmiston finished the last note of the postlude as Henry approached, hat in hand. She turned on the piano stool and looked into his blue eyes. "Have you come to any conclusions, Henry?"

"No ma'am. Ezra Palmer suggested the Odd Fellows Orphanage up in Liberty but—"

"You know, that's exactly what my mister suggested. I hear it's a fine place. That would probably be best for him."

Henry's gaze fell to the floor along with his hopes. "I thought perhaps he could stay here in Walker—with someone. Maybe even with you all."

Mrs. Edmiston rose and cleared her throat as she put her hand on Henry's arm. "I'd like nothing better but—but we can't take on any more mouths right now. I'm sorry. It's just—well, that's all I can say." She added quickly, "I'd be glad to write a letter of recommendation. He's a fine lad. I'll be around with the soup I made for you in a few minutes."

"Thank you, ma'am. We appreciate your kindness." He turned and hurried out as his throat tightened. How would he tell David? Was this really the solution God had in store?

Henry found David in the churchyard and motioned to him. "Let's get home, little buddy. Mrs. Edmiston is bringing us some soup."

By the time they washed up, the Edmiston's pulled into the drive with their dinner. Henry fell silent through the meal, trying to find the words to tell his brother about Liberty. Maybe they wouldn't have room for him there. If not, where? He decided not to bring up the subject until he knew if indeed they would accept him.

Sunday afternoon he reluctantly paid a visit to Mr. Sampson, the leader of the Odd Fellows, to inquire about membership and the orphanage. The man assured Henry his membership would be welcome in the lodge. He also offered to write a letter on his behalf to inquire about available space for David in Liberty.

"Thank you, sir." Maybe they would turn down his request. Maybe there was yet another way.

Chapter 5

Harriet headed for her folk's house while her mother and Pops delivered the soup to the Freeman boys. She pulled the traditional Sunday dinner of roast, carrots, and potatoes from the oven before she set the table. When her folks arrived, Harriet made the gravy. Pops went out to check on the livestock. She watched his slow hitch toward the barnyard.

"Did Pops ever hear about his loan?"

Glessner put on her apron and tied it before she answered. "No, he hasn't heard yet." She paused, leaned toward the window over the sink, and glanced toward the barnyard. "We had a visitor the other night."

"Visitor? What's that got to do with the bank loan?"

"Maybe everything and maybe nothing. A strange man showed up at the door. Not one of those bums from the rail line in the north pasture, mind you. This was a gentlemen's gentleman. Very nattily dressed. Bowler hat, double-breasted suit, with a quite nice overcoat."

Harriet frowned and quit stirring the gravy. "I still don't understand. What did he want?"

"He said he was a representative of Mr. Lipton of the Lipton Tea Company. Said he was looking for land to buy and wondered if he might come in and talk about the possibility of buying our farm."

"Did you let him in?"

"Yes. I asked him in to have a cup of tea so he could talk to Pops when he came in from the corn crib."

Harriet gritted her teeth at the thought of what might be coming next. "And?"

"Well, since it was near supper, I invited him to stay so we could discuss his proposal over a meal. This might be the very thing we should do. Then we could move to town on a paved street and forget trying to make a go of cattle ranching."

"And what would Pops do? Sit in a porch swing and watch the world go by?" Harriet's stomach churned as she poured the gravy into a bowl.

"Now hear me out, Harriet. Jim T. was surprised to learn who he represented and all. When he got through with his proposal, it was quite late. He said he'd give us some time to think it over and would be in contact with us directly."

Harriet set the bowl of gravy on the table. "What did Pops think about it?"

"Well, he wasn't as excited about it as I was. In fact, we stayed up almost all night discussing it. That would solve the money problem. Then we wouldn't need a loan for feeder cattle."

"Mother, listen to yourself. Are you asking Pops to move to town after twenty-five years? Look at all the work he's put in on this place—all the sweat and tears. All the improvements."

Glessner glanced out the window again. "Well, if he doesn't get that loan, that's what's going to happen anyway."

"Did you ever hear back from the Lipton man?"

"Not yet. I'm praying if that's what we're to do, Jim T. will be agreeable."

Harriet shook her head. How could that be any kind of workable solution in Pops' eyes? Her heart went out to him as he entered the back door.

Monday morning Henry sent David off to school and went out to seek work. Maybe that was his answer. He walked to several farms, the blacksmith shop, and the general store to no avail before David came home from school. The answer was the same everywhere. They would all be pleased to have Henry work for them. But with the Depression and several years of crop failures they could only pay a pittance—not enough to keep them in their mother's rented home.

Every day he got the same answer. On Saturday, he saw Mr. Sampson at the post office. "Any word on your inquiry yet?" Henry asked.

Mr. Sampson turned from his post box with a letter in hand. “Well, it looks like this might be what we’re looking for.” He pulled out his pocket knife and carefully sliced the letter open. After he gave it a quick look he handed it to Henry with a smile. “Looks like they have one spot available and can take him right away.”

For a brief moment, Henry felt relief which quickly turned to guilt. How would he tell David?

The following week, Mr. Sampson saw Henry on Main Street and mentioned the Odd Fellows were scheduled to meet a week from Monday. He could join then and pay his two dollar dues. Mr. Sampson added he’d send notice to the home in Liberty of David’s arrival.

When Henry got home, he checked his pockets. He had four dollars and seventeen cents left after he paid for his mother’s funeral. How in the world would he buy David some clothes and pay their train fare to the orphanage—let alone his ticket to Iola? The rent was due soon, too. He guessed it was time to face facts. The orphanage was the way it was going to be.

He looked around his mother’s kitchen. Was there anything worth selling? Perhaps they could rake together enough to meet their bills by disposing of her few belongings. She only had a few possessions she’d brought from Denver after the boy’s dad died. Perhaps he could engage Mr. Harrison, the local auctioneer, if he wasn’t already booked. He headed down the road to his best high school friend Lloyd Harrison, to ask Lloyd’s dad if he was available.

When he entered Harrison’s front gate, Lloyd spotted him. Henry was surprised to see his friend back from the city.

“Henry, old buddy! Good to see you!” Lloyd put down the scythe he was sharpening and shook his hand. “Sorry ’bout your Ma.”

Henry took a quick breath to steel himself against his sorrow simmering beneath the surface. “Thanks, Lloyd. Didn’t know you were here. What brings you back to these parts?”

“Oh, just came to see the folks. Dad wrote he needed some help. Don’t get back very often. What brings you to see us?”

Henry paused a minute to put words to his idea of a sale. He'd keep the news about David and the orphanage quiet for now. Didn't want word to get back to his little brother before he had a chance to tell him. "Well, I need to get rid of Mother's stuff. Thought your dad might be able to have an auction for me."

"Oh. Movin', huh? Well, Dad's in the house. Just knock on the back door."

Henry felt like his feet were in wet concrete. Each step seemed harder than the last. Putting his plans out there didn't make this any easier.

Mr. Harrison invited him in for a cup of coffee.

"How are you boys making out since your mother passed?"

"Not too good, sir. I found Mother's ledger book in the kitchen cabinet. It didn't look like she was going to be able to make the rent payment this month if she didn't get any sewing jobs. She's had a real struggle since Dad died."

"How long's your dad been gone now?"

"Four years last May."

"She thought it would be easier to move back to Walker to be among familiar folks after Dad passed. Out there, she pressed men's suits in a factory twelve hours a day. Made five cents on each one. Didn't put much food on the table, though. She couldn't have made it if some folks hadn't taken her in. My brother, Homer and I helped out by setting pins in a bowling alley, but at four cents a line it didn't help much."

"Well, we were glad she came back. I wonder if we'll ever see good times again. What can I do to help you all?"

Henry swallowed the lump in his throat. "I, uh, I came to see if you would do an auction for us. We need to scratch up some money to meet our bills."

The elder Harrison nodded. "I understand. Be glad to do the sale for ya, son."

They set the date for the next Saturday, November 11.

On the way home, Henry had a funny feeling about the date. What was it? It wasn't anybody's birthday that he could remember. Then it hit him. That was the day his second little brother, Albert D., died of burns twelve years earlier.

The scenario played in his head how he had thrown the football in the kitchen. Homer missed it and the ball hit the pot of boiling water on the stove, spilling over his four-year-old brother. He'd died on Armistice Day.

Henry didn't think he could handle the sale of his mother's things on that date. Besides, how could you hold a sale with an Armistice Day parade marching down Main Street? He turned and went back to Mr. Harrison's.

The auctioneer agreed with Henry. They moved the sale to the following week.

"That'll give me more time to advertise the auction in the surrounding area."

Henry was grateful Mr. Harrison had the week open. Now he would have more time to get things ready for David as well as sort through and clean out the house. The immediate task of telling David loomed like a mountain before him. This was the hardest thing he'd ever done. "Lord, give me the words."

Chapter 6

At supper, David seemed quieter than usual.

Finally, Henry asked him, “Something bothering you?”

He put down his sandwich and looked at Henry. Tears brimmed his blue eyes. In a voice just above a whisper, he said, “Why didn’t you tell me I was going to the orphanage?”

How did he know? Although Henry waited for the right time to break this news, he’d waited too long. His heart pounded in his ears. Darn these small towns! News travels faster than words over a telephone wire. Henry sat silent for a long moment, then took a deep breath.

“Well, for a long time I hoped something else would pop up. Guess I didn’t want to admit it to myself, let alone you. Hard as I’ve tried, I can’t figure out anything else, little brother. I can’t leave you here all alone and I sure can’t take you with me. You’ve got to get your education. There’s no steady work here. For now, that’s just the way it is. I’m sorry. I don’t like this any better than you do.”

The boy examined his peanut butter and jelly sandwich. “When?”

“Sometime after the 18th.”

“Why the 18th?”

Henry took a deep breath and said a silent prayer. “It’s when Mr. Harrison can do the auction.” His mouth went dry.

David’s chair scraped against the wood floor as he pushed back from the table. He stood in front of the calendar on the wall and counted off the days. Henry heard him mumble, “Fifteen days,” as he wandered into the bedroom.

Henry sat with his head in his hands wishing there was another way.

When David went to school the next morning, Henry began the task of going through drawers and disposing of all unnecessary paper. He put other stuff in the sell pile and allowed only one box of goods for the keeping pile. Perhaps Mrs. Edmiston would store it for him until he could somehow wangle a place for them to live.

After a week, he had everything sorted. The keep box contained his mother's Bible, a soup tureen with a base given to his parents on their wedding, the butter churn, and a few pictures. His mother loved to take photos. Those were the hardest to sort through. So many memories. So much lost.

Mr. Harrison stopped by on his way to the parade on the 11th to make sure everything was ready for the sale. He said he posted sale bills in Harwood, Nevada, Schell City, and Walker. He hoped for a good crowd. Before Mr. Harrison left he handed Henry one of the bills. He opened it and a new reality set in. This part of his life in Walker was over. Would he ever return? He didn't see that as a real possibility.

The auctioneer was pleased. People swarmed in as if the sale was being held on the grounds of the governor's mansion, but bidding was slow and most things sold at a pittance.

After the sale, Mr. Harrison tallied up the totals and handed Henry the money. His voice echoed in the empty kitchen. "Here you are. Maybe you'll have enough to get you all to Liberty. Sorry it wasn't more. People just don't have much money to spend these days."

Henry looked at the account sheet. "I understand. Thank you, Mr. Harrison. How much do I owe you?"

He patted Henry on the shoulder. "Not a thing, son. I want you Freeman boys to have it all. If the situation were reversed, I know your folks would have done the same for my boys."

Henry had no words. How could he thank this good friend? The only words coming through his tight throat was, "Thanks."

The next morning Henry, David, and Oscar sat in the pew at church together. Henry wondered how long it would be before the four remaining Freeman boys could sit together again. Henry knew they had a bond stronger than the unity of this common place. They enjoyed an unbreakable love for one another—no matter the number of miles separating them. The thought was reinforced as Mrs. Edmiston played the closing hymn of "Blessed be the Tie that Binds our Hearts in Christian Love."

After the service, Henry asked Mrs. Edmiston to keep his box of keepsakes for him until he could return to reclaim them. She accepted them willingly. "They'll be safe with me."

She handed him a small sack. "Here. I made you some sandwiches for the train. Figured you'd need something to eat on the way."

"Thank you, Ma'am. You're so kind."

As he turned to go, he almost bumped into Harriet who stood directly behind him. He gathered his courage and asked, "Harriet, may I write to you?"

Her smile made his heart swell. "Yes. I'd like that. I'll look forward to your letters."

Henry felt a new warmth he'd never felt before. He waved to her as he gathered the lunch, his carpetbag, and David's small suitcase and a small sack. He called to his little brother in the churchyard. "It's time we got over to the train station."

As the train rocked along the tracks northward to Liberty, Henry reflected over the past six weeks. How life could change so quickly. His brother's head rested on the window as he slept.

Curious, Henry looked into his brother's small sack. It contained a picture of their mother standing outside the house, a tin car, a nickel, and three pennies. So few possessions. So much grief. He looked at David. What would life hold for him at the orphanage? Would he really ever be able to bring him home again? So many questions—so few answers.

Chapter 7

The question of the Lipton man burned inside Harriet while she and her mother did the dinner dishes. She waited until Pops was asleep on the couch, then she whispered, "Any more word?"

Glessner turned from the sink. "Word about what?"

"You know. About the Lipton man?"

She shook her head. "Oh, that. Well, we never heard any more from him. I keep hoping, but I guess it's a lost cause now, anyway."

Harriet frowned. "Why do you say that?"

Drying her hands on her apron, Glessner sighed. "Pops got the loan yesterday from the Harwood bank. He'll be out tomorrow scouring the countryside for some more feeder cattle."

Harriet drew in a long breath, grateful he'd gotten the loan. This farm was where he belonged. He was as married to the soil and his cattle operation as much as he was to his wife. She fell silent, deciding she'd better let the subject drop before Pops awoke and heard their conversation.

After they finished the dishes, Harriet headed back to Nevada to ready for another busy week at the Edmiston Clothing Store. As she drove, she wondered if she really would hear from Henry. After all, in school, he hardly noticed her. She thought about sharing this news with her roommate, Bernice, but decided against it, since he might not write.

David awoke when the train slowed through Kansas City. "Where are we?" He rubbed his eyes and looked through the window at the city streets.

"We're in Kansas City. We'll be in Liberty soon."

The boy took a fresh grip on the small bundle. He clenched his teeth while a scowl set his face.

"It's going to be OK. It's just another adventure. Like when we moved to Denver." Henry hoped he sounded convincing. In reality, he was afraid for David and said a prayer asking God to protect him. He also prayed for the orphan staff to care well for his brother.

Before another hour passed they pulled into the train station in Liberty. On the platform, they were approached by a man with a kind face dressed in a modest but threadbare suit.

"Might you be the Freeman boys?" The man stuck out his hand.

"And you are . . .?"

"Pardon me. I'm Mr. Thornton, director of the Odd Fellows Home."

The word *home* rang in Henry's ears. This place was an orphanage, no matter what they called it. The stark reality of their predicament settled another foot deeper into his heart. "Yes. We're the Freeman boys. This is David and I'm Henry." He returned the handshake.

"My pickup is over there. Our place is only a couple of miles south of here." He took his watch from his vest pocket, popped the lid, and glanced at the time. "Ah, yes. You've arrived just in time for supper. Let's be going. We don't want to be late."

A cool north wind pushed at their backs and enveloped them in a cloud of gritty dirt. David rubbed his eyes as Henry dropped their bags in the back of the old Ford pickup before they slid onto the seat. David watched in silence as rolling hills dotted with bare trees flew past the window. He sat mute between Henry and Mr. Thornton.

As they crested a hill Mr. Thornton pointed to a complex of huge, three-story brick buildings on the left set far back from the road. Farm fields, a large barn, and other outbuildings surrounded the brick buildings. An ornate iron gate guarded the entrance of a long lane which led to the main building.

"There's where we're going, my lads." Mr. Thornton pulled up in front of the center building and set the hand brake. "Grab your bags."

They followed him up the long granite stairs to the double wooden doors. Inside, Henry noticed the words I.O.O.F. HOME in black hexagon tiles set in the white tile floor at the base of another staircase leading to a large entry hall.

The director pointed to the room beyond. "That's our reception room where our orphans meet their new families. Put your bags in there. I'll show you to your room after supper."

David's wide-eyed glance darted toward Henry as he set his bag inside as directed.

Mr. Thornton led them down a long hall to a staircase to the basement dining hall. Every room in the place had fifteen-foot ceilings with almost ceiling-to-floor windows. About a hundred boys and girls along with a great number of adults sat at long tables on bench seats. All heads were bowed as an adult male voice blessed the food.

With the blessing finished, Mr. Thornton announced, "Everyone, this is David Freeman and his brother, Henry. David is the newest member of our family. Henry saw his brother take a step back when Mr. Thornton said, *family*. Hand to his back, Henry directed his brother to the seats at the end of a table where the director stood. How could these people become family?

Henry began to relax a bit as some of the children talked with David during the meal.

Between bites of vegetable soup, Henry asked Mr. Thornton, "Who are all these adults? I thought this was a home for children."

"Well, with these hard times many Odd Fellow members have lost their homes. We furnish them a place to stay in exchange for their work here on our farm. Hopefully, they'll be able to get back on their feet soon."

Henry said a silent prayer, grateful his brothers at least had a roof over their heads and food on the table.

Immediately after supper, they fetched the bags from the reception room. Mr. Thornton directed them to a long hallway with a left turn at the end. He led them down this side hall. "This is our north wing—for boys. The south end is where the girls stay."

He continued, "These used to be individual rooms but we've had to double up in here since the needy families moved in." David's small room sat at the end of the hall. His window opened to the west. A small dresser with three drawers sat beside the narrow bunkbed. His head hardly moved as his gaze darted around the small room like a frightened bird in a cage.

"I'll leave you for a few minutes while you say goodbye."

As soon as Mr. Thornton left, David blurted out, "Am I gonna get adopted?"

"What makes you say that?"

"Is that why I'm here? Mr. Thornton said the orphans get adopted."

Henry sat on the bottom bunk and drew his brother to himself in a big hug. "You are *not* an orphan. No one is going to adopt you. You have a family. Never forget that. When I can figure out a way, I'm going to make a home for you."

"Promise?"

"Promise."

After a long silence David spoke again, "But there are so many kids here. More even than in all of Walker school."

"All the more people to make friends with." Henry's words echoed hollow and tinny, even in his own ears. "I know you'll make the best of this, little brother. I'll write you often and come see you when I can."

He nodded in silence as a tear rolled down his cheek.

Mr. Thornton's voice echoed in the hall. "Mr. Henry, we need to leave now or you'll miss your train."

Henry gave his brother another quick hug. The boy's boney body felt as stiff as a board. Henry turned quickly before David could see his tears.

As they drove the long driveway to the main road, Henry looked back and saw David watching them from his bedroom window. Henry whispered, "Oh God! Help us!"

Mr. Thornton shifted the truck gears and turned onto the main road. "Don't worry about your brother. We'll take good care of him."

Henry was without words.

Henry seated himself on the train just in time to hear the conductor call out, "All Aboard!" During the long ride to Mr. Pickerell's farm in Iola, he slept on and off between transfers. His brother's thin face appeared each time he closed his eyes. As thoughts of guilt assaulted him, he repeated, "This was the only way."

The first evening after supper, Henry penned a letter to David in the bunkhouse. He told him about the train ride back to Kansas, but could think of little else to say. He avoided any mention of adoptions for fear it would stir more worry. By the time he finished he decided he'd better hit the hay. Morning came early with twenty cows to milk. He'd have to write Harriet later.

Chapter 8

Each day Harriet rushed to her apartment on her lunch break to check the noon mail. After a week, she decided Henry hadn't really meant what he said when he asked to write her. Had he said that just to be polite in front of her mother? After eight days she took her lunch and ate in the alteration room with her Aunt Merrie who served as the alteration lady. If she did have a letter from him, it would just have to wait until evening.

Aunt Merrie laid a wet cloth on a pair of pants she had finished hemming and applied a hot iron. Steam rose from the wet cloth. She smiled and said, "Been missing you at lunchtime the last few days, girl. Where you been?"

"Oh, I had some errands."

She applied another pass of the iron. "Sure must have a lot of errands."

"Um-huh." Harriet wasn't about to tell her maiden aunt she hoped for a letter. If she did, she'd never hear the end of prying questions.

Several days later, Harriet discovered a letter from Iola in the mailbox after work. With shaking hands, she grabbed the letter opener and drew out the single sheet of lined notebook paper. It read:

December 1, 1933

Dear Harriet,

Sorry I haven't written sooner. I'm not much of a letter writer as you can tell. Mr. Pickerell keeps us pretty busy. Got David settled at the Odd Fellows Home. Haven't heard from him yet, although I sent him one letter as soon as I got back. I'm sure it was a big change for him there. Besides children, they have about 250 adults who need a roof over their heads. They work the farm for food and shelter.

David got it in his head I took him there to place him for adoption. Don't know how long he'll have to stay there. Hopefully, someday I'll be able to return to Walker and bring him home.

Things are pretty bad here. The wind continues to carry off all the top soil. Dirt sifts into everything. Is it still bad there, too? I doubt Mr. Pickerell will have much of a crop come next fall. He may not have need of extra hands. Guess I better wrap this up and go to bed. Write back if you care to.

Sincerely,
Henry

Two days later, Henry received a letter from David.

December 1, 1933

Dear Henry and Homer,

I'm getting to know some of the kids. Most of them are real nice. Everyone has chores. I help milk the cows morning and evening.

My room is on the same floor as the music room but it's in the girl wing. That's where the radio is. After supper, if we've finished our chores, we can go in there and listen to Amos and Andy, but we have to be quiet.

Mr. Harold is my music teacher. He wants me to try out for the boys' choir. We go to school in the building north of where we sleep. There are twelve kids in my class. We have 5th and 6th grade together. The teachers come out from Liberty to teach us.

There are a lot of rules to learn here but I only got in trouble once. Before supper I walked down the girls' staircase instead of the boys'. I had to do dishes after supper for my punishment.

We had a nice Thanksgiving dinner.

Love,
David

Henry folded the letter and shoved it in the envelope and sighed. Poor kid! Must be tough to learn all those rules.

Harriet waited a few days to answer Henry's letter. She didn't want to appear too anxious.

Homer saw Harriet's letter at Henry's place at the table. He peered at the return address. "What do you think this is about?"

Henry snatched it from his plate, afraid Homer might grab it and tear it open. "I asked Harriet Edmiston if I could write to her." He shoved it in the front pocket of his overalls to read in private.

"So are you sweet on her?"

"None of your business."

Later in the evening, Henry put on his coat, took a lantern, and went to the barn to read the letter.

December 15, 1933

Dear Henry,

Like you, I have been busy. I've been helping Mother with practice for the Christmas play at church. They will perform on Christmas Eve. Will you be back in town then? I hope to see you if you are.

Whatever would make David think he was going to be adopted? It must be so hard to live with so many people. Glad he's got a place to be.

There are some kids in Nevada about his age who don't seem to have any folks. They come in the store often just to get warm. If Uncle Vernon sees them he chases them out, poor things. Says it's bad for business. But then, that's Uncle Vernon—always has his eye on the business. Not on people.

Sincerely,

Harriet

Henry let out a long sigh, folded the letter, and stuck it in his pocket. He too was glad David had a place even though it had so many rules.

Chapter 9

Henry didn't have money for train fare to Walker and had nowhere to stay. He wrote Harriet he'd be in Iola for the holiday.

A couple of weeks later Henry and Homer lay on their bunks after a particularly cold day outside. The wood stove crackled and sent a weak glow into the bunkhouse.

Homer said, "Do you think we're about done here?"

"I was kinda thinking the same thing. Hardly enough for one hired hand, let alone two."

After a long silence Henry said, "Where do you think we should go?"

"Don't know. Hadn't really thought about it. Sure don't want any part of city livin'. Kind'a thought about goin' west. California, maybe. At least it would be warm there."

Henry didn't want any part of California. Besides, he'd be awfully far from David—and Harriet. He let the subject drop for now, but it did give him cause to think on the possibility in the coming days.

By late January, Homer began to talk again of leaving. "I'm going to pull up stakes here and go on out West. Comin' with me?"

Henry eyed his brother as he sat near the fire to warm his hands. "Naw. I think I'll stay here. At least for now, anyway. You told Mr. Pickerell yet?"

Removing his work boots, Homer moved his chair nearer the stove, to warm his frozen feet. "Figure I'll tell him tomorrow. Wanted to know what you're going to do first. You're welcome to come along."

Henry shook his head. "California doesn't interest me much. Think I'll stick around these parts."

"Too far from Harriet?"

Henry eyed his brother and shifted in his chair. "Maybe. David too. We can't all go running off. You go on. I wish you well, my brother."

Homer got his final pay the next Saturday morning and boarded the afternoon train for California.

Henry watched the train slowly pull out of the station. Bums who had no money for tickets dived like rats into the open doors of the lumbering boxcars until it picked up speed. How long would it be before he saw his next youngest brother again? Within a couple of minutes nothing was left but the belching smoke. The engineer gave a final, fading whistle—then silence. Henry turned and trudged the snow-filled road back to Mr. Pickerell's place. Without their mother, this family seemed to be drifting further and further apart.

The next month, Mr. Pickerell approached Henry as he pitched hay from the loft. "Henry, we need to talk."

"Okay. I'll be down in a minute."

Mr. Pickerell eyed Henry, shoved his hands in his jacket pockets, then stirred the loose hay on the barn floor with his foot. "Henry, I've decided to pack it in. Had someone make me a pitiful offer for my place. Figure I better take it while the takin's good. Most folks are walking away from their land—don't get the blessing of an offer to buy. Don't know if this new owner needs help, but I wanted you to be the first to know so you could plan what you'll do next."

Henry leaned the pitchfork against the wall. "Guess I could talk to him. Thanks for the information."

When Henry talked to the new owner, the man offered only half what Mr. Pickerell paid. Henry decided to visit the Army Recruiting office in Kansas City to see what they had to say. At least he'd have room and board and clothing if he signed up. He'd stop by to visit David, too. It might be the last time he'd be free to see him for a while.

Henry wrote Harriet sporadically. In the early part of March, she received a letter from him in the afternoon delivery. She noticed the postmark from Fort Leavenworth, Kansas. She waited for the milk to heat so she could pour it over white bread for supper for her and her roommate, Harriet read the letter.

March 10, 1934

Dear Harriet,

Notice my new return address? Mr. Pickerell sold out and Homer left for California. I went to Kansas City to look for work. So many men were standing in soup lines. There didn't seem to be any work there so I decided to sign up with the Army. As a new recruit, I'm signed on at $20 a month which is what I made working for Mr. Pickerell, but I do get my clothes plus room and board. Today I learned I have to pay for my laundry and dry cleaning, though.

I've been in basic training for a week now. Hard work but not any harder than I'm used to. We spend a lot of time cleaning our weapons. The danged dust blows into everything. I'm getting so I can clean my rifle about as fast as the best of them.

After I signed up I went to see David. He seems to be doing OK but I think he's having a hard time adjusting to so many new people. The folks are from all over Missouri. I could only stay for one evening before I had to leave for Fort Leavenworth.

His roommate is a boy about his age although he's a lot bigger than David. Billy Joe Martin is his name from near Marshall, Missouri. I guess his father couldn't afford to feed him so he brought him to the orphanage. He and David seem to get along pretty well. I'm glad they're friends.

I had hoped leaving would be easier this time than it was before, but in a way it seemed harder. Maybe because I'm not free to show up anytime. Now, I'm under somebody else's orders.

I'll have to finish this letter later. I'm on KP duty.

Sorry. I haven't had time to get back to finishing this letter till now. Can't believe it's been a week since I started on it. Seems like my Sergeant is always barking orders at us. We spend a lot of time marching.

I'm going to try real hard to make Private First Class, but there doesn't seem to be much chance for advancement because the Army is so small right now. Nobody moves up in rank unless somebody retires, gets busted, or dies.

We just got word President Roosevelt cut the pay of federal employees by 15% so my paycheck next month will only be $17.85.

I haven't heard anything from Homer. I hope he's found work out there in California. If worse comes to worse, he could set pins in a bowling alley. Of course, he's a good farm hand.

How are your folks? From what I hear an awful lot of farms are going bust. Are things any better at the store? Write when you have time. The address on the front of the letter will be where you can write me for a little while until I get out of basic training. I'll write again when I know where Uncle Sam sends me.

Regards,
Henry

Harriet laid the letter on the table.

During supper, Bernice noticed the mail as she tapped cinnamon on her bowl of bread and milk. "Hear from Henry again?"

"Yes. He's joined the Army."

Bernice slammed the cinnamon tin on the table. "The Army? Why would he do such a thing?"

"Said it was better than standing in a soup line. Guess he's right. Don't think he's one to be idle all day, for sure."

Sucking air through her teeth, Bernice said, "Hope he doesn't want to make it a career."

"You and me both."

Chapter 10

At odd times, Harriet found herself thinking of Henry—like when she was supposed to be going through the racks to hunt down just the right dress to make a certain customer look "less fleshy," as her Pops would say. Most of the time there wasn't such a dress, but she eventually would find one which satisfied the customer.

One day in the alteration room while she munched her peanut butter and jelly sandwich, she wondered if Henry looked as forward to her letters as she anticipated his. This letter-writing was fine, but she preferred face-to-face conversations. Henry had not been back since he left over five months ago. She wondered if he would be stationed anywhere near Nevada after his basic training. As she thought about it, Fort Leavenworth was probably the closest active Army base around. That seemed a world away.

A few days later, she saw a man in the men's department who looked like Henry from the back. Had he finished his training? Had he come to visit? Her heart beat faster. She made a beeline for the men's side of the store and took a deep breath to call his name. Before she could get it out, he turned. He looked nothing like Henry.

"Hello. Can I help you?" he said.

"Uh. No. I—I thought you were someone else." She felt heat creep up her neck and into her cheeks. She turned to hide her embarrassment just as he stuck out his hand.

"I haven't met you yet. I'm Gerald Grimes, the new salesman Mr. Edmiston hired yesterday. I saw you earlier. Someone told me you were Mr. Edmiston's niece, but I didn't catch your name."

She turned and looked down at his hand but was too embarrassed to shake it. “Oh. Well, I’m Harriet Edmiston. Pleased to meet you, Mister, Mister . . .”

“Grimes, ma’am. I guess we’ll be working together.”

“Uh, yes. I guess we will.” She turned on her heel and made a quick exit to the alteration room on the women’s side of the store.

Aunt Merrie looked up from her sewing machine. “Has the customer returned for her dress already? I’m almost finished. See if you can stall her for ten minutes while I press it.”

“No. She’s not returned. I told her it wouldn’t be ready till tomorrow. Take your time.”

Aunt Merrie cocked her head. “What’s got you so flustered? You rushed in here like a bear was after you.”

“Nothing. Nothing at all.” Harriet headed for a fitting room—the one with a chair so she could sit to collect her thoughts. That one was occupied so she headed for the bathroom, slipped in quick, and latched the door. She sank onto the toilet seat. Harriet hadn’t realized how much she wanted to see Henry again until she’d been surprised by Mr. Grimes. Maybe she had been daydreaming too much about him. After all, Henry hadn’t said anything in his letters indicating he cared for her as much as she suddenly realized she cared for him. She’d force herself to think of other things when he popped into her mind.

Now if she could just master that knack.

Chapter 11

David and Billy Joe soon became fast friends at the orphanage. Besides a common love for music, they both had a passion for gadgets. The science teacher, Mr. Bales, formed a club for boys to make simple projects. They first voted to make crystal radios out of wire and junk found around the home. Billy Joe and David made one for their room so they could listen to Amos and Andy there instead of the music room. Then they wouldn't have to be so quiet.

One day near the end of school in May, Mr. Thornton came to their classroom during the last hour and whispered in Mr. Bales ear.

When Mr. Thornton left, Mr. Bales cleared his throat. "Billy Joe, Mr. Thornton wants to see you in his office. You may be excused."

"What's all this about?" David whispered to his roommate across the aisle.

With a scowl, he shrugged. "Dunno."

"Did you break a rule?"

"I don't think so. Geesh!"

Henry scowled. "Suppose it's about our radio?"

His friend closed his book and put it in his desk. "Radios aren't against the rules, are they?"

"Don't think so."

David raised his hand. "Mr. Bales, can I go with Billy Joe to Mr. Thornton's office?"

"No, son. This doesn't concern you."

As soon as the bell rang, David gathered his books and headed for his room. As he opened the door, he heard soft sobbing. Billy Joe lay on his bed, his head buried in his pillow.

He closed the door behind him. “What happened? Did you get in trouble?”

His roommate sat on the edge of his bunk and wiped his eyes with his sleeve. “Dad’s dead.”

David sank beside him. “What happened?”

“Mr. Thornton said our horse kicked him in the head. Neighbors found him in the field.

David’s heart pounded in his ears.

“Now I’m an orphan like you, ‘cept I don’t have any brothers—no one’s gonna look out for me.”

The sick feeling from last fall returned in David’s stomach. The day Doc Liston straightened from his mother’s bedside, looked straight at him with a shake of his head, and said, “Your mother’s gone, son.”

He had no words for his friend. He slipped his arm firmly around Billy Joe’s shaking shoulders.

The next few weeks were tough for both boys. Often during the night, David heard his roommate’s muffled sobs. Billy Joe’s grief seemed to re-open his own wounds. Both boys went about their daily chores in a daze. The relentless summer heat filled with the ever-present blowing dust offered no consolation to these grieving almost twelve-year-old’s. Even the evening radio programs didn’t prove to be a helpful distraction.

Near the middle of July, Mr. Thornton knocked on the boy’s door just after breakfast.

“Billy Joe, please follow me to the reception room.”

“Wonder what that’s about?” he said as he headed for the door.

David shook his head. Fear tightened his throat. After he left, David crept to within earshot of the reception room near the front door.

“Billy Joe, meet Mr. and Mrs. Northrop. They’re looking for a son to adopt. Mr. Northrop is an Odd Fellow in good standing. They live on a farm near Randolph, Missouri. I thought you would be a good fit for this family."

Edging closer to the doorway, David tried to peep through the open door. When he couldn't get a clear view he walked past as if going to the music room.

Billy Joe, eyes wide, sat in a chair next to the settee on which an older couple sat.

Mr. Thornton continued, "You need to go to your room and collect your things. They want to leave directly so they can be home by nightfall."

In a panic, David ran out the door of the girls' wing on the south side, around to the other end of the building and in the north side door. He didn't dare go back down the hall by the way he came. They'd see him for sure. He had to get to their room before Billy Joe left.

David's heart pounded in his chest. Adoption. The very word made him shudder. His greatest fear had befallen his friend. He looked around their room for something to give him before he left. In his drawer of their dresser, he found the little tin car he brought from home.

The door opened. He whirled to see his friend's pale face. Billy Joe opened his mouth to say something but David's words were quicker.

"I heard. Here. Take my car—and our radio. I can make another. Then you can listen to Amos and Andy like we always do."

Without a word Billy Joe pocketed the little car and began to empty his clothes into a paper sack from his drawer in their shared dresser.

"Write me, okay?"

Billy Joe's only response was a slight nod as he placed the cobbled-together radio in the top of the sack.

David searched for words but there were none.

"Tell the others goodbye," his roommate whispered as he turned and shuffled out the door in a daze.

Watching through the window of their room, David saw the three of them leave out the long drive in a rattletrap pickup belching smoke out the exhaust. David turned to look at Billy Joe's bunk. He shoved the empty drawer closed.

Will I be next? Will Henry keep his promise?

Chapter 12

The new hire, Gary Grimes, asked Harriet out after a few weeks. After several invitations, she finally went. Mr. Grimes displayed his prideful attitude by everything he said, and his wild driving made her sorry she went. After several more fruitless invitations, his asking became more infrequent. Harriet measured every man she met by Henry Freeman. They always came up woefully short.

If only Henry would write more often. Although he wrote with some regularity, Harriet questioned his interest in a more serious relationship. Perhaps he didn't want to get too involved in these hard times.

Harriet felt fortunate at twenty to have a job which met her needs. She was also grateful for her roommate, Bernice, who worked as a secretary at a law office on the square. They were both from Walker and knew the same people. Bernice dated Ben, a sharecrop farmer near Walker.

One morning over a quick breakfast together, Bernice sighed as she spread lard on a piece of toast. "Harriet, I so wish Ben could scrape together enough to buy his own place. Then we could marry."

"Any idea when that might happen?"

Bernice wrinkled her nose and shook her blond curls. "With the failing crops every year I don't see it happening anytime soon. We'll probably have to wait till the cow jumps over the moon."

Stifling a little laugh Harriet said, "I think the whole world is holding its breath waiting for a better day."

"You're right, girl."

Harriet shoved her purse under one arm, plopped her straw pancake hat on her head, and charged for the door. "Maybe one day everyone will be able to sing President Roosevelt's campaign theme song, 'Happy Days Are Here Again'.

"Don't count on it," Bernice mumbled at the slamming door.

By the end of May, 1934, Henry finished basic training and received orders to stay at Fort Leavenworth. His summer was spent supervising the swimming pool. He also worked hard on a promotion to Private First Class and beyond. Henry shined his shoes, passed inspections, and volunteered for any extra duty that came along. Sadly, no promotion appeared.

When fall arrived, Henry's superiors chose him for a squad to travel to the military academy at Booneville, Missouri, and another at Alton, Illinois to demonstrate marching and marksmanship. From there they went to the Cavalry at Fort Riley, Kansas. With all this touring they had little free time to themselves.

He heard from David occasionally and made it a point to answer him quickly. Henry's leaves were few and far between—usually only twenty-four hours long.

In August, on David's twelfth birthday, Henry got an unexpected two-day pass and hitched a ride with a fellow soldier to Kansas City. From there, he took the train to Liberty. Stopping in a small shop, he bought his brother a birthday card, then walked the couple of miles to the orphanage. Henry arrived just in time to join the ragtag bunch of hungry residents for a supper of tomato soup and rye bread.

David was overjoyed to see him. During the evening, their conversation turned to Billy Joe.

"Ever hear from him?"

David looked away. "No. Can't figure it out. Thought for sure he'd write."

"Have you written him?"

"Don't have his address. Mr. Thornton says I don't need it. Said it's better this way."

Henry thought that a little odd, but let it pass. "Guess he has his reasons."

At bedtime, Henry headed back to Kansas City. He found a room at the YMCA at 10th and Oak. The next morning, he explored the downtown area. As he strolled, he wondered if there were any jobs available in these fine clothing stores, restaurants, or office buildings. His reenlistment wouldn't come up for over two years, but it never hurt to think ahead.

He left for Fort Leavenworth on the afternoon train. As he rode, his thoughts turned to memories of the home he and his brothers had shared. It didn't seem possible it had been almost a year since their mother died. Yet, in a way, it seemed like a lifetime ago. So much had changed. His little brother was another year older, and Henry was no closer to his goal to make a home for him—not on his current salary, or position, for sure.

A year after his enlistment, he wrote Harriet.

February 11, 1935

Dear Harriet,

I finally made Private First Class. Now I'm up to $30 a month. It's a long way from where I planned to be at this point, but I guess with the times, I should be grateful for a roof over my head and clothes on my back.

How are things at the store? Maybe this year won't be so dry, and farmers will have a better crop than the last few years—if only it would rain.

I hope I'll be able to get a three-day pass soon. Maybe I could come see you. We could go to a movie or something. So far they've only issued twenty-four-hour passes, except once when I got a two-day pass and went to see David. They keep shipping us all over the place to demonstrate our shooting abilities. Seems like a bunch of busy work to me, but what do I know?

I guess it's better than working for the government employment programs like the WPA or the CCC. One guy from Fort Scott told me the WPA set his dad to work on the brick streets there. They're turning over every brick on every street! He said another bunch is building a swimming pool and a band shell for outdoor concerts in the summer. Others are being paid to dig ponds on outlying farms. From the looks of the skies, I doubt any ponds will fill up soon. Guess it's better than sitting on the corner spitting in the street or standing in a soup line.

David is doing well, but he misses his friend Billy Joe. Some folks near Randolph adopted him. David hasn't mentioned making another close friend, although he has a new roommate, Jonas Moses.

I'll let you know if I get a three-day pass. How late do you work on Saturday night? Suppose I could take you to dinner someplace on the square, or would you rather go to a movie?

Sincerely,
Henry

As soon as Harriet read the letter she knew what she preferred. Who wanted to sit in a movie house and waste time watching actors prance through some musical? She wanted to talk with Henry—to hear first-hand and in person all about his life. What he thought about the Army. What his future plans were. Hopefully, he wouldn't make a career of the service. If he did, he'd have to travel anywhere some General chose to send him. Not her plans for a life, for sure. At least it was a time of peace—not like in the Great War when she was a small child.

On the other hand, if he chose that path, she would have to accept it or look for another man. The thought of settling down with someone other than Henry made her shudder.

Was he dating someone? From the sound of it, Uncle Sam kept him pretty busy. On his salary she doubted there was much left over for movies, dating, and such.

She was probably thinking too far ahead. If only he would come for a visit, maybe she would have a clearer picture of how things really were.

During the fall of 1935, although Henry spoke of a visit, he hadn't given her an actual date. Had he lost interest? His letters still came at his regular pace—far too few to suit her. In late October, Harriet received another letter.

October 10, 1935

Dear Harriet,

I think I might be able get a three-day pass to come home on Thanksgiving. Would you be able to get off work early Wednesday, the 27th, before Thanksgiving Day? Let me know as soon as possible so I can get my bid in for those three days.

Sincerely,

Henry

Harriet was thrilled. Finally he was able to get a pass.

The next morning Harriet asked Uncle Vernon, "Would it be possible to get off early Thanksgiving Eve?"

He folded his arms then rubbed his chin. "Hmm. I suppose you want to help your mother get ready for her traditional dinner."

Harriet held her breath. She didn't want to lie to him, but if his assumption was the ticket for him to let her off work, she would go with it.

"Yes. I guess we can get along without you that evening. We'll need you for sure the day after the holiday. We have new merchandise coming in for Christmas." He chuckled. "'Gotta make hay while the sun shines,' like my brother says."

She turned with a quick "Thanks" and scurried into the alteration room to dash off a short note to Henry. On her lunch break, she ran to the post office. Before she dropped the letter in the slot, she hesitated. Would he think her too anxious? But he did say to let him know as soon as possible. She let go of the letter before she over-thought this one.

The next month Harriet busied herself getting ready for Henry's visit. Near Thanksgiving she received another letter from him.

November 18, 1935

Dear Harriet,

I'm so sorry. I'll not be able to come to see you this Thanksgiving. They have us scheduled for maneuvers again. According to the old hands around here, we've been more active than in previous years. I wonder if the government is worried about Germany re-militarizing the Rhineland.

Sincerely,
Henry

Harriet tossed the letter on the table and exclaimed to her roommate. "If only he weren't in the Army! Those big wigs must enjoy ruining everything. Especially holidays. I wish he'd never joined that rotten outfit!"

Chapter 13

In the late fall after David turned thirteen in August of 1935, he thought he heard something like a pebble hit the brick wall outside the open window. There it was again.

He crawled out of bed, stuck his head out the window, and looked into the cool, moonless night. Several feet below stood Billy Joe, his former roommate. In the past year, the boy had grown much taller. His bowl-cut hair appeared darker and his overalls hung on his scarecrow-like frame.

In a hoarse whisper, David said, "Billy Joe! What are you doing here?"

He put his finger to his lips. "Shhhh. Throw me your sheet so I can climb up. Quick! Before someone sees me."

Pulling the top sheet off his bunk, he tied one end around the steam heat register standing near the window, then threw the other end down. Billy Joe caught the end of it, pulled himself up, and tumbled into the room.

"Shhhh. You'll wake the dead."

Jonas, David's roommate, rolled over in his bunk and began to snore.

"How did you get here? And why?" A hundred and one questions pulsed through David's head.

Billy Joe whispered, "Ran away. Northrop nearly worked me to death. Didn't feed me much. Only reason he adopted me was for a free farm hand."

"Why didn't you write?"

"I did. But every time old man Northrop found the letters he tore them up. Then he whipped me within an inch of my life with a razor strap. I'll never go back there."

"We need to tell Mr. Thornton."

"You crazy, boy? He'd ship me back there faster than you could say 'sickum.' The ole buzzard always told me, 'I'm an Odd Fellow in good standing. Try to run away and you'll be back here the next day.'"

"What are you gonna' do?"

"Just came to tell you what happened to me. Don't let anyone adopt you. Oh, and I brought you this." Billy Joe dug in the pocket of his overalls and handed him a tiny object.

He recognized it immediately—the little tin car he gave Billy Joe the day he left.

"I know this little car was special to you. Sometimes it was the only thing that kept me going—knowing someone out there cared about me."

Jonas rolled over and called, "Mama?"

David touched Jonas's shoulder. "Go back to sleep. Your mama's gone."

"He do that often?" Billy Joe whispered.

"'Bout every night."

"I gotta get out o' here 'fore someone sees me."

"Where'll you go?"

"As far away from that old man as I can git. I'll hitch a train somewhere."

"Be careful." He held out the tin car. "Want to take this?"

"Naw. Thanks anyway. Maybe we'll meet again someday." Suddenly, he turned, scrambled out the window, and shinnied down the sheet.

David squinted into the darkness, but his friend was gone. He yanked the sheet in and untied it. He lay awake for a long time and heard the lonesome whistle of the train through the leafless trees—then drifted off.

When daylight streamed in the window, He wondered if he'd dreamed it all. Then he saw the tin car on the dresser and knew for sure. He took a deep breath and said a prayer for Billy Joe. He tucked the toy in the corner of his dresser drawer quick before Jonas could see it and ask questions.

Henry's letters didn't come any more frequently through Thanksgiving and Christmas. When it came time for Henry to re-up the next year, would he choose another hitch in the Army? Surely he wouldn't if he didn't advance.

In February, Harriet received a letter from Henry which read:

February 12, 1936

Dear Harriet,

I have some good news. I attained the rank of Corporal. Now I'll be making $42.00 a month. It's been a slow go, but I've doubled my pay in the past couple of years. I could earn $12 more a month if I could make Sergeant, but doubt it will happen—even if I continue to spit-shine my boots and keep out of trouble. At times, this soldier deal seems like a dead-end. I'm not complaining, you understand. It could be worse.

I'm a bit concerned about things in Europe. Hitler seems to have something up his sleeve. We heard the other day he's reforming Germany's air force. But enough of military talk.

Finally heard from Homer. He's working on a rice farm for a fella. He's not making as much as I am—of course he's warmer out there, but that's about all. He said Oscar has decided to move out there, too. The fella he worked for in Walker lost his farm to the bank.

I've been picked to play the snare drum for the Drum and Bugle Corps. We wake the camp every morning.

David seems to be doing well, in spite of his situation. He still asks occasionally if I'm sure he'll not be adopted. Guess some others have been.

Sounds like he's got some friends. He said he especially likes science and music. Told me he'd love to have a guitar, but there's no way I can afford to get him one. Guess he'll just have to use the instrument God gave him. At least a singing voice doesn't cost any money. Did I tell you he was in the Boys Choir for the home?

How is business at the store? Maybe this will be a better year for crops—if we can get some rain. Tell your folks hi for me. I miss you. Hope I can get a three-day pass sometime soon.

Still thinking about whether to re-up in February.

Sincerely,
Henry

Harriet laid the letter on the kitchen table and prayed a very specific prayer. "Lord, you know how I feel about Henry making a career of military service. Please help him make the right decision."

Days melted into weeks. Henry wrote in June he had saved enough money for a three-day pass so he could make a trip to see her.

He arrived just in time for wheat harvest. At Pop's request, he spent most of his leave helping Pop harvest with the threshing crew, much to Harriet's disgust.

Was Pop's need genuine, or a means to keep him busy and away from her? The word must have leaked about Henry's visit. Harriet had kept the news pretty much to herself, except for Mother and Bernice. She wondered which one blabbed.

Henry managed to wrangle a three-day pass a week before Thanksgiving. He called Harriet at the store.

She could hardly believe her ears. "Maybe David could come too. I'm sure Mother wouldn't mind."

"I'll see what I can do."

She hung up the phone and whispered, "Now if some General doesn't mess this up and cancel his pass, it will be great."

Chapter 14

When Harriet shared the news with her mother, Glessner said, "Wonderful. I'll write to Henry and tell him he and David are both invited."

"You sure it's okay?"

"Of course I'm sure. What's two more around the table? One of my prized turkeys will feed us all."

Henry wrote a quick response to Glessner's letter.

> Dear Mrs. Edmiston,
>
> Thank you for the Thanksgiving invitation. I contacted Mr. Thornton at the Odd Fellows Home. It took some fast talking but I finally got him to let David come too. He will arrive in Walker by train. Our former neighbor, Mrs. Hammond will pick him up.
>
> See you soon.
>
> Regards,
>
> Henry

Harriet waited at the station in Nevada with a little nervous tap to her foot for Henry's train to arrive late Wednesday afternoon. She couldn't wait to see him again. This time, it was too cold for harvest. Hopefully, Pops hadn't dreamed up some other chore to take Henry away from her. She rose from the bench and peered through the snow flurries when she heard the locomotive. Harriet's heart beat faster and her knees felt weak. She pulled her coat collar up as she took a deep breath when Henry got off the train. How could this man have such an effect on her? He looked very sharp in his uniform.

His face lit into a wide smile when he saw her on the platform. She felt his arm slide firmly around her waist as he steered her up the hill toward the town square.

"Have a good trip?"

He grinned and gave her a little tug. "This is the best part."

Harriet felt his smile all the way to her toes.

After a simple dinner of ham sandwiches and potato salad and a lot of small talk they caught the last train to Walker. She couldn't believe he was finally here. When they reached Walker, Harriet's father picked her up from the station. As Pops turned his pickup toward home, she watched Henry through the back window as he headed through the snow toward Mrs. Hammond's to share a room with David. How she wished they could spend more time together.

Henry found it hard to get to sleep, even though he was tired from his travel. Memories of his folks, his brothers, and how life used to be for them in this town battled for his attention with the recollections of his all-to-brief meal spent with Harriet.

How could the woman he'd written to for three years be more beautiful than the last time he'd seen her? How would he ever be able to support a wife and family on what he made in the service? Would she wait for him until he made enough if he chose that path? Maybe she was dating someone else. These and other thoughts chased in his head well into the night.

He awoke with a start, afraid he had overslept until he smelled bacon and coffee from Mrs. Hammond's kitchen. David still slept soundly beside him. He pulled on his shirt and trousers and crept into the kitchen.

Mrs. Hammond cracked eggs into the hot grease in her iron skillet. "You up already? Thought you might sleep a little later." She poured a cup of black coffee and set it before Henry.

"Thank you. Too much going on to waste time in sleep."

"I agree." She turned from the stove and propped one hand on her hip. "Did you and Harriet have a good supper last night?"

"Oh, yes, ma'am."

Henry noticed her quick glance and slight smile before she pulled the toast out of the oven and plated the eggs. Had he said too much? Why did she grin?

Setting the plate before him, she asked, "How old are you now, Henry?"

"Twenty-six. Why do you ask?"

"Just wondered. Mr. Hammond and I were married with a baby on the way by the time he was your age."

Nodding, he said, "Those were better days." He scooped a forkful of over-easys.

"Does that mean if times were better, you'd marry now—or is Harriet Edmiston not the one?"

How did Mrs. Hammond always know when something was up? Like the time he and Homer stole the watermelon out of the old timer's patch just outside of town. They had no more than gotten it home when Mrs. Hammond called to them from her kitchen window, "Nice watermelon, boys. Where'd you get it?"

Not only did they have to return it with apologies. Their dad made them clean out the stalls in the barn *and* the chicken house before breakfast the next morning.

Why did she want to know if he thought Harriet was the one anyway? Most every conversation in this town was fair game for news, as the locals put it. He really didn't want to be the latest headline on the grapevine.

"Harriet is a nice girl. For the rest, we'll just have to see." He hoped his answer would satisfy his hostess because the subject was closed between them as far as he was concerned. He wasn't even sure Harriet felt the same as he felt about her. He thought she did by the way she smiled at him last night, but she hadn't said so with words. But then, neither had he.

David shuffled into the kitchen and Henry mentally sighed in relief.

"Good morning, little brother."

"You hungry, sonny? I'll rustle you up some eggs here in a minute." Mrs. Hammond said.

Henry went to shave so they could leave for Edmiston's farm as soon as his brother finished breakfast.

From the bedroom, he heard Mrs. Hammond humming a tune. He couldn't place it at first—then he recognized it. "Here Comes the Bride." He'd have to check the train schedule for the earliest ticket to Nevada for tomorrow morning. No use sticking around here for her to ask more questions. Maybe he could meet Harriet for an early lunch there before he caught the train to Fort Leavenworth.

Everything was a flurry of activity at the Edmiston farmhouse. Harriet popped the last pumpkin pie in the oven while Glessner stirred gravy and called for Pops to come carve the turkey. Glessner asked Henry to sharpen the butcher knife, and David played checkers in the living room with Janie. Harriet's aunts, uncles, and cousins gathered to enjoy the day of relaxation and rest.

As luck would have it, Henry's place at the table was between Harriet and Aunt Merrie. Everything went without a hitch until Aunt Merrie asked Henry the dreaded question.

"So how old are you, Henry?"

He replied respectfully, "Twenty-six, ma'am. David, it looks like you need more potatoes. Can I pass you some?" Henry nearly shoved the bowl of mashed potatoes into the boy's chest.

"Sure. Thanks."

"Isn't this a wonderful dinner, David? Thank you, Mrs. Edmiston for inviting us."

She smiled sweetly and said, "It's good to have us all together today."

Henry heard Aunt Merrie mutter, "That's how old Dr. Murphy was when he asked me to marry him."

He pretended he didn't hear her. He wanted to avoid the word marriage at all costs. Who knew what dinner table conversation might grow from that one little word.

Soon the carved bird was nothing but a pile of bones and the last spoonful of mashed potatoes disappeared. Harriet rose to help her mother clear the table for dessert.

When Henry tasted Harriet's pecan pie he had to fight the urge to ask for a second piece. He hadn't tasted pie so delicious since his mother died.

Late in the afternoon he and Harriet took a walk out by the barn lot. Snow from the day before lingered in little skiffs. He'd had a thousand conversations in his head with this girl. Now she was beside him and he was as tongue-tied as a village idiot.

After his several attempts at conversation, Henry looked her in the eye, gently put his arm around her waist, and drew her in for a kiss. Just then, Pops rounded the corner of the garage with two buckets of slop for the pigs. Henry took a step back, loosen his grip, and cleared his throat. Heat crept into his cheeks.

Pops appeared not to notice and threw the contents into the pig trough. He turned quickly and headed back to the house.

"I—I guess David and I better be going," Henry muttered.

"Not yet, Henry Freeman." Harriet slipped her hands up his chest and encircled his neck to give him a lingering kiss.

In grateful surprise, he wrapped his arms around her to return the affection.

They both exploded in gales of laughter.

"Did you see the look on Pops' face?"

"I thought he might throw the slop on us and forget the pigs."

"Pops is so very shy. He doesn't even kiss Mother in front of anyone. I'm sure he's embarrassed beyond words."

Harriet convinced Henry to walk with her through the frozen pasture. Arm in arm, they talked. By the time they got to the far north pasture, Henry paused and cleared his throat near a clump of evergreens. He turned to Harriet and said, "Mrs. Hammond really gave me the business. Wanted to know if I thought you were—the one. I really didn't have an answer for her. It set me to thinking. We need to talk."

Harriet drew in a deep breath. Was this conversation really happening? She started to pinch herself but thought better of it. "No, we haven't, really."

"I don't know if I even have the right to discuss a future with you now. I mean, I've still got a while before I have to decide if I'll stay in the Army. And I have no idea what I'll do if I don't re-up. It's a little foolish to speak, but I feel like we need to—to—Harriet, are you willing to wait for me? I mean could we be—um—could I speak for your hand?"

Joy welled in Harriet's heart and overflowed in an ever-growing smile. "Yes!" she whispered. "Yes, Henry!" She touched his warm cheek.

He grabbed her in a bear hug and twirled her around. "Harriet, those words have made me the happiest man in the whole world. I promise I'll do everything in my power to be the best husband I can be."

She kissed him and buried her face in his chest. "I know you will, Henry. Let this be our little secret—for now."

Henry smiled. "Agreed. No use feeding the rumor mill just yet."

The next morning Henry got David up early so they could catch the first train out headed for Nevada. When they arrived in Nevada Henry realized the boy hadn't spoken a word all the way from Walker.

"Something on your mind, little brother?"

He scuffed the snow with the toe of his worn shoe. "Just wish I didn't have to go back."

Henry plopped his hand on his brother's head. "One day, little brother. One day."

David nodded and looked Henry in the eye. "Promise?"

The train whistle cut their conversation short. Henry put his arm around his shoulder and guided him toward the passenger car. "Promise."

When the train pulled out, Henry headed for the square to see if he could have an early lunch with his sweetheart. If he left on the one o'clock train, he figured he could still get a connection in Kansas City to make it back to Fort Leavenworth by the time his leave expired.

Harriet met Henry at a new little lunch place near the train station. He guided her to two empty stools at the end of the high bar. They ordered a hamburger and Susie-Q potatoes. While they ate, Aunt Merrie's comment popped into his head.

"Tell me about Aunt Merrie. Who was Dr. Murphy?"

"What brought that up?"

"She mentioned him yesterday at dinner."

Harriet wiped her mouth and took a sip of Coke. "Well, he was sweet on her and asked her to marry him after he got out of medical school. Grandmother Edmiston refused to hear of it. Said Merrie was the only one of her seven children still single so she had to stay with them and look after them in their old age."

"Did she?"

"Yep. Still does. They're pretty much house-bound now. After a few years, Dr. Murphy finally gave up and married somebody else." Harriet paused, then continued, "He and his wife lived across the street from Aunt Merrie and her parents until the day he died. I think that's why she's always so interested in her nieces and nephews since she doesn't have any children of her own."

"How sad. I didn't respond to her yesterday. Didn't want to speak of marriage to anyone but you."

"Henry, you know as well as I, what the old gals don't know they just make up. Even though we're not going to say anything, I imagine we'll be an item around Walker—and Nevada, too, since Aunt Merrie saw us together yesterday."

He squeezed her hand under the counter. "Well, let them yammer on. The truth will come out soon enough."

She tried to hide a giggle as she wiped her mouth with a napkin. They held hands as they made their way to the station.

All too soon the one o'clock train chugged in. Henry grabbed one more kiss before he stepped onto the train stairs.

"All aboard!" the conductor called. The train began to move as the conductor disappeared inside the passenger car.

Henry remained on the stairs.

She blew him a kiss.

A pain ran through his chest as he watched her on the platform. How long would it be before he saw her again?

Chapter 15

As Henry's three-year commitment drew to an end in February of 1937, the Army promised him a rating of Supply Sergeant if he would re-enlist. He considered it but felt he could do as well being a civilian. He'd had enough of someone else ordering his life.

The first place he went was Nevada. He didn't tell Harriet what he had decided or that he was coming. He just walked into the store about closing time on a Saturday.

Harriet looked up from tallying her daily tickets and let out a shriek. "Henry! You're here!"

He glanced at Uncle Vernon who wore a severe frown.

"Good grief, girl, you nearly scared me to death. This a business establishment, not the state hospital for the mentally deranged."

Aunt Merrie shook her head as she ambled out the door—but not before she gave a disapproving glance at her brother, Vernon.

Harriet left her sales tickets on the counter, grabbed her coat, and made a beeline for the door. "Let's get out of here before I get in more trouble than I already am."

He grinned from ear to ear as he drew her snugly to his side to shield her from the frigid wind, pleased with her reaction to his surprise. "Know anyplace I could get a warm supper?"

With tears clouding her vision, she said, "I think I can arrange that."

As soon as they entered her apartment she closed the door and threw her arms around his neck. "I can't believe you're really here!" A deep satisfaction swept over her in his strong embrace.

Henry kissed her tenderly and whispered in her ear. "Neither can I."

While she dumped spaghetti into boiling water and fried the last quarter pound of hamburger, she fired questions like a machine gun.

"Where's your uniform? Did you re-enlist?"

Henry sat at the kitchen table and feasted his eyes on her. "Nope."

Her shoulders relaxed as she let out a long breath.

"Does my decision make you happy?"

She paused, glanced his way, and said, "Yes. I hoped that would be your decision. But what will you do? Do you have a job?"

"Don't know what I'll do yet. Figure I'll go to Kansas City to find something. I've looked around here but found nothing."

She poured a can of tomato soup into the meat. "I'm not surprised. Uncle Vernon had ten people show up the other day in response to his ad in the paper for a two-hour-a-day job."

Henry cleared his throat. "I saw Lloyd at the train station today. He's been looking for work for weeks all over the county. He's back in Walker now. His dad isn't doing well. He's come home to help him."

Plating the spaghetti, she said, "You'd think he could find something to do. Didn't he make a lot of furniture in high school?"

"He did, but no one's in the market for furniture when their bellies are empty. His dad tried to talk him into taking over his business. Lloyd said he couldn't talk fast enough to be an auctioneer. His dad's going to retire."

Harriet set two forks on the table and took a seat across from him. Feasting her eyes on Henry, she smiled. "Let's eat before you starve."

The next day, Henry headed back to the city. Soon he landed a job at an office supply company. The $12.50 a week sounded passable, but after he paid his lodging, eats, and laundry, he barely had enough for the trolley car back and forth to work.

He needed to make more so he could visit David and Harriet.

After two months, Henry visited Nevada again. He and Harriet spent Sunday discussing their future plans.

Harriet poured them a cup of depression coffee. "Wish I had real coffee to serve you. This will have to do."

"Oh, well, it's hot. It works. I got a letter from Lloyd last week. He says the filling station owner in Walker wants to sell it. It comes with an International pickup with a 300-gallon tank on the back for farm deliveries."

Listening intently, Harriet sat and sipped her bitter brew. "So are you going to throw in with him?"

"Well, I don't know. With the money I've managed to save from the Army and the money he's got, I figure we'll still need about $350.00."

"Where will you get it?"

"Well, there's the rub. The seller won't loan us the money and neither will the bank." He smiled. "I considered robbing one, but doubt that would work either."

"Good thought. Didn't work out too well for Bonnie and Clyde, did it?"

Henry chuckled as he lifted another fork of spaghetti. "Nope. That's for sure. Well, we'll have to pray on it." Henry reached for her hand.

She smiled. "Yes, we will, my dear."

The next Monday during Harriet's lunch break, Aunt Merrie leaned back from her sewing machine and took her feet off the treadle.

"How are things going with Henry?"

"Oh, you know. Kinda hard times—but what's new?"

Merrie shoved her chair back from the sewing machine and snipped threads from the dress she'd finished altering. "Does he like his job in the city?"

Harriet wondered what the latest information was on the grapevine. Aunt Merrie seemed rather persistent in her questions. "Well, as a matter of fact, he'd like to buy into a filling station in Walker with his old buddy, Lloyd Harrison. But they're having trouble getting the financing."

She'd probably said too much but now the cat was out of the bag. Aunt Merrie didn't say anything. She just nodded a quiet, "Hummm," as she turned to the ironing board.

Chapter 16

A few days later as Aunt Merrie entered the store, she paused by a table where Harriet folded ladies' undergarments.

"When you get a chance, I'd like to talk to you alone."

Now what was on her mind? Harriet shrugged it off but instead of going home at noon, she grabbed a sandwich at the lunch counter down the street and brought it into Aunt Merrie's alteration room.

"You wanted to talk to me?" Harriet perched on the tall stool by the ironing board.

Aunt Merrie threaded a needle. "I did. I wondered if I might act as a banker for Henry and Lloyd."

Harriet frowned, her turkey sandwich halfway to her mouth. "A what?"

"You heard me. A banker. You know. Someone who loans money to people—like for a business loan."

Shifting on her stool and resting her sandwich in her lap, Harriet took a hard look at Aunt Merrie. "But you're a seamstress—not a banker. Besides, Henry and Lloyd need $350.00. That's a whale of a lot of money—especially in these times. I can't ask you to be their banker."

"You didn't ask me. I volunteered. And I *do* know how much money that is. Surprised they don't need more. I've got faith in those two young men. They'll pay it back. They're hard workers."

Harriet struggled to keep her jaw from hanging open. Would Henry accept a loan from her aunt? "I—I, don't know what to say."

Aunt Merrie smiled. "You don't have to say anything. Look at it this way. What do I have to spend my money on besides coal for my furnace and food for my belly? I have no children to spend it on. Been saving for a rainy day for years. Might as well help you young people along. That's the least I can do. Now you go write Henry a letter and tell him to buy the filling station. We'll draw up an agreement later. You better go off to work before my brother finds you in here lollygaggin'."

Harriet slid off the stool, hugged her aunt with a quiet "Thank you," and made a quick exit.

Henry could hardly believe his eyes when he read and reread Harriet's letter. He never dreamed the money would come from such an unlikely source. He called Lloyd long distance from the pay phone in the drug store.

His next stop was the office of his boss.

"Mr. Forrester, this will be my last week here. Thank you for the opportunity to work for you."

His boss frowned as he sat back in his chair. "And what are you going to do for employment? Work for my competitor?"

"No sir. I'm buying a filling station."

Mr. Forrester leaned forward with his elbows on his desk, hands clasped. "Filling station, huh? Well, I wish you well. Too bad you couldn't stay with this company. You could have gone far."

Henry shook his employer's hand. "Thanks again, Mr. Forrester."

As he rode the train to Walker on Friday afternoon, his worldly possessions in his bag, he pondered his former employer's words. Given enough time, he truly might have gone far. But he didn't want to dance to someone else's tune. He had tunes of his own to play. Right or wrong, he wanted to work hard—for himself. Not contributing to someone else's pocket. Now he was one step closer to his goal to bring David back to Walker.

On Friday night, He and Lloyd met with Aunt Merrie at her home to sign the loan.

Henry read through her hand-written agreement. "Wait a minute. This paper says the loan is interest-free. That can't be."

Lloyd peered at the document over Henry's shoulder.

Straightening her four-foot-ten frame at her desk she said, "It most certainly *can* be."

Lloyd stepped forward, "But Miss Edmiston, that's not the way it's done."

Aunt Merrie grinned and winked. "It is when I'm the banker."

Henry's gaze swiveled between Aunt Merrie and Lloyd.

Handing a pen to Henry, she said, "Just sign here, boys. Then you're off and running. What'll you call your new company?"

"We hadn't had a chance to talk about it yet, ma'am," Lloyd said.

"What about, H & L Oil Company?" she said.

The guys looked at one another and Lloyd said, "Sounds good to me, Ma'am."

Henry shook Lloyd's hand. "Sounds good to me too—partner."

After the men signed, Aunt Merrie added her name to the agreement. "Now I know you fellas will work hard and pay back this loan in good time."

"Thank you, Miss Edmiston, for your trust in us," Lloyd said as he shook her hand. "We surely will see to it your money is returned quickly."

Henry silently vowed, When Aunt Merrie receives her final payment, I'll marry her niece—but not until.

Word spread quickly about the new owners of the filling station in Walker. Everyone seemed eager to support the two home-town boys who had come back to run a business.

The 300-gallon tank on the truck, orders kept them busy delivering gas to the outlying farmers in the area despite the depressed times. After all, if a farmer was going to produce a crop for a living in these times, he had to plow more ground than a team of mules could cover in a day. Even old time farmers yielded to the newer ways of tractors, which increased the sales of the H & L Oil Company.

There were a few holdouts, however—like Harriet's dad.

"I've no use for tractors. Broke down most of the time. I can get half a day's work done with mules in the time it takes to fix those dad-blamed tractors."

Henry was grateful most folks didn't agree with Pops.

Henry tallied up the receipts from April just as Lloyd came back to the station from delivering an order to a farmer west of town.

He sat on the edge of the desk. "How does it look, Henry?"

"Not bad. If we keep this up, we'll be able to pay our loan back by September or October. Have a few due bills here, but nothing we can't handle. Too bad we can't expand our business somehow." Henry stuck his pencil behind his ear.

"Like what?"

Henry strode to the door and saw a crop duster fly overhead. "Oh, I don't know. Too bad we're not closer to an airport. We could sell gas to planes."

Shaking his head, Lloyd gathered the receipts and said, "Henry Freemen, you're always thinking! Let's keep this business going at a good speed before we think of branching out."

"Think about it, Lloyd. It's what makes things click."

It wasn't a week later when a hydrogen airship, the Hindenburg crashed. When Lloyd heard about the disaster the next day he looked at his partner and nodded. "Well, Henry, I've thought about it. I doubt too many folks will line up for much air travel after what happened. Let's just stick to selling fuel to things on the ground."

"Perhaps you're right, my friend. Guess we'll have to convince the old timers to use tractors so we can drum up more business."

Chapter 17

With each week, the filling station showed a steady profit so their repayment fund for Aunt Merrie grew. Out of Henry's salary every week, he also put some aside for a ring for Harriet.

An old timer came into the station one day driving a 1930 Model A Ford.

"I notice you have an old car, young man. Wonder if you might be interested in this one."

Henry frowned. "Why are you selling it? Something wrong with it?"

"Nope. I'm moving to Des Moines to live with my widowed sister and it's too far for me to drive up there. Figure I'll just use her car when I get there."

Henry looked under the hood. Everything seemed to be in good working order. "What do you want for it?"

"I figger thirty dollars oughta do it. I'd ask more, but she's pressing' me to come right away. Deal?"

"Deal." Henry didn't hesitate. He figured he'd better strike while the iron was hot—before the old guy changed his mind.

By late May, they had more than half the money to repay the loan. Henry was tempted to officially ask Harriet to set a date for their marriage but waited for the accounting nearer the end of June before making his move.

On June 26, Henry could wait no longer. He left the station early so he could clean up before he headed for the florist shop in Nevada.

"What can I do for you, young man?" the lady behind the counter asked.

"I've come for a corsage. Got any suggestions?"

"Special occasion?"

The heat of embarrassment crept into his cheeks. "You could say that. Going to ask my girl an important question."

The lady smiled and moved to the glass front refrigerator. "Well then, we need something very special. Roses?"

Henry hesitated. "No, she's not a rose kind of a girl. What else you got?"

Reaching inside the refrigerator, she drew out a white flower. "Gardenias are nice. On sale too." She brought it near his nose.

Henry sniffed, taking in the sweet fragrance. "This will do nicely, thank you."

She went into the back room. "I'll just be a minute."

Henry's heart fluttered. The moment he'd waited for so long had finally arrived.

The lady emerged with a little white box. "Here you are sir." He peered inside. A white gardenia surrounded by forest green ribbon nestled inside.

The florist gently placed the lid on the box and handed it to him. "Good luck."

"Thank you." Henry paid for his purchase and headed for Edmiston's Department Store. He hid the box behind his back as he watched Harriet through the front glass. The late afternoon shadows lengthened around the square. Soon she would be his own—his bride.

Harriet saw him through the window and motioned him inside.

"Know anyone who would like to enjoy dinner and a ride?"

She straightened the dress on a mannequin and squared the necklace. "Aunt Merrie might like to go."

"I had someone else in mind."

Harriet gave a coy smile. "And who do you have in mind?"

"Oh, someone with red hair and a beautiful smile. One who would like to wear this." He extended the box to her.

Harriet's eyes widened as she received the box, pulled the lid, and looked inside. "Henry! It's beautiful!" The sweet aroma filled the store. She blinked back tears as she lifted the corsage from the box.

The lady at the front desk followed the sweet scent. "Oh, my! Someone is in for a special evening."

"Indeed," Harriet whispered as she drank in the flower's sweetness.

Henry drove Harriet to her apartment as a hot afternoon breeze blew through the open car. He visited with Bernice at the kitchen table as he waited for Harriet to change into her best brown frock.

Bernice turned from the stove to see Henry pin the gardenia to Harriet's lapel. "So what's the occasion?"

Henry reached for the doorknob and said, "We'll tell you later."

As they drove to the restaurant Harriet said, "What *is* the occasion?"

"We'll talk later—after we eat. I'm starved."

Harriet nodded as she slipped her arm into his.

They ducked into a little place on the west side of the square for a pot roast supper. Through the meal, she caught Henry looking at her in a most peculiar way. Was he ready to set a date for their wedding? He certainly must have something up his sleeve because he'd never bought her flowers before. Her stomach flipped—in a good way.

After they finished their apple pie with a slice of cheddar cheese on top, Henry suggested they go to Radio Springs, the city park. By the time they arrived, dusk had settled into night. Dim bulbs outlined the building set on a small island in the middle of a pond. The sound of quiet conversation and occasional laughter drifted across the water from inside the shelter. Lightning bugs blinked in search of a mate. The two found an empty park bench situated on the dry, crunchy grass near the water's edge. They sat listening to the night sounds. Her gardenia gave a sweet fragrance to the otherwise sun-scorched surroundings.

Henry turned to Harriet. He took her hand and looked into eyes. "Harriet, from the day I visited your folk's house when my mother died, I've hoped for this day. I've hesitated to commit to a marriage date because I wasn't sure what path my life would take.

"When your aunt loaned Lloyd and me the money for the station, I made a vow that when the loan was paid off, I'd make our commitment official with a marriage certificate."

"And when might that be?"

"As soon as the loan is paid in full. Don't want any debt hanging over our heads. It should be before fall. Will you? Marry me, I mean?"

She blinked back tears and her hands gripped his a little tighter. A smile graced the corners of her mouth as she whispered, “Oh, yes, Henry. How I’ve waited for this day.” She yielded to his loving embrace.

“I can hardly wait until the day we are one.” He took a deep breath and continued. “There’s one other thing we need to talk about.”

Harriet hoped he wasn’t going to bring up the subject of children—something she hoped would be far, far into the future. If they were to marry, she’d have to take measures to make sure babies didn’t happen until *she* was ready. She leaned back. “What?”

“It’s about David.”

Relieved, she said, “David?”

“I promised to bring him back to Walker. Are you willing to bring him into our home? He’s got three more years of school left.”

After a long silence, Harriet nodded. “Well, I hadn’t figured on starting married life with a husband *and* a teenager, but if that’s the deal,” she nodded, “then that’s the deal.”

Henry let out a long sigh. “Thank you, Harriet. He’s a good boy. At least if he’s with us he won’t be haunted with the constant fear someone will adopt him. Guess we better start looking for a place to rent in Walker.”

August business was even more brisk than July. Henry couldn’t wait to tell Harriet the news. He drove in for a quiet supper at her place near the end of August. While he munched his bacon and egg sandwich, he said, “Are you ready to be a married woman? I figure we’ll have the total payment ready for Aunt Merrie by the end of this month.”

She rose from her chair and sat in his lap. “You bet I am, Mr. Freeman. Where are we going to live?”

He chuckled. “You mean we can’t just live here?”

“You think Bernice would like that? Might be a little crowded in our bed, don’t you think?”

They enjoyed a good laugh at the thought of three in a bed.

“No Harriet, I located a place. I want to take you to see it tonight after we finish supper. It’s the nicest place in Walker.”

“Oh? What’s the rent?”

"Only $7.00 a month."

"Wow! Sounds like a bargain. Let's get out there before dark. I want to see this place."

When Harriet saw Henry's find, she understood why the rent was so cheap. The structure of the house was in good shape, but it had no running water, no inside plumbing, and it burned coal for heat.

She held her tongue until she saw the three-burner wood stove in the kitchen. "Oh my. I wonder if I can manage this."

Henry stopped in the doorway. "What's the problem?"

"I grew up cooking on a coal-oil stove. I guess I can learn to cook on a wood one."

"Of course you will. Women have been doing it for years. Other than that, what do you think?"

Harriet strolled to the living room and put her hands on her hips. "Well, with one bedroom David will have to sleep in here on the couch. Will he mind?"

Encircling her small waist from behind, he kissed her neck. "It'll work fine, my love."

She had an idea. "Bernice and Ben think they will move to Walker when they get married. Perhaps we could rent my apartment in Nevada when they marry next month. The rent there is only a little more than here."

"But then David would have to go to school in Nevada. I promised him a home in Walker so he could finish here."

Harriet took a deep breath and nodded. "Guess I better get some boxes tomorrow so I can start packing." Maybe she could ask Mrs. Dennis, her mother's neighbor, how to cook on a wood stove. She used one and people from far and wide raved about her cooking.

In the night, Harriet woke up worried about using an outside privy. It was going to be an adjustment—but then, so was married life. She remembered one of her grandmother's favorite sayings. "Life is full of surprises. It's how you take them that makes the difference."

Harriet guessed her grandmother, Lucy Edmiston, spoke from experience. After all, when Grandmother married in 1886, she not only cooked on a wood stove and used a privy, she came to this place as a new bride from Russellville, Kentucky in a covered wagon. Harriet hoped that was the end of the similarities. Grandmother Edmiston bore seven children—not Harriet's plan, for sure.

The next weekend the almost-newlyweds moved Harriet's goods from her apartment into their rental house. Now she could work on wood stove practice before she had two men to cook for.

Within the month Henry and Harriet stood up for Bernice and Ben when they got married. A little butterfly flip tickled her stomach as she watched her friends tie the knot. One day soon she and Henry would be the bride and groom.

Chapter 18

On Wednesday evening, September 1, Henry and Lloyd paid a visit to Aunt Merrie. Lloyd twisted the crank on the bell in the middle of the front door, to signal their arrival.

Aunt Merrie opened the door. “Well, look who we have here. Come in and make yourselves at home. Can I get you all some coffee?”

“No, ma’am,” Lloyd said as he and Henry stepped inside the parlor and sat on the couch. “We’re here on official business.”

“What business?”

Henry pulled a stack of bills wrapped in a piece of paper from his pocket. He grinned. “Aunt Merrie, we’ve come to pay our debt.”

“Oh.” She sat in the chair by her writing desk. “So soon? It’s only been five months.”

“We don’t like owing anyone. Business has been good.” Henry counted out the bills on her desk. When he laid the last bill on the stack he beamed and said, “Thank you for your trust in us. It’s been a pleasure doing business with you.”

She pulled out a letter from one of the desk drawers. Well, I have a confession to make. I didn’t rely on my own judgment alone. I wrote to your commanding officer and asked for a recommendation. Here. Read it.”

Henry drew the letter from the envelope and read:

> To Whom it May Concern:
>
> I have known Henry S. Freeman since February 15, 1934. During this period, he was directly under my command for one year.
>
> I have always found him honest, faithful and loyal. He has many attributes which made him a very fine soldier.

G.E. Isaacs,
Captain, 17th Infantry,
Commanding Officer

"But how?" Henry glanced at Lloyd.

Aunt Merrie sat straight and smiled. "I have my ways." She rose and shook Henry and Lloyd's hands. "I wish you all the luck in the world, boys."

Henry handed the letter back to Aunt Merrie. "Thanks again." They left as quickly as they had come. Henry felt a little extra spring in his step. Not only had he been given a high recommendation by his commanding officer, he was debt free, and he was about to marry the girl of his dreams.

Henry swung by the local jewelry store and picked out a simple octagon gold band for Harriet as a symbol of his undying love before he picked her up at the store. He'd surprise her with it on their wedding day.

Harriet and Henry kept their impending marriage a secret. Harriet didn't want to cause a stir—especially from Gary Grimes since he still occasionally asked her out. Henry said he figured the invitations were more of a joke on Gary's part since it was very evident he and Harriet were definitely an item. Henry said Gary would probably quit his little charade when Harriet became Mrs. Freeman—at least he hoped so.

Henry picked Harriet up from work on Thursday before Labor Day. He turned onto the highway and headed for Walker. "I've been thinking. Why don't we drive to Fort Scott and get married tomorrow night?"

"What?"

"I told you I was going to marry you when the loan was paid off. It's paid—so let's get married. It's a perfect time."

"How do you figure?"

"Well, if we got married tomorrow night, we could go to work Saturday and not tell anyone. Then no one could give us any razzmatazz about getting married. We could leave after work and head out for a honeymoon on Sunday and Monday, since the store will be closed for the holiday. What do you think?"

Harriet didn't know what to say. Of course she wanted to get married, but she surely thought she would have at least a week to plan the whole affair. But then again, there wasn't any money to for anything fancy. She wondered if life would always be this seat-of-the pants, married to Henry. He certainly was full of surprises.

"Well—is it okay with you?"

She threaded her arm through his, nodded with a grin, and said, "Yes. I think it is."

"Good. I'll call the Presbyterian pastor tomorrow to ask him to do the service."

The wheels in Harriet's head began to whurr. "Who will stand up with us?"

"Oh, I'll ask Lloyd. Maybe Pastor Young's wife could fill in. We could ask Bernice and Ben, but the less people who know about this, the better."

"You're right," Harriet said as Henry pulled up in front of the house which would soon be their home.

True to form, the next day, Gary Grimes began his familiar line. "Hey, Harriet. How about a night on the town with ole Gary? We could hit the honky-tonk north of town and have a high old time. Tell Henry Freeman to get lost. I could show you what a *really* good time is."

It was all Harriet could do to keep her mouth shut. She wondered why her uncle kept him on. Judging from what she saw of the daily receipts, she didn't think he was a very good salesman. She wondered if he knew something was up, because he kept on with his foolishness all day. She certainly hadn't told anyone and didn't think Henry had either—unless Lloyd said something.

When five o'clock rolled around, she was extremely grateful to leave work and hopped into Henry's waiting Model A.

"Where's Lloyd? You did ask him, didn't you?"

Henry grinned. "Of course. He'll be along after a bit. Had to make a delivery to a farm way north of Walker. He'll meet us over there."

Harriet took a deep breath as they headed for Fort Scott, twenty miles to the west. The strain of the constant heckling all day had made her weary. As Henry drove, the sound of cicadas, the drone of the engine, and the country air caused her to lay her head on his shoulder and doze. Before she knew it, they pulled in front of the pastor's home in Fort Scott.

"Have a nice rest, my bride?"

Her heart skipped a beat at the word bride. Was this really happening? "Yes, I did, my groom."

Henry put his arm around her for a long, lingering kiss. Someone honked behind them. They turned to see their best man.

"Somebody gettin' hitched tonight?" Lloyd said as he stepped out of the oil truck and shut the door.

Henry got out and opened the door for Harriet. "I think so, if we can find a best man."

"Glad to oblige you, sir," Lloyd said with a low bow.

The pastor performed the union in front of the fireplace in the living room of his home. It was over almost before it began. In less than ten minutes, Harriet Edmiston became Harriet Freeman—a name she hoped to carry for the rest of her life.

She mused to Henry on the way home, "Funny what a few words can do."

He put his arm around his wife and gave her a gentle squeeze. "So true, my beautiful bride."

This time the word seemed to fit.

The next morning Harriet barely made it to work on time—and she forgot to take off her wedding ring. By ten o'clock Mr. Grimes discovered her mistake and put on quite a performance.

"What am I gonna' do? The girl I had my cap set for has gone and married another." She heard him carrying on several times through the afternoon. By now half the town must know Harriet changed her name to Freeman. So much for secrecy!

By four, Uncle Vernon told her she was free to go for the day. He slipped her a five spot and wished the newly-weds a good trip.

"Oh, thank you, Uncle Vernon."

"You're welcome, he said with a grin. "Now get out of here."

Harriet didn't think he let her go early because he was being generous—he probably just wanted to shut Grimes down.

For whatever the reason, Harriet called Henry at the station. "I've been able to get off a little early. Please come pick me up immediately at the store. Don't forget our bags at the house."

As the sun made its way for the western horizon, Henry turned their car to the south and headed for Roaring River State Park in southern Missouri for their two-day honeymoon.

Chapter 19

The newlyweds arrived home late Monday evening. In the night, Harriet had to go to the bathroom. She stumbled out of bed and made her way to the outhouse. The overcast sky gave little light to guide her on her way. She didn't see the outhouse door left ajar and ran right into it.

"Ow!" Her head throbbed. Angry tears trickled down her cheeks. After she sat in the privy for a while, she wiped her face with the sleeve of her gown and headed back to bed. She was too tired to light the coal oil lamp to see the damage.

At first light, Henry stirred. He put his arm around his wife and drew her close. "My Lord! What happened to you?"

Harriet opened her eyes. She could only see out of one of them—the other one was swollen shut. She leaped from bed and looked in the mirror. "Oh, no!" A black eye.

"Did I smack you with my elbow during the night? Oh, Harriet. I'm so sorry."

Harriet moaned. "It wasn't you, Henry. I ran into the privy door in the dark last night. How am I going to go to work like this?"

If Harriet thought Mr. Grimes was obnoxious on Saturday, he took the all-time prize on Tuesday. Every person who came in the store offered her sympathy and wanted a full account of what happened. She wasn't about to tell anyone she ran into an outhouse door, so she merely said, "a door."

Mr. Grimes popped in a couple of times ready to give a blow-by-blow account, adding his own special touch at the end. "She says she ran into a door. But I think the truth is, her new husband socked her. She should have married me. I know how to treat a woman."

By afternoon, Harriet had all she could take. The next time he opened his mouth, she whirled on him raising her fists and said through gritted teeth, "Mr. Grimes, open your mouth one more time and you'll have two of these."

Later, she wished she'd done this months ago because she didn't hear another peep out of him. From that time on, he steered clear of her, obviously afraid she'd deliver on what she promised.

Harriet expected Henry to make a trip to Liberty any day to get David since school had started. By the next week, she asked about it.

"I think I'll leave him there for a while. From his letters, he seems to be getting along pretty well. I hate to make him sleep on the couch when he has a bed there. Besides, I think we need to have time alone while we get adjusted to married life. What you said about taking on a husband and a teen at the same time made me rethink my plan."

Harriet was grateful for his decision. She did want to provide a home for her brother-in-law but hoped she and Henry could enjoy these first few months without a third party around. Besides, she was still trying to figure out how to cook even the simplest meal without burning it on the wood stove. Perhaps they could bring David for a visit at Christmas.

Later in the fall, Harriet found Henry hunched over the kitchen table going through a pile of receipts from the station.

"Something wrong, Honey?"

He looked up with a scowl. "Sales are down. Those farmers who gave up and left for California or lost their farms to the bank hurt our business. Those who are still farming are late paying their bills. The station profits are really down."

Harriet stood behind him and rubbed his shoulders. "I know you'll figure out something."

"I wanted to move David here by January, but I don't think our finances will allow it. Without the loan payment, I thought we'd have enough to feed the three of us. Now I'm not so sure."

She pulled a chair beside him and sat. "It'll get better."

He put his arm around her. "I hope you're right. Even some of the old timers are getting rid of their mules. We'll see what spring brings. Maybe then we can send for him."

Harriet didn't say it, but she was grateful for her job. At least her salary could help keep them going in the lean times.

Near Christmas, Henry wrote a letter to Mr. Thornton requesting permission for David to come to Walker for the holiday. The director agreed. Henry was to pick him up on Friday and return him on Monday.

A heavy snowstorm blew in on Thursday night, so Henry called the orphanage and asked them to put David on a train instead.

The fifteen-year-old arrived in Walker Friday around noon. Christmas morning, the drifts were too deep to drive a car. Pops brought a wagon to Walker pulled by his mules to pick up the three of them.

Henry mused, maybe those mules *were* good for something, after all.

By Monday, the drifts were still too deep to safely drive David to Liberty. Henry got him up for breakfast. "I think we better wait a day or two to drive you back. Sure wouldn't want to get stuck in the snow."

A wide grin spread across his brother's face. "Maybe it's a sign I'm supposed to stay here."

The lump in Henry's throat kept him from responding to his brother's suggestion. He plated the eggs, ruffled David's hair, and went to the bedroom. Should he tell his brother of their financial situation? He didn't want to plant doubt, still . . . .

Thursday the roads were passable. The two set out in the early morning for Liberty. He didn't want the boy to have to go both ways on the train. As Henry drove they made small talk until there was only one subject left. Henry turned into the long drive at the orphanage.

He decided to share the money problem and said, "David, I had hoped to move you with us in January, but there isn't enough money. Perhaps by summer . . . ." He stopped at the front door and pulled the hand brake.

David sat, hands in his lap. He stared out the window at the frozen landscape. Finally, he spoke over the idling engine. "Okay. I know you'll do what you promised when you can."

"I'll try my best, my brother."

The boy grabbed his bag, bolted from the car, and charged up the stairs through the front doors.

To Henry, this parting seemed harder than all the others. He felt as if his heart would break. When he returned home, he grabbed a sandwich before heading to the filling station. He noticed a small object on the floor by the couch. It was David's little tin car he'd taken with him when he first went to the orphanage. He picked it up and set it gently on the end table and vowed, "By God, I'll do everything I can to get him home before this next school year."

Chapter 20

"Henry, you got your nose in the newspaper again?" Lloyd asked as he came into the station after making a delivery. "Here. Put this in the safe. Mr. Baker finally paid his bill."

"Good." Henry stuffed the money in his pocket and went back to reading the paper.

"What's got your attention? You look like a hound watchin' a badger hole."

"Oh, this guy, Hitler. I've got a bad feeling about him."

Lloyd sat on the edge of the desk and took a look at the article. "What makes you say that? What's it to you anyhow?"

"Maybe it's my military training but I think he's up to something. With all the rearmament he's done, he's broken the Versailles Treaty."

"Aw, Henry, you think too much. He's a whole ocean away. What he does over there doesn't matter here."

Henry closed the paper and folded it carefully before he stuck it in the desk drawer. "That's what everyone thought before the Great War back in '14. Before it was over, we were in it up to our necks. I feel things are heating up the world over."

"How so?"

"Well, Japan may be a half a world away too, but I have an uneasy feeling when I think of them invading China last summer. Mark my words. No good can come of it." He bent in front of the safe, tucked the payment securely inside, and twirled the combination lock.

During 1938, Henry continued to keep an eye out for articles on the German leader when he sent troops into Austria and added that nation to his territory. No country in Europe did anything to challenge him. Henry carefully clipped articles from the *Kansas City Star* and wondered what else the German dictator had on his grocery list, not to mention Japan.

Spring brought a series of rain storms—and turned the dirt roads to mud. By the time the rain quit, it was almost too late to plant. Slowly their business began to improve. Henry was careful to put every spare penny aside so he could bring David home.

By June, he felt he could wait no longer. They'd just have to make do. He made a call to the headmaster to arrange to fetch his brother.

As he drove to Liberty, memories flooded his thoughts. Had it been almost five years since he brought David to the Odd Fellows Home? He would soon be sixteen and in two years he'd be old enough to go to college, if they could scrape together enough to swing it. But where?

He turned into the long drive and past the big iron gates in front of the home.

Mr. Thornton seated Henry in the reception room while he went to get the lad.

While he waited, Henry studied the room David had always feared. It didn't look so bad today, for this was homecoming day—not an adoption day. He noticed the simple furniture and polished wood floor and wondered how many children had been adopted from this orphanage. He whispered, "Thank you, God, I'm finally able to make good on the promise I made." He was grateful this place had been there for his brother.

Mr. Thornton stood in the doorway with David. Henry was struck by how tall his brother had grown in the past few months—almost as tall as the director. They'd have to get him some new pants, first thing. Although he almost outdid Henry in height now, his build seemed very slight. Hopefully, they could fatten him up when he got home.

"Well, young man, we hate to see you go. It's been a pleasure to have you here," Mr. Thornton said as he shook David's hand. "I wish you well. May God be with you in all your endeavors."

"Thank you, Mr. Thornton. I appreciate what you've done for me here."

"Remember to use your voice for good, young man. It's indeed a gift from God."

He flashed a toothy grin as he picked up his bag. "Yes, sir. I will."

Henry reached for a shake. “Thank you, sir. You all have been a lifesaver.”

“Godspeed. Remember us in your prayers.”

“We will, sir,” Henry said as they descended the stairs and headed for the front door.

David waved to some boys playing ball in the side yard as he and Henry rode the long drive.

Henry glanced at his brother. “Sad to leave?”

He sat in silence for a long moment. “Learned a lot there, but I’m not sad to leave. That part of my life’s over. I look forward to being home again.”

Shifting gears, Henry said, “Perhaps we’re both ready for the next chapter in our lives.”

In an attempt to fatten David up a little, Harriet worked on her cooking skills on the wood stove. Both he and Henry were very forgiving.

Henry spoke often of his mother’s bread, so for a special treat, Harriet decided to bake them a loaf in the wood stove on one of her rare days off.

When she read the recipe, it said to proof the yeast. She didn’t know what proof meant, so she put some water on to heat. When it was bubbling, she poured it into the yeast and proceeded to add the required amount of lard, salt, and flour. She kneaded it until it no longer stuck to her hands like the recipe said, and covered it with a tea towel to rise.

After a couple of hours, she looked at it. It hadn’t risen at all, so she decided it must need heat to rise. She stoked the fire, put the dough in a bread pan, and set it in the oven. Soon the aroma of baking bread filled the house.

When the required minutes passed, she grabbed a couple of hot pads to draw it out. To Harriet’s dismay, it was as flat as when she put it in. In fact, it was a heavy brown blob of crusty dough.

When Henry came home for supper, he grinned and said, “Hummm. Is that bread I smell?” He took one look and his face fell.

She fought, unsuccessfully, to hold back the tears.

Enfolding her in his arms he said, "Oh honey, don't cry. We can always use it for a doorstop."

That was the last time Harriet attempted to bake bread. She decided the previous Mrs. Freeman would have to be the legendary bread maker of the family. Her young brother-in-law would just have to stay skinny.

David worked at the station when he wasn't hiring out to bale hay or do odd jobs around town.

One day about a month after he returned to Walker, the funeral director saw him on Main Street. "Say young man, I hear you have quite a voice. I wonder if you might sing for a funeral tomorrow."

"A funeral? I've never sung at a funeral before."

The mortician chuckled. "Well, it's no different than singing in church. Same songs. I'll pick out a couple if you'd like to give it a try. It pays fifty cents."

David's smile faded. "Oh, sir, I couldn't take money for singing. It's my gift from God. I couldn't charge for it."

"Suit yourself. You can come by my office later to see the songs. Deal?"

"Yes. Sir. By the way, whose funeral is it?"

"Old Ezra Palmer. Remember him?"

"Ezra? He used to pitch me pennies to sing for him in front of the general store when I was little." He was the same old fella who suggested David go to the Odd Fellows Home when his mother died—but he kept that to himself. Funny how things work out.

It wasn't long before the young man sang regularly at funerals in the area as well as solos at church. He even sang a few weddings, but he was careful to never take a penny for his service.

Chapter 21

Despite the worrisome news on the world front, the economy began to grow in small ways. People in the cities had a little money to buy whatever beef, pork, and chicken meat, the farmers could spare.

One day in late September, shortly after their first anniversary, Henry came home for a bite of supper before he headed back to the station. Harriet made bacon and tomato sandwiches for them.

As they sat, Henry said, “Pops came in the station today. Said he was going to buy the Presbyterian Church that closed last fall.”

Harriet scowled. “What does he want with the church? He’s not going to preach is he?”

Chuckling, Henry sat back in his chair. “Nope. Says he’s going to tear it down and use the lumber to build your mom the new house he’s promised her for twenty years.”

Harriet stared at him. “Are you kidding?”

“Nope.” David chimed in. “I heard Jim T. say it, too. Said the church cost him only ten percent of what new lumber would cost.”

Giggling, Harriet said, “Pops. Always making a deal.”

Henry smiled. “He’s a sharp horse-trader, for sure.”

“I can’t wait to talk to Mother. She’s been drawing house plans for as long as I can remember. She always said I could help her choose wallpaper and curtains whenever Pops got around to building it. When is he gonna start?”

Henry opened and salted his sandwich. “From the way he talked, it’s going to be right away. He’ll have to move fast if he’s going to get the house done before winter.”

As soon as they finished their meal, Harriet put the dishes in the dishpan. “David, would you mind doing these, please? I really want to get out to see Mother before dark.”

"Sure. You go ahead."

"Thanks," she said as she dashed out the back door and ran to the car.

After he finished the dishes, he settled on the couch to study geometry.

As Henry read the newspaper, his eyes fell on an article about something called the "Munich Agreement." Neville Chamberlain, Prime Minister of Great Britain, said this new document would assure "peace in our time." The Munich Agreement gave Germany permission to take big chunks of Czechoslovakia for German territory—without any objection from Great Britain and France. He mumbled, "Oh my Lord."

David looked up from his book. "What's the matter?"

"Oh, just reading some stuff about Europe."

To Henry's surprise, his little brother wanted to know more. Henry relayed his thoughts about Germany and their seeming lust for more territory. He went on to tell him about an article he'd read recently. In Germany, you had to have a permit for a gun and Jews were not allowed permits.

"What do you suppose that's about?"

"I don't know, but it doesn't set too well with me. Can you imagine our government telling us we couldn't own a gun?"

"It'd be kinda hard to enjoy a good rabbit stew without one."

Henry smiled. "For sure."

When Henry told him about the part about "Peace in our time," David made another comment.

"Remember when Brother Frazier used to quote that scripture in church?"

"Which one?"

"They will say peace, peace, but there is no peace."

Henry shifted in his chair and let this truth sink in. His little brother had a deep understanding—even beyond some grown men. "You're right. I'm afraid this peace thing is going to blow up into war. Hopefully, it won't come here."

Church demolition and building the new house went quickly. Several who weren't otherwise occupied applied to work for Jim T.

Harriet and her mother spent several lunch hours at Moore's Dry Goods store in Nevada picking out curtain material for each room, shopping for rugs, and selecting wallpaper. Janie wasn't as available since she was in her first year at Cottey College in Nevada.

Even though there was no electricity for Walker's rural residents, Jim T. surprised Glessner with a generator to supply power to the house. He even bought a kerosene-fired refrigerator. It didn't fit in the kitchen, so they put it on the back porch.

Every spare minute the women worked to finish the curtains by Christmas. Just before the family left to go to Christmas Eve services in Nevada, Harriet and Glessner hung the last kitchen curtain.

At dinner on Christmas Day, Harriet noticed her husband tearing up. That night when they lay together in bed she whispered, "Are you all right?"

"Why do you ask?"

"You seemed awfully quiet at dinner."

He took a deep breath and rolled toward her. "For the first time since Mother died, I felt like a little part of my family was together again. I'm so glad David's here with us. Thank you for agreeing to bring him home."

She snuggled into his chest. "I'm glad he's with us, too."

"Without you, I couldn't have done it."

Harriet smiled. "What do you think he'll do after he graduates?"

"We haven't talked about it much, but I hope he'll go to college."

"Where?"

"About the closest place would be over in Fort Scott. Don't know where he would live, though."

"Well, it's a worry for another day. We've got time to think on it."

He yawned, stroked her hair, and sighed. "Yes, we do, my love."

Just before Christmas, David asked Henry at the supper table one night, "Remember when we talked this fall about Jews not being able to own guns in Germany?

Henry nodded. "What about it?"

"Our World History teacher told us today that last month Hitler ran gun raids on Jews all over Germany. Said it was for public security. They tore up their businesses and houses and even hauled a bunch of 'em off to jail. They even arrested Jews who had knives."

With a heavy sigh, Henry said, "Public security, my foot! That snake Hitler, bears watching. I think if I were a Jew there, I'd be finding another country to live in."

In late February of 1939, the Freemans awoke to someone banging on the front door.

Henry grabbed for his trousers.

Sitting up in bed Harriet said, "Who could it be at this hour?"

"Don't know. Suppose it's some drunk? Sounds like they're about to beat down the door. David, look out and see who it is!"

As Harriet put on her robe, he yelled back, "Looks like your folks, Harriet."

"What? I thought they were going to the movie in Nevada tonight, but it's too late for them to be coming home at this hour."

David said as he opened the door, "You all don't look like you've been to a movie."

Harriet scurried to the living room and lit a lamp. "Mother, what happened? You smell like you've been to a bond fire. "Didn't you go to the movie?"

"Janie and I did, but Pop stayed home. Said he was tired. On the way home when we got east of Walker, Janie and I saw a red glow in the east. Oh, Harriet! Everything's gone! Burned to the ground."

Jim T. sank into a chair with a wracking cough, his body black with soot. "Couldn't save anything except our twin beds. Managed to get them apart and out the window before the fire got to our bedroom. Sure glad I woke up in time."

Harriet helped her mother to the couch. "Your new house! I'm so sorry. Pops, what caused it?"

"Not sure, but I think the fool kerosene-fired refrigerator started it."

Janie stood beside the front door as if in a daze.

"Here, honey." Harriet pulled on her sister's elbow. "Come sit on the couch with Mother."

Janie whispered, "It's all gone, Sis. Everything."

Harriet put her arm around her sister. "But we still have you. That's the important thing."

Glessner buried her face in her hands and sobbed. "I hadn't even gotten the stickers off the windows yet. If only Janie and I hadn't gone to Nevada, maybe we could have saved it."

"Now Mother, don't blame yourself. That's not going to fix anything. Henry, get some blankets out of the cedar chest. I'll get some wash rags and warm water so you can get the soot off.

Later, Harriet directed her folks to sleep in their bed. She and Henry made pallets with blankets on the floor in the living room.

Harriet's last recollection of that horrible night was the sound of her mother's muffled cries from the bedroom as Jim T. let loose with another series of wracking coughs.

Pops didn't waste any time. He arranged for his family to move into an empty house not far from the charred remains. He heard of a lumber yard closing in Harwood and arranged to buy all the building material at a rock-bottom price.

Harriet went to visit her mother the next week. On the way there, she rehearsed encouraging phrases she might say to Glessner to cheer her. When she arrived, her mother met her at the door with a smile and a yardstick in hand.

Glessner hugged her and said, "Come on in. I've got something to show you."

Harriet followed her to the kitchen where there was a large piece of butcher paper on the floor with marks on it.

"What's this?"

"You know when you build a house, there are things you wish you'd done differently? Now I have the opportunity. This time, I'll make the kitchen big enough to hold a refrigerator and I think I'll enlarge the dining room."

On the way home, Harriet marveled at her mother's ability to bounce back, even in the face of such great loss.

Janie had a little harder time of it, however. The only dress she possessed was the one she wore to the movie that night. It became a joke around campus. People called her "One Dress Edmiston," which didn't please her in the least. When Harriet heard it, she invited Janie to their uncle's store to pick out two more. To have an Edmiston in Nevada with only one dress would *never* do.

Four months after Henry and David had their last discussion about Hitler, Lloyd laid the Kansas City Star on the filling station desk. "Here you go, worrywart."

The headlines read: "NAZIS TAKE REMAINDER OF CZECHOSLOVAKIA."

"Didn't waste any time, did he?" Henry said with a frown.

"You worry too much. There's no way Nazis will pose a threat to us."

Henry tilted his head and said, "Don't put any money on it."

"Roosevelt will keep us out of the mess."

He hoped Lloyd was right but didn't put much stock in his partner's opinion. His fears were confirmed when Germany and Italy joined in a pact called the "Axis Powers" after Italy took over Albania.

The pot was beginning to boil.

Chapter 22

Harriet planned a simple dinner for their second anniversary in September, 1939. She turned on the radio as she mashed potatoes. On the world scene, the news hadn't been good for the past few months. Just two days before, Hitler's armies invaded Poland. This caused France, England, and their allies to band together to declare war on Germany.

Henry came in the back door just as the smooth baritone voice of Edward R. Murrow announced President Roosevelt would host a Fireside Chat in a few minutes.

"What do you suppose it's about?" she said as she spooned the mashed potatoes into a bowl.

Turning up the volume on their Emerson radio, Henry sat to listen. President Roosevelt's familiar voice began:

"My fellow Americans and my friends, tonight my single duty is to speak to the whole of America. Until four-thirty this morning I had hoped against hope that some miracle would prevent a devastating war in Europe and bring to an end the invasion of Poland by Germany."

Harriet's stomach flipped. Surely, the President wasn't going to involve the United States in this mess. She thought of all the young men who would have to go to war. That couldn't happen. She turned her attention back to the radio. As she listened, she tried to read Henry's expression, but he gave no clue as to his thoughts.

The President continued. "Every ship that sails the sea, every battle that is fought does affect the American future."

Tension rippled across her shoulders. Would President Roosevelt yield to the war-monger's voices?

"At this moment there is being prepared a proclamation of American neutrality."

Harriet let out her breath in a great sigh and whispered, "Thank God."

Henry put up his finger to silence her as his attention remained glued to the radio.

"I myself cannot and do not prophesy the course of events abroad. Those wars today affect every American home. It is our national duty to use every effort to keep those wars out of the Americas.

"This nation will remain a neutral nation. I have said not once but many times that I have seen war and that I hate war. I say that again and again."

Harriet saw her husband relax a bit.

The President concluded with, "As long as it remains within my power to prevent, there will be no blackout of peace in the United States."

Harriet gazed into Henry's eyes and took his hand. "Do you think Roosevelt will truly keep us out of the war?"

"I hope the President will keep us at peace—but don't know if he can. Only God knows. Sure glad I got out when I did. My Army buddies, like Hilton, will be in for a rough ride if we do go to war."

During the fall, Glessner borrowed a sewing machine from a neighbor to make curtains for their new house under construction. She also bought some dresses at a second-hand store and made them over to fit Janie for her second year in college. Before winter set in, Pops moved them into Glessner's second new house within twelve months. Harriet took the day off to help them settle their few possessions.

By dusk, neighbors from the surrounding area arrived in twos and threes.

Glessner looked out her kitchen window from the sink. "What do you suppose all this is about?"

"Don't know, Mother. Let's find out."

From the front porch, they noticed each person carried different items.

"What's going on here?" Glessner asked as Harriet slipped her arm around her mother's waist.

"We decided to bring you some things you might need. Guess you might call it a shower of sorts," the closest neighbor said.

Glessner beckoned, "Well, come in and sit a spell."

As the neighbors gathered in the kitchen, Harriet put a pot of coffee on to boil.

One brought a spare mixing bowl. Another gave them hand-tatted sheets. A third had sewed a gingham table cloth—complete with a simple wooden table her husband made to put it on. A fourth brought a blanket.

Tears brimmed as Glessner looked over the gathering. "We are indeed blessed to have such dear friends."

One spoke up, "But you have always been there for us when we had a need. Now we have the opportunity to return the favor."

She whisked away a tear and whispered, "Please know it is greatly appreciated."

As they disappeared into the darkness, Glessner unfolded her new tablecloth, lit a coal oil lamp, and placed it on her new kitchen table.

Harriet took her mother's hand as they stared in silence at the flickering flame.

In October, Henry was surprised to get a letter from his brother Oscar, who had gone to California.

October 14, 1939

Dear Henry,

Sorry I haven't written sooner—but you know I'm not much of a letter writer.

When I got out here, I got a job at Lockheed Aircraft. We're extra busy. Putting on more workers all the time because of the trouble in Europe. Sure hope Roosevelt can keep our dog out of this fight.

I lived for a long time with Al and Sylvia Lauderback who moved from Walker to Culver City. They have a niece, Myrtle. She has a sweet little daughter, Marilyn, who is two. Myrtle and I got married last month.

How are you and Harriet doing? Homer told me you all got married. He's still working for the rice farmer up in Lincoln, California.

We'll try to get back there to see you all sometime. I can't say when. Write when you can.

Love,
Oscar

Henry handed the letter to Harriet. "Here's some news from my wayward brother."

"Sure took him long enough to write. Glad we finally have an address for him." Harriet read the letter as she sipped her coffee.

He waited until she finished it, then said, "Sounds like he has a pretty good job, doesn't it? Bet this job pays more than the bowling alley."

"Looks like the Freeman family tree is growing. Think they'll come soon?"

"Doubt it. I'll believe it when I see him pulling up in front of the house."

Before many days passed Henry made time to reply to his brother.

October 20, 1939
Dear Oscar,

You old rascal! Congratulations on your marriage. We can't wait to meet her and Marilyn.

We were able to bring David from Liberty to live with us. He's doing well in school. He'll graduate next spring.

Can't believe Mother's been gone 6 years.

Things sure don't look good in Europe. From the radio broadcast the other night it sounds like President Roosevelt isn't spoiling for a fight. Hope they get it settled over there soon. Sure doesn't look good.

Lloyd Harrison and I own the filling station in Walker now. Harriet still works at her Uncle Vernon's Department Store. Hope you can come soon.

Love,
Henry

Henry continued to keep a close eye on the unsettled conditions in Europe. One Saturday in early spring, David returned to the filling station after delivering gas to some outlying farms.

When he entered, Henry said, “Come sit a spell. We need to talk about your future.”

“What about my future?”

“I think you should go to college.”

David sat forward. “College? I hadn’t really thought about college.”

“I have. I want you to get more education than I did. Besides, if this mess in Europe heats up anymore you’d be a likely candidate for service. If you’re in college you might not have to go.”

“I doubt we’ll go to war. Leastwise not as long as long as Roosevelt is President. I appreciate the offer, Henry, but we can’t afford it.”

“Well, Fort Scott has a two-year junior college. Residents can go there for free.”

“Where would I live? That alone would cost a lot.”

Henry hesitated while he placed his newspaper on the desk. “I went over there the other day and took the mail carriers exam.”

“What did you do that for? You got an ache to carry the mail like Dad?”

“I might sell the filling station to Lloyd if I could get on at the post office. Then the three of us could move over there. Then you could get a college education. What about it?”

He sat silent studying his shoes. “It’s a lot to think about, for sure.”

“Well, we don’t have to decide today. There're lots of hurdles to jump. I may not pass the exam and Lloyd may not want to buy the station. I haven’t asked Harriet if she wants to quit her job, either. Guess she could drive to Nevada every day to work if she wanted.”

“That’s twenty miles from Fort Scott. You better think about this some more.”

“Okay, little brother. I will if you will.”

Chapter 23

After they went to bed, Henry told Harriet about his plan to be a postman and the discussion he and David had earlier. After he laid out his thoughts, he waited for Harriet's response.

Silence.

"Well, what do you think?" He finally ventured.

"I'll need some time. It's a lot to digest all at once. Are you sure you want to be a mailman? I hadn't considered a move since you mentioned it a while back."

"Don't you want him to go to college?"

"I do, but—well, I love my job. Not sure I want to leave it. Twenty miles is a long way to drive to Nevada from Fort Scott every day." Harriet rolled away from him and drew the covers around her neck.

Henry spent the next couple of hours wondering if his idea was crazy since no one seemed excited about it. Finally, he took a deep breath. If it was to be, all the loose ends would have to fall in place. At least he had time for it to happen.

At lunch the next day, Harriet mentioned Henry's idea to Aunt Merrie as they sat together in the alteration room.

"I don't want David to miss out on more education. Guess I could drive from Fort Scott every day."

At that moment, Uncle Vernon breezed in the door with a pair of pants marked with tailor's chalk over his arm. "Did I hear something about Fort Scott?"

Harriet wished she had kept her lip zipped. She wasn't ready to share this news with anyone but Aunt Merrie.

"Did you say you were going to drive from Fort Scott to work? Are you and Henry moving?"

"No. Well. I don't know. It was just something Henry mentioned. Nothing's been decided."

"Wouldn't want to lose my best sales girl." Uncle Vernon smiled and turned to Aunt Merrie. "You need to hem these pants right away. The customer is waiting. He says he has to have them for his wedding."

Aunt Merrie laid her sandwich on her lunch sack and wiped her hands on a small towel. "When is the wedding?"

"Two o'clock today."

She shook her head. "So much for planning ahead." Merrie laid the pants on the ironing board and plugged in the iron.

Harriet waited until Uncle Vernon left, then said, "Aunt Merrie, keep this under your hat for a while. We're not making any decisions yet. Just tossing around a few ideas."

She nodded as she drew out her scissors from her apron pocket.

"I understand."

When Harriet headed out the door after work a few days later, Uncle Vernon called to her. "Stick around a minute. I want to talk to you before you leave."

Harriet wished she had chosen to go out the back door instead. She didn't like confrontations, especially with Uncle Vernon. Everything was usually his way or else—no matter the subject.

He directed her to the stock room. "Have you decided about moving to Fort Scott?"

"No. We've not discussed it any further. Why?"

"Well, for the past six months I've been working on an idea to open a store there. I need a manager and a storefront somewhere on Main Street. I'm meeting with the owner of a building tomorrow. You could be my main saleswoman for the lady's department if you and Henry moved there."

Harriet was speechless. She didn't want to tell him about Henry's thought of selling the filling station or his possible job change. She wasn't even sure if Lloyd knew of Henry's plan—if indeed it was a plan.

She managed to nod and mumble, "I'll talk to Henry about it."

At supper, Harriet hardly ate. As Henry took his last spoonful of tomato soup he glanced up and scowled. "You all right? Why aren't you eating?"

David looked from one to the other.

Harriet stirred her soup. "I'm fine. David, do you want another grilled cheese?"

"No. I'm good, thanks. Is it all right if I go play basketball at the high school tonight?"

"Sure. Be back by ten," Henry said as he continued to eye his wife.

As the door clicked behind his brother, Henry laid his hand on Harriet's arm. "Okay, what's with the silence?"

Harriet felt the sting of tears. She spilled out the conversation with Vernon and his idea for a new store in Fort Scott—and his plans for her.

"And that's why you're upset?" Henry put his arm around her shoulder.

"Yes. I don't like change. After eight years, I know just about everyone who comes in the store in Nevada. I'd have to learn all new people."

"But wouldn't you like to find a house with an indoor bathroom? We might even rent one with a gas stove instead of a wood one. Wouldn't that be nice?"

Harriet nodded as she cast a disparaging glance at the wretched wood stove.

He continued. "I'm sure we could find something to fit the bill."

"But we're close to the folks here."

"Well, it's not like we'd be moving to the moon. We could still come over for Sunday dinners, just like always."

"Thirty miles seems like a long way to me just to come for a visit."

"I'll bet we could even find a two-bedroom place so David could have a bed instead of the couch."

"Perhaps. Guess it would beat driving the ten miles from Walker into Nevada every day."

"That's right. Oh, and I heard from the post office in Fort Scott. They have a route coming up. Maybe this is the way we're to go. Looks like the doors are opening, don't you think?"

"But what about the filling station? And David? He won't graduate until May."

"I spoke to Lloyd today. He's willing to buy me out. What do you think? We wouldn't have to move till after graduation."

Harriet took a deep breath. "Let me get used to this idea."

"Okay. But I have to let the post office know soon. Don't want the route to get away."

Chapter 24

David wasn't too excited when Henry talked to him again about the move.

"What's the problem?" Henry said. He set two cups of coffee on the kitchen table.

"I want to be out on my own. Don't get me wrong. It's not like I don't appreciate all you and Harriet have done for me. It's just, well, it's time for me to stand on my own two feet."

"What does that mean to you?" Henry took a seat.

David reached for his cup of coffee, leaned against the counter, and took a sip. "I've been thinking of going out to California. Maybe I could get on with Oscar at the airplane factory. He said they're hiring."

Henry took a hard look at his little brother. His life had been a series of moves. First from Walker to Denver when he was six. Then the death of their father, months before the stock market crashed. When he was seven they moved back to Walker with their widowed mother. When he was barely eleven, he moved to the orphanage—then back to Walker to live with them.

Scraping some crumbs off the table Henry said, "I really hoped you would get more education before you set out on your own."

"What more do I need? I learned about radios and plumbing and woodworking at the orphanage. I could earn a living at any of those three." He planted his hands on the table and leaned in. "Henry, I don't want you to upend your life and move to Fort Scott because of me."

"Well, it looks like we'll be moving anyway since Harriet's job has opened up."

"But what about you? I don't want you to sell the station. You've worked so hard to make it go." David shoved his hands in his pockets.

Henry dumped the crumbs into the trash. "I have, but I feel like it's time to move on."

"We can both agree on the moving on part. But I feel my place is in California, not Kansas."

Maybe David had farther to go than Henry thought. Perhaps it was time to let the young bird fly. Henry sighed. "Okay, little brother. It's your choice. Just know our door's always open to you if you ever want to come back."

David's toothy grin spread across his face. "Thanks for understanding. And thanks for all you've done for me. I do appreciate it."

Henry felt like a father watching his son launch into a new chapter. What would the future hold for them both?

In Walker, life shifted into a flurry of activity unimagined months before. David graduated high school in Walker as planned in the class of 1940. The next day, Henry and Harriet put him on the bus for California.

On the world front in May, the word wasn't good from Europe. Hitler's armies invaded France and five days later the Netherlands surrendered to Germany.

By June, Italy entered the war siding with Germany, and France fell to the German forces.

Henry sold his interest in the filling station to Lloyd. The Freeman family found a small bungalow on National Avenue in Fort Scott and moved in before the end of July 1940. It even had an indoor toilet—and a gas stove. Although Henry expected to become a mail carrier, his best-laid plan went awry when the postmaster gave the position to another.

Uncle Vernon took advantage of the opportunity. He offered them a chance to purchase stock in the new Fort Scott store and appointed Henry as the manager. What Henry didn't know about the retail clothing business, he learned quickly from Harriet. The store opened before fall and was off to a good start.

More storm clouds appeared on the horizon when Japan joined the Axis Powers in late September 1940. Before two months passed, Hungary, Romania, and Slovakia fell in lock-step with the Nazis.

Congress passed a bill shortly thereafter requiring all men from 21 to 45 to register for the draft. If their name was chosen in a lottery, they would have to serve one year—not something Henry would ever choose to do again. He was relieved to discover he was classed 4-A because of his prior military service, which made him an unlikely candidate to be drafted.

Unlike his brothers, David wrote more frequently.

October 30, 1940

Dear Henry and Harriet,

I've been able to get on at Lockheed Aircraft with Oscar. We're building Hudson bombers for the Royal Air Force. The way the Brits are going through planes, they must be in a heck of a fight with Germany. We're slapping them together as fast as we can.

Doesn't look like things are any better since Germany took over northern France. I wonder who else will fall to them before Hitler is satisfied.

Hey, that's swell you're a 4-A. Doubt they'll ever get around to taking someone as old as you, though. Some of the guys at work who are 21 and older have received their letter from the Selective Service Agency to report for duty. If they pass the physical and don't get a deferment they'll have to go into the service for two years now instead of one.

Those guys in Washington must not think Great Britain is going to be able to whip the Germans. Maybe that's why they're drafting guys even in peacetime. Doubt we'll be able to stay out of this war. It's the talk around here anyway. Is it the same there? Glad I'm not 21 yet!

Hope you all are doing well.

David

Henry rubbed the back of his neck as he laid the letter on the kitchen counter.

Looking up from the stove, Harriet asked, “Bad news?”

“Yes and no. David’s working at Lockheed with Oscar.”

She turned down the burner under the fried potatoes and slipped her arms around Henry’s waist. “And the bad news?”

“Looks more and more like we’re going to get sucked into this war, regardless what Roosevelt says. David says some of the guys at his work are being drafted.”

Harriet rested her head on her husband’s chest and said a silent prayer those predictions wouldn’t happen.

During the Christmas holidays in 1940, there was little time to dwell on those thoughts. Business boomed at the Fort Scott store. Henry took advantage of the better times and bought a new two-door Chevy. It was a great improvement over their 1930 Model A.

By March 1941 Henry’s apprehensions grew deeper when Bulgaria joined the Axis Powers.

Chapter 25

In April, 1941, David wrote he would like to come home for Memorial Day the end of May. Henry was delighted. Perhaps he would stay and decide to attend classes at the junior college.

Harriet planned a party for him with some of the college students. "Perhaps then he will decide Kansas is better than California."

Henry responded, "Swell idea. Hope it works."

When David stepped from the bus, Henry was surprised at his tan—and look of maturity. How could a year change a person so?

The planned party proved to be a great success. David took particular interest in Lucilee, one of the very beautiful students from the college. They discovered they had a common interest in music. She played the piano and violin.

Over the next week, they spent all their spare time together.

Henry confided in Harriet one evening, "From what I see, I think David might be falling for her. Perhaps your plan succeeded."

"I hope so. Lucilee would make a lovely sister-in-law. Guess time will tell."

"He's getting serious earlier than I did, for sure."

Harriet eyed him. "Well, not much. What were you when we finally *saw* one another? Twenty-three?"

He cleared his throat. "Yes. But that was different."

A sly smile crept onto Harriet's lips.

The next morning at breakfast, David said, "Can you drop me at the bus station this evening? If not, I can walk."

With her spoonful of oatmeal in mid-air, Harriet said, "Oh. I thought you might stay awhile longer."

"I'd love to, but I need to get back or I'll lose my job."

With a raised eyebrow Henry said, "No chance you might stay and go to junior college? I'm sure Lucilee wouldn't mind if you did."

David wiped his mouth, grinned, and shoved back from the table. "I wouldn't mind it either if that's all that was at stake. But I need to keep my job. Pays more than anything around here."

As quickly as he came, he was gone again. They heard by the grapevine, Lucilee received very regular letters from him.

In the fall, they learned several young men in Fort Scott received draft notices. The *Kansas City Star* and *Times* ran articles of the war with alarming regularity. Reports of Japan's increasing aggression were disturbing as well as the news from Europe.

After all, even if the U.S. did get sucked into the war, Henry had already served his military obligation. The one they had to worry about was David. He would for sure be called up for service at his age.

Harriet wished they didn't take newspapers. It was easier to stick her head in the sand if she wasn't confronted with daily reports on the world front. Hopefully, Roosevelt would find a way to avoid war like he said. After all, with his guidance they had made it through the roughest days of the Depression. Surely he wouldn't fail them now.

Henry tried to talk about having a child a couple of times, but Harriet made some excuse to put him off yet again. In her words, "There will be plenty of time in the future for children."

He didn't understand his wife's reluctance. After all, they had both come from families with several children. Anytime her mother mentioned grandchildren, Harriet changed the subject, now that he thought about it.

At first he was grateful they hadn't added a baby to the mix when they were in the small house in Walker. Now, they had the room and the finances.

Perhaps she didn't want children at all. He tried to remember any discussion in which she said anything like that, but didn't recall any. Still, they *had* been married over three years. He whispered, "Oh God. Help her change her mind if my suspicions are true!"

In the late fall when Henry got home from the store, Harriet said, "The mail is on the kitchen table. Looks like we got a letter from Oscar."

He read it and laid it on his chairside table in the living room without a word. Harriet wondered at the contents and waited until Henry had gone to bed before she dared read it.

November 15, 1941

Dear Henry and Harriet,

Wanted you to hear the news from us before you heard it elsewhere. We're having a baby in May. Hope it's a boy! Marilyn is excited about having a brother or sister.

David is still living with us. He's a great help to have around. He reworked the bathroom plumbing last week. Would have cost me a bundle to have a plumber do what he did.

We're really busy at work. News from Japan sure doesn't sound good. Europe either, for that matter. Some of the guys at work have been called up, even though our boss tried to get them a deferment. I don't think we're prepared for any kind of war here in the States, if worse comes to worse. From an article I read the other day, sounds like our Navy is really lacking. The shipyards can't crank out a ship as quick as we spit out those planes. England is keeping us busy with orders for more all the time.

Love,
Oscar

Harriet knew this would cause another discussion. After all, Henry was the oldest. Now his younger brother would have the first blood grandchild in the next generation of the Freeman family.

When she tried to imagine their home with a screaming baby, she shuddered. That would mean she'd have to stay home from work. Of course, not all babies were like her younger sister, Janie, but they *could* be. How would she get out of this?

Leaving the letter on the table, she decided not to bring the subject up until Henry said something. A couple of days later, the letter disappeared.

"Did you see Oscar's letter?"

Harriet glanced up from her mending. "I think I saw it beside your chair when I dusted the other day. Is it missing?"

"No. I filed it." Henry disappeared behind the pages of the *Kansas City Star*. Silence lingered like a heavy fog.

She broke the impasse with, "What would you like for dinner tomorrow night?"

With a flat tone, Henry said, "Whatever you fix is fine."

Harriet went to the kitchen. Another round down. Sometime she was going to have to yield but hoped it would be at least a couple more years—if she could put him off that long. Maybe she could hire a nanny. That might work—if Henry would agree to it.

She finally had to admit the real problem was labor. Those memories of her mother bearing Janie in the bedroom, made her stomach roll. She remembered as a seven-year-old vowing to avoid this part of life if at all possible. Harriet wondered how Henry's mother had managed to face labor six times.

Chapter 26

The first Sunday of December 1941, Harriet picked up the last dish from the Sunday dinner table. She carried it into her mother's kitchen while Henry and Pops headed for the living room. Pops turned on the radio to hear "The World Today" on the CBS network.

The announcer's words caught them off guard. "We interrupt this program to bring you a special news bulletin. President Roosevelt just announced the Japanese have attacked Pearl Harbor, Hawaii by air."

Henry called out, "Mom! Harriet! Get in here quick. Don't know if this is another 'War of the Worlds' prank or the real thing!"

The women rushed into the living room to hear the broadcast in progress. They gazed from one face to another in disbelief at the reports about the attack by the Japanese.

"Where is Pearl Harbor, anyway?" Glessner asked.

"In Hawaii—out there in the Pacific somewhere," Henry said.

Harriet sank into a chair and whispered, "Oh, no!"

"What do you think the President will do?" Pops asked.

Henry stood with his hands on his waist. "Not much he can do, now. This means war."

Their usual Sunday afternoon activity ceased as they waited for any more news bulletins into the evening. Finally, Harriet and Henry left for the silent thirty-mile drive home.

All Harriet's hopes seemed dashed for a peaceful resolution. War threats seemed to pop up like a relentless smallpox epidemic.

By the time they got into bed, she asked Henry, "Do you think the Japanese will invade us?"

"I hope not," he said.

His response left little comfort for a restful night's sleep.

The next morning, Henry carried his Emerson Strad radio to work so they could listen. By eleven o'clock, the announcer said they would carry President Roosevelt's address to the joint session of Congress from the House of Representatives within the hour.

Employees and customers alike gathered around the radio to hear the President say, "Yesterday, December 7, 1941-a date which will live in infamy-the United States of America was suddenly and deliberately attacked by naval and air forces of the Empire of Japan."

He went on to say the attack had been planned for days or even weeks. He added the Japanese government deliberately sought to deceive the United States by false statements and expressions of hope for continued peace.

A murmur of fear went through those gathered around the radio when he told the people additional American ships had been reported torpedoed on the high seas between San Francisco and Honolulu. Silence fell as he went on to tell of attacks in various places the night before including Manila, Hong Kong, Guam, and the Philippine Islands with an early morning attack on Midway Island.

One woman whispered, "Are we next?"

Someone shushed her as the President concluded his short speech with, "There is no blinking at the fact that our people, our territory, and our interests are in grave danger. With confidence in our armed forces, with the unbounded determination of our people, we will gain the inevitable triumph—so help us God."

He then asked Congress to declare war on the Japanese Empire.

Before the afternoon was out, Congress granted his request. What they had feared for many months was upon them.

Within the week, young men from all walks of life showed up at recruiting centers to volunteer for the Army, Navy, and Marine Corps.

In the next couple of days, Harriet noticed every customer who entered the store, what few there were, seemed to have an anxiousness about them. If they looked at dresses or hats, most only tried them on without a purchase. They were more eager to talk about the President's speech and speculate what he would do next. Each day brought more rumors—most of them unfounded but they added to the fear.

On December 11, a customer entered as soon as Harriet unlocked the front door.

"Have you heard the news, Mrs. Freeman?"

Harriet shook her head. "What news?"

"Germany and Italy declared war on the United States a little while ago! Now we're not only going to fight the Japs but the Germans and Italians, too."

She stepped back. "Are you sure? Where did you get this information?"

"It's on the radio. I heard it with my own ears."

Soon every person who entered had the same report.

Before the day was out, the United States declared war on Germany and Italy. The fight was on.

As she made dinner that Thursday night, Henry came in the door with a handful of flowers and held them out to her. "Happy birthday, sweetheart."

Harriet blinked back tears. "Oh, Henry. You remembered."

"I never forget, do I?"

"No, but I didn't think you would remember with all the bad news today."

He put his arms around her in a tight hug as she sobbed. "It's going to be all right. We'll get through this."

"Oh, honey, you sound just like my mother."

He reached for his handkerchief in his back pocket and dabbed at her eyes. "Dry those tears. Crying isn't going to help." He planted a kiss on her forehead.

Taking a raggedy breath, she said, "This is definitely a birthday I'll not forget—ever—as long as I live."

"Well, it does make for a memorable twenty-eighth birthday, for sure. Better put your flowers in some water before they wilt."

As she did the dishes that night, she admired her flowers and pondered the state of things. Two world wars in her lifetime. What were things coming to? Hopefully, this plague wouldn't reach U.S. soil.

The next evening as Henry read the paper he let a swear word slip.

Harriet exclaimed, "Henry! What on earth brought that on?"

"Hitler is really something. He told the Reichstag the reason they had to declare war on us was because of the failure of Roosevelt's New Deal supported by rich people and Jews. Can you believe that?

"He goes on to say about Roosevelt, and I quote, 'First he incites war, then falsifies the causes, then odiously wraps himself in a cloak of Christian hypocrisy and slowly but surely leads mankind to war.' It says here that when the Reichstag heard this statement they leapt to their feet in thunderous applause."

He folded the paper and slammed it on his chair-side table. "That old snake. Talk about the pot calling the kettle black. That's exactly what *he's* done. Is his legislature blind? Why can't they see what he's doing? Why aren't there any dissenting voices? This can't be happening!"

Harriet sighed. "You're right. The whole world has gone nutty. I wonder where it will all end?"

He rose from his chair and stared out the window into the inky night and murmured, "I wonder if anything will ever be right again."

No matter how everyone tried, Christmas held little joy. Henry heard of many young men receiving their draft notices who had not yet volunteered.

A surprise awaited those already in the service who had expected their commitment to be short term. They learned their time of service would be extended until the end of the war—plus six months—whenever that might be.

Harriet asked, "Do you think they will ever call older men?"

He quickly responded, "I really doubt it. With my three years of service, they'd have to be pretty desperate to call up a thirty-one-year-old with a wife."

His words echoed in her ears over the next few days. What if he was wrong? What if they *did* get that desperate? What if they *did* call men who'd already served? Those questions hounded her like a hungry fox, day and night.

In January of 1942, Henry received a letter from his old partner, Lloyd.

> Dear Henry,
>
> Betty Brown and I got married last month. Remember her? I dated her in high school." When we came home from our weekend honeymoon in Kansas City my draft notice was in the mail. Guess you were right in your suspicions about that old devil, Hitler. Uncle Sam doesn't waste any time when he says, 'I want you' does he? I've had to sell the filling station.
>
> We've heard rumors our outfit will be headed somewhere overseas after basic training.
>
> Regards,
> Lloyd

Henry folded the letter and didn't mention it to Harriet. That would start another firestorm, for sure. How long would it be before one of those notices appeared in his mailbox?

Chapter 27

By late January 1942, the war took on a new reality when one of the employees told Harriet her son was one of the first U. S. soldiers to be shipped to Great Britain.

When Harriet awoke early the next morning, her mind filled with fear of Henry being drafted. Cold sweat covered her body. Suddenly, she knew what she had to do. It was time for a baby. Her resistance to Henry's pleas made him more vulnerable to a possible draft.

How could she have been so blind? She remembered how Henry hated being under a Sergeant's orders night and day. By her resistance, he could end up in the South Pacific facing Japanese soldiers or on some battlefield in Europe. God forbid!

All day she wrestled with her decision. On her lunch break in the back room between bites of bologna sandwich, she rehearsed the words she might use to tell Henry of her decision.

At supper, Henry said, "You're awfully quiet tonight. Something wrong?"

She rested her forkful of spaghetti on the plate. "I've made a decision."

"About what?" he said as he buttered a piece of bread.

"We need to have a baby. It's time."

Henry nearly dropped his knife. "What brought this on?"

She cleared her throat. "I'm not getting any younger. Besides, Mother keeps asking me when we're going to give her grandchildren. She keeps reminding me what a wonderful father you'd be."

"There must be more to it than that. She's been feeding you that line since before we got married."

Harriet ran out of words. Tears welled.

He took her hand. "Are you sure about this? You seemed so against the idea."

"I don't want you to have to go to war. I don't know what I'd do if—if you weren't here."

"And that's why you're upset?" He gathered her in his arms. A happy little smile tickled the corners of his mouth. "When do you think this might happen?"

She snuggled into his embrace. "The sooner the better. Before I change my mind."

Easter Sunday Harriet rushed to fix breakfast so she'd have extra time to make sure her new suit had the correct accessories before they left for church. As the bacon sizzled, the aroma caused her to gag. Barely making it to the bathroom, she called for Henry.

"What's wrong? Are you sick? Can I get you something?"

Harriet grabbed a wash cloth, bathing her face in cool water. "No, I think you've already given me something, thank you."

With a puzzled look he said, "Uh, what did I give you?"

She blinked back tears. "A baby."

His face was a quick study in expression. First, jaw-dropping shock, then spreading joy, with a shout of "Hallelujah!" He grabbed her and swung her around the bathroom, almost tripping over the toilet. Before another whirl, she broke away from his embrace, retching again.

He finished making himself breakfast while she rested in bed. The Freemans were absent from their usual place in church that Easter Sunday.

By late morning, Harriet felt she could get dressed so they headed to Walker for their usual Sunday dinner with her folks.

On the way, she took out her compact, pinched her cheeks, and said, "Do I look all right?"

"You look just fine," he said with a grin.

The minute they entered, Glessner took one look at her daughter and said, "Are you ill?"

Glancing away she said, "No. What makes you say that?"

"Well, from the looks of you, you're either sick or in a family way."

Harriet's bottom lip quivered. "Do I look that bad?"

Glessner smiled. "No. Not bad. Just—pregnant. Guess you better get to work knitting some of those wool soakers. Babies tend to leak, you know."

Knitting anything seemed beyond her abilities at the moment. She did however make a mental note to work on her makeup so others wouldn't guess until she started to show—if her mother could keep a secret that long.

Henry watched his wife with empathy as, each morning, she made at least one trip to the bathroom to empty her stomach. How could a tiny baby make someone so sick?

Perhaps something was wrong. He didn't remember his mother being sick like this—but then again, he wasn't as tuned into his mother's pregnancies as he was his wife's.

The middle of April, he received word from his brother about their new baby—a boy. Born March 13. They called him Jerry. Immediately, he wrote back to congratulate them and scribbled a p.s. on the bottom of the letter which read:

We're expecting the end of November.

He hoped Harriet didn't mind his postscript. She had been very careful not to tell anyone in town. He didn't know how long she intended to keep the secret. Then again, she *was* very slender. That wasn't a surprise since she ate very little and never before noon.

How she managed to go to work every morning was beyond his understanding, but then as much as she enjoyed the store, he doubted a stampede of buffalos could keep her away.

Henry kept a close eye on the progress of the war but avoided making comments about it aloud because it seemed to upset Harriet so.

There were certain things you couldn't ignore like the day Henry went to buy a new tire for the car in June.

"Sorry young fella," the mechanic told him at the shop. "You'll have to get you a bunch of those ration stamps now before you can buy a tire. Government's clampin' down on rubber for the war effort. Japs captured our source of rubber in Southeast Asia."

Henry drove without a spare for three months before he could get enough ration stamps to buy one.

The Germans began a drive toward Stalingrad, Russia, by early July. More young men were being called by the lottery. How long would this mess continue? Thank goodness David was still under twenty-one. Maybe the war would be over by next year when he'd be old enough for the draft.

The next week he saw Lucilee at the front counter in the store.

"Have you heard from David?"

With a shy smile, she cleared her throat. "Oh yes. He writes almost every day. He told me of your news."

Henry gave a quick glance to see if Harriet was in earshot. "Shh. It's not common knowledge yet. Should be soon, though."

"My lips are sealed."

"Tell him I said hello."

"Will do," she said as she headed for the door with her package.

That night he took a hard look at Harriet as she got ready for bed. "Shouldn't you be showing more?" Even in her nightgown she was hardly out of shape.

"Oh, it will come soon enough."

"How much weight have you gained?"

Harriet tried to change the subject.

He repeated his question.

She squared her shoulders and lifted her head. "Nothing yet."

"What does the doctor say?"

"He tells me to eat more, but I'm not hungry."

"When are you going to tell people about the baby?"

"When I have to, I guess."

He'd have to make a point to see she ate more. He hoped she would tell about the baby soon—before word got out otherwise.

By early September, Harriet could hide her secret no longer. Henry thought she seemed both excited and embarrassed when someone mentioned it. Whenever he questioned her about her weight she brushed it off referring to him as a worry wart or a mother hen.

As the weeks wore on, Harriet seemed to be more irritated.

"Are you all right? You like kinda pale," Henry asked one morning at the breakfast table.

Harriet straightened and ran her hand along her back at the waist. "Well, I—I seem to have a pain in my back. Probably nothing."

"You need to have it checked out. Better call Doc Wilkening for an appointment."

"It'll probably go away. You worry too much."

Henry reached for her hand. "Promise me you'll call today. Okay?"

"Oh, all right. If you insist."

That afternoon Harriet got an appointment and walked to the doctor's office around the corner from the store. An hour later she called Henry from the doctor's office. "Can you come pick me up? Doc says I need to go to the hospital right away. I have a kidney infection."

"Be right there."

Henry had never remembered her missing a day of work. "This must be bad," he whispered as he pulled up in front of the doctor's office.

The infection kept her in the hospital for a week.

The second week she was able to go home but was still confined to bed. He called Glessner to come stay a few days. Some of her mother's good chicken soup and tender care might just do the trick.

After a few days, Harriet was able to be up. At the end of the week, she was dressed when Henry came home, much to his relief.

At the doctor's suggestion, she limited her work to a few hours a day during early November. By evening, she was ready for bed when she got home.

How would this play out when birthing day came? Henry redoubled his prayers for his wife and soon-coming child.

Chapter 28

After work in mid-November, Henry sat at the kitchen table reading the *Kansas City Star*. Harriet peeled potatoes.

"Uh oh. Wonder how long it will be before David gets a knock on the door from Uncle Sam."

"What are you talking about?"

"Says here that President Roosevelt issued an executive order lowering the draft age from 21 to 18."

Harriet wiped her hands on her apron and rushed to look over Henry's shoulder. "Are you sure?"

"Says right here. See?"

She squinted at the page and sighed. "Oh dear. Maybe he can get a deferment."

"Don't know. Doesn't work for most guys. Now if he was in school, it might be a different story."

"But he's not. Let it go."

Henry knew by her short retort she was worried too. He guessed he better back off. He didn't want to upset her even more.

The same week Henry received another letter from his old partner, Lloyd. From his mention of sandy desert, he surmised Lloyd was fighting somewhere in North Africa at the moment. He also mentioned he had been trained as a medic.

The next day Lucilee came in the store to look at dresses.

"What exactly are you looking for?"

Lucilee smiled and said, "Nothing too fancy. I'm looking for a dress to wear to California."

Harriet turned from the rack. "California? Wouldn't be going for a visit to a certain young man, would you?"

Lucilee took a deep breath, then said, "I'm going out to marry him in a few days."

With a raised eyebrow Harriet said, "Oh really? We hadn't heard about this. Congratulations."

"He called last night and we made the decision. What with the President changing the draft age, we decided not to wait any longer. Dad wants me to stay here, but I just can't. I need to be with David."

Harriet hugged her future sister-in-law. "Welcome to the family. We wish you well."

"Thanks."

Lucilee chose a dress and held it up as she looked in the nearby mirror. "I think I'll try this one on."

As soon as David's fiancée made her selection and left, Harriet took a few minutes to digest the news. She didn't know Lucilee well, but what she did know of her, caused her joy. When Harriet had watched Lucilee and David together, they seemed to be a very compatible couple.

Soon she and Henry would have a new sister-in-law. Hopefully, the couple weren't too young. The Freeman family tree was growing, in spite of the trials of the past.

As soon as Henry finished marking a suit for alteration in the men's department, Harriet told him the news.

"Hmmm. I wondered if a marriage might be in the works when I read that news in the paper last night. Hope he can stay out of the service, or at least not be sent overseas. I'd hate for him to have to leave his bride."

A few days later they received a letter from David.

November 14, 1942

Dear Henry and Harriet,

Just wanted you to know the news. After much prayer, I've asked Lucilee to come to California to be my bride. I know we're young, but I don't see much use in waiting any longer. Everything's so uncertain in these times. Like my supervisor says, "Life is short. Grab it while you can."

Hope all is well with Harriet and the baby. Let us know when it's here.

Monday nights were reserved for dressing the windows with fresh merchandise. With four display windows, it usually took all evening.

Near five, Henry said, "Honey, why don't you pick out the things you want for the displays and I'll drive you home. I can come back and finish while you rest. You look pretty tired."

A light snow fell as they drove home. He glanced at Harriet as the illumination from the streetlights flashed across her thin frame. Even though she was full term, she still had a tiny belly—not like his mother looked when she was about to have another. But then again, his mother outweighed his wife considerably.

He directed her to sit while he rustled some eggs, bacon, and toast for their dinner.

"Honey, I think I'll just go lie down instead of eating supper. I feel awfully tired."

"You need to eat."

She called over her shoulder as she headed for the bedroom, "I need to rest more than I need food."

"Suit yourself." Henry ate quickly, pulled a blanket over her, and kissed her forehead before he left. "Rest well, my dear."

After he had three of the four windows finished, the phone rang at the front desk.

It was Harriet. Her voice sounded strangely far away.

"I think you better come home and take me to the hospital. It's time."

"But you're not due for a few days yet."

"I don't think anyone told the baby that."

"Okay. I'll be there as soon as I finish this last window."

She moaned. “I think you better come now. Better call Doc Wilkening, too.”

“Okay. Be right there.” Henry looked at the unfinished window with naked manikins, detached arms littering the floor He muttered to himself. “Guess I’ll just have to finish this later.”

He made a quick call to the doctor’s home.

No answer.

He called the hospital and told them they were on the way.

“Who is your doctor?”

“Wilkening.”

“Oh dear. We’ll have to give him a call. He left for Thanksgiving at his daughter’s in Kansas City this morning. Perhaps he can catch the last train to Fort Scott tonight.”

He’d not tell that bit of news to the mother-to-be. No need for more tension. He grabbed his hat and coat, locked the door of the store, and glanced at the naked manikins as he started the car.

Chapter 29

Doctor Wilkening did indeed catch the last train and arrived by one a.m., two days before Thanksgiving. By four, he met Henry in the hall as he took off his mask.

"Congratulations, Mr. Freeman. You have a tiny little girl. Five pounds, twelve ounces."

Henry beamed as he grabbed the doctor's hand for a shake. "Thanks, Doc. Is Harriet all right?"

"It was touch and go there for a while. We had to take the baby with forceps. Your wife was very weak from that kidney infection. It's going to take her some time to recover. She could use some help when she gets home. But that won't be for a couple of weeks or so."

"I'll call her mother to come. Can I see her?"

"You can go look at her, but I doubt she'll know you're here. We're going to keep her sedated for a couple of days. Want to see your girl?"

Henry nodded.

The doctor motioned him to the nursery room door. "I need to warn you, the baby's head is quite bruised because of the forceps, but I think she'll be all right." Through the window, he pointed to a nurse tending to a very skinny howling baby.

Chuckling, Doc said, "Guess she's announcing her arrival with gusto. What she lacked in weight she made up for in length. Twenty-one inches."

Henry's heart felt as if it would burst.

"What's her name?" the doctor asked.

"Well, since we got a girl, it's Sally Margaret—after both her grandmothers' middle names. May I see my wife now?"

"Certainly. Follow me."

Henry crept into the room lit only by a dim goose-neck light on the gray metal nightstand. "Harriet?"

Her eyes fluttered open. She ran her hand down her torso. "Baby gone yet?"

"Yes. It's a girl," he said as he squeezed her hand and kissed her forehead.

A slight smile passed her lips before her head lolled to the side. He walked back to the door of the nursery alone and watched the tightly wrapped bundle until morning light crept across the hospital hallway.

Taking one more peek at his wife, he left the hospital to go home and change clothes. He put in a call to Glessner and Pops to tell them of their new granddaughter. He was sure the Walker operator heard every word of the conversation from her living room switchboard—as was her custom. Nothing was ever a secret if it went through the telephone lines in that little town.

He headed for work early so he could get the naked manikins dressed before the store opened.

True to Doctor Wilkening's words, Harriet didn't awaken enough to track mentally for a couple of days. Glessner and Pops brought Thanksgiving dinner to Fort Scott that Thursday and were permitted to peek at their new granddaughter through the nursery room door.

The next Monday evening Henry picked out the mail from the box and thumbed through it while he ate some leftover turkey hash before heading to the hospital. One letter was from the Selective Service Agency. He tore it open. Inside was a card on which was written:

> Notice of Reclassification
>
> Henry Sanford Freeman has been reclassified from 4-A to 1-A.

It was signed by the local draft board member and postmarked on November 25, 1942.

Henry whispered, "My God. The day after Sally was born! Wonder how long it will be before they call me up? How Harriet will take this?"

When he visited her after supper, he said nothing of the draft notice.

Two weeks later when the doctor made his evening rounds he said to Henry, "You can take your family home tomorrow—*if* you have arranged for temporary help. She's still very weak."

Henry grinned from ear to ear. "Yes, sir. I'll be here bright and early."

The next morning, he arrived before breakfast. While Harriet ate, Henry went to the business office. He paid the $75.00 bill in full with a fist full of two-dollar bills he had saved for the occasion.

The next week Harriet found the letter from the Draft Board in a stack of old mail. She opened it and gasped.

That evening at supper she said, "What did that letter mean from the Draft Board?"

Knowing the jig was up, he wiped his mouth with a napkin and cleared his throat as he glanced at her. "Well, I guess I'm no longer 4-A. They've reclassified me. If they draw my name in the lottery, I'll have to go back to the service."

"And when were you planning on telling me this?"

"I got it when you were in the hospital. I wanted you to get back on your feet before . . ."

Harriet's voice rose to a wail. "How can they do this? You've already given them three years of your life! What are you supposed to do—walk away from the store? Who will run it if you're gone?"

He shoved back from the table. In a quiet tone he said, "I don't think they care about the store, sweetheart. They just want warm bodies."

With wide eyes she said, "Is there no way to get a deferment?"

"I doubt it. If we make waves, it may draw attention to me. Just let it drop. Maybe they won't pick my name."

Silent tears answered his remark. Sally began to cry.

Near Christmas Henry noticed an article in the *Kansas City Times* as he ate his cereal at the breakfast table.

It read, "British Foreign Secretary Eden tells the British House of Commons of mass executions of Jews by Nazis. U.S. declares the crimes will be avenged."

Those words made his stomach roll. Was this report real? Surely not. If it was true, that must have been why Hitler didn't want Jews to have guns or knives. Those poor souls were left with no defense. Why did Hitler hate the Jews so? He surely must be a madman. Henry took the paper to work so Harriet wouldn't see it. He didn't want to set her off. She seemed overly emotional since the baby's birth. Perhaps she needed more rest.

The bruises on Sally's head finally disappeared in time to meet the extended family at Harriet's folks on Christmas.

A few days later, they received a Christmas greeting from California. One paragraph read:

> David and I got married in North Hollywood on the 14th of December.

Henry smiled and said, "Well, I guess the little bird has built himself a nest. Best wishes, my brother."

As the new year of 1943 approached, Henry sat in his easy chair as he savored his now-rationed coffee. He reflected on how their life had changed more than they could ever imagine in just thirteen months. What would the next year bring?

By the end of January, Americans conducted bombing raids on Germany. There was no hiding this news from Harriet. Henry glanced up from his easy chair, *Kansas City Star* in hand. "Maybe things are looking up. Says here the Russians defeated Hitler at Stalingrad. Perhaps this is the beginning of the end for that old devil."

Harriet took the paper, folded it, and laid it aside as she sat in his lap. She leaned her head on his shoulder and said, "Tomorrow couldn't be soon enough for me."

Chapter 30

Harriet didn't have much time or energy to worry about world affairs. The baby took most of her attention and energy. Her fears of a crying baby materialized as Sally howled day and night. Often this brought Harriet to tears also. Was there no end to this? By the time the baby was three months old she only weighed nine pounds.

Harriet watched as the doctor took Sally off the scale. "Is there something wrong with her?"

"Let's try a different formula—one without iron. That mineral irritates some little ones."

On the way home Harriet stopped at the grocery and picked up the new formula.

When Henry came home that night, he opened the door and wondered what was different. Then it clicked.

Silence. Blessed silence.

He tiptoed into the kitchen and whispered, "Is everything all right?"

"Shh! She's sleeping."

They enjoyed a quiet dinner for the first time in months.

By mid-May, 1943, German and Italian troops surrendered in North Africa.

From March through July of that year, the British conducted air raids on the Ruhr Valley in Germany. As a result, Germany was unable to produce steel and weapons. These raids also halted their production of aircraft and locomotives.

Henry and Harriet took heart. Perhaps this war would be over soon.

Now, when Harriet went to the store, she had to make sure she had her ration stamps. Besides sugar, coffee, and tires, the ration list now included all kinds of processed foods, meats and canned fish, cheese, canned milk, and fats. Supplying the troops brought about changes in the nation's eating habits.

Because Harriet's folks lived on a farm, the Freeman family was fortunate. On Sundays when they went for their weekly dinner, Glessner made sure they went home with an extra supply of butter and milk from their cow. They always had plenty of beef to share since Pops was a cattle rancher. Her mother saved her canned milk ration stamps to help buy formula for Sally. Henry hunted rabbits on Sunday afternoons and occasionally fished the farm ponds.

Harriet breathed a sigh of relief when Sally weighed in at eighteen pounds at her six-month checkup the end of May. She had doubled her weight in just three months.

As the doctor lifted the baby off the scales, Harriet remarked, "Well, I guess that new formula did the trick."

The doctor grinned as he handed the baby back to her mother. "She's well-fed, that's for sure."

Near the end of June in the morning delivery of mail, Harriet thumbed through the letters. One from her sister, Janie, one from her mother, and on the bottom, a letter from the local draft board. She sliced it open as her heart pounded.

The letter said Henry had been chosen by the lottery to assemble with other individuals at the bus station on July 13, 1943. He was instructed to meet the Fort Leavenworth bus to report for a physical examination prior to induction.

Harriet called Henry immediately at work and asked him to come home for dinner.

"What's the matter? You sound upset. Is Sally okay?"

Trying to steady her voice she said, "She's fine. I'll tell you when you get here," and hung up the phone.

Sally awoke from her nap and began to wail.

Henry wasted no time leaving the store as soon as he hung up. Was something wrong with her folks? Had she received bad news about David?

As he came in the back door he found her seated at the kitchen table, her head resting on her arm. Sally sat in the highchair gumming a piece of dry toast. The open letter lay on the table. His glance caught the letterhead "Bourbon County Draft Board." With a sinking heart, he read the contents.

His wife looked up, silent, with an expression that sliced his heart. All his reassurances to her played in his mind in hollow echoes. He took a deep breath and encircled her in his arms as she sobbed.

Chapter 31

On Henry's last day at work, Uncle Vernon came to Fort Scott to see Henry.

"Meet me in the stock room," he said as he breezed in the front door.

Henry followed.

Folding his arms, Vernon said, "You've done good work here, young man. I hate to lose you. Perhaps they'll reject you for some reason. Then you can come back to work."

With a weak smile, Henry said, "That's a nice thought, but I can't think of a reason I could be rejected."

Vernon shifted from one foot to the other. "Well, you're color-blind, aren't you? Maybe that'll save your bacon."

"Maybe, but I doubt it."

"Well, whenever you can get back here, know you have a job waiting."

"Thank you, sir. That means a lot." Henry shook Vernon's extended hand.

Heading home, he wrestled whether to tell Harriet about Vernon's remark about his color-blindness, but decided not to. The reassurances he'd given her to date had turned out to be nothing but false hopes.

He pulled in front of the house, took a deep breath, and gripped the wheel. Short of a miracle, he'd be in for another hitch in the Army, like it or not. This time, he'd likely be shooting at Germans or Japs rather than demonstrating his shooting skills to military school students. His stomach did a flip-flop at the thought.

The next day, July 13, 1943, arrived too soon. They went to the bus station early to get a place with a good view of the departure.

He found it hard to say anything as he cradled his baby. All these years of waiting for a child and now . . . .

Harriet snuggled into him. It was as if she wanted to soak in each moment before he left. How he wished this moment could last forever. Since they'd been married, they had never spent any time apart. Even when he went fishing with his buddies, he always came home at night.

They watched the other Fort Scott men arrive to catch the same bus—"Fatso" Graves, Glenn Maupin, Don Hewitt, Harry Royer, Harold Sinn, Dan Madison, Willard Baker, Kennon, Babcock, Brownie, Hall, and Depew. So many familiar faces—so much uncertainty about the future.

All too soon, the collection bus arrived—a school bus pressed into service. Henry kissed his wife and child one last time, picked up his suitcase, and headed for Fort Leavenworth. He took the last available seat over the wheel well. Thirteen men headed for service. Foul exhaust fumes belched out the back as the driver pulled away. In a flash they were gone.

Harriet forced back the tears as she drove to her parents' home in Walker to drop Sally off. As yet, she had found no one suitable to care for the baby. Uncle Vernon wanted her to take Henry's place as manager of the Fort Scott store as soon as possible. She interviewed several women as sitters, but she felt ill at ease with each of them. Harriet thought one of the women might work, but the baby took one look at her and wailed, holding out her arms to her mother.

Perhaps the war would be over before Henry got out of basic training. The news sounded somewhat hopeful with Patton's 7th Army landing on Sicily's south coast. But then, that was a long way from Hitler and Germany—and a lot of casualties, she was sure.

As she drove, she mumbled, "Oh, God, be with those dear soldiers on the battlefield. Protect them and bring them home safe."

It took several days for Henry to go through endless processing and placement tests at Fort Leavenworth. No one cared he was color-blind—much to his chagrin. Recruits poured in from everywhere. By July 23 they were ready for induction.

The Sergeant's voice boomed over the assembly. "We're not taking anyone thirty-three or older."

Henry's heart flipped. Was this his chance? He shot his hand into the air. "Sir, I'll be thirty-three tomorrow."

The Sergeant frowned and barked. "You're thirty-two today, soldier. Welcome to the Army."

The words echoed like a crashing cymbal. Now he'd be jumping to some commander's orders and likely dodging enemy bullets until the war was over—plus six months according to the newest regulation. If he'd stayed in the Army back in '37 like his Army buddy Hilton, he'd have some stripes on his sleeve. But now, he would have to start at the bottom—again.

Much to Henry's surprise he and the other recruits were allowed several days' leave in early August. He relished every minute with his family. He and Harriet took long walks in the park together as they pushed Sally in the stroller.

On Sunday, they went for their usual dinner with Harriet's folks. He held Sally even while she napped, unwilling to let her out of his sight. He marveled how his daughter had grown since he last saw her.

Harriet still had not found a sitter for Sally. No one was too anxious to keep a very active eight-month-old. She arranged for her parents to keep Sally until she could find a sitter.

The night before he left, as they lay in bed, he said, "What do you think about coming to stay where I'm stationed when I get out of basic—if I'm not shipped overseas?"

Harriet took a deep breath and let it out slowly. "And where might that be?"

"I haven't a clue. Rumors fly around like a swarm of bees." He waited for what seemed like an hour.

Finally, she said, "Well, let's see where you end up first."

He didn't press it. If he pushed, she'd dig in her heels and the whole idea would never have a chance to even get off the ground. He knew she didn't like the idea of getting so far away she couldn't spend Sunday afternoons with her folks. It was probably too much to hope he'd be stationed anywhere near Walker, Missouri.

Perhaps with the Allies bombing Rome and the British bombing Hamburg, Hitler would give up soon. Palermo had just fallen to Patton's 7th Army. With Mussolini's arrest and his Fascist government in shambles, things looked good for a shortened engagement.

The next morning, Harriet put Henry on the train for Fort Leavenworth.

A few days later, one of the employees, Mrs. Willey, approached Harriet.

"I heard Henry left for the Army on the 13th of July."

"Yes, Mrs. Willey, that's right."

"I read in the paper where thirteen of 'em went together on that same bus."

Harriet ran through the names in her head. "Yes. I think you're right."

Mrs. Willey wagged her head and clucked her tongue. "That's just bad luck, for sure." Shaking her finger in Harriet's face she continued. "They'll not be coming back. Mark my words. They'll not be coming back."

Fighting for composure, Harriet took in a deep breath as she pondered how to answer the old busy-body. An anger rose from deep in her belly. She cleared her throat, squared her shoulders, and with all the control she could muster said, "You're wrong, Mrs. Willey. They *will* come back—everyone." Harriet turned on her heel and stalked away.

She decided not to tell Henry of the woman's prediction. At least not now, anyway. No use giving the old biddy's words any more power. Better to let them drop.

A couple of days later Harriet received a letter from Henry dated August 13, 1943.

> Got to Fort Leavenworth midnight Friday. Up at 5:00 a.m. Long day. I.Q. tests, radio aptitude and mechanical tests. Had to watch a venereal disease movie—again.
>
> The next day we were issued small New Testaments. Didn't take one. Still have the one from when I was in before. Went to one of the seven church services Sunday. Each one packed. The chaplain who spoke was at Pearl when the Japs bombed the place. He was real good.

In the next letter she received Harriet learned,

> Didn't get chosen for flight training. It was either color-blindness or my age—not sure which. They said I'd be attached to the Quartermaster Corps since I have experience in clothing stores. I'll be handing out food, clothing, and supplies to the troops in foxholes part of the time.
>
> By the time I took out insurance and authorized buying compulsory war bonds every month, I'll have $9.45 for cigarette money.
>
> Some of the fellows I knew from my last time here are now Master Sergeants drawing $138.00 a month. One said it would go well for me because of my previous service. Hope so.

Harriet shook her head. His current salary certainly was a far cry from their recent earnings in the store.

Farther down in the letter she read,

> We still have no idea where we're going for basic training. A Corporal told us when there are Pullman cars available we'd be shipped somewhere. Maybe Texas. Maybe Nebraska.

> There are so many men coming into Fort Leavenworth we ran out of room in the barracks. The new ones sleep in tents. The mess hall lines are double and extend for a quarter mile.

She marveled at how one man with a greed for power in Germany could disrupt so many lives, a half-world away.

Henry wanted her to come to Fort Leavenworth the next Sunday for a visit, but by Thursday, he had received his shipping orders. He would be gone on the train within twenty-four hours.

On Saturday, August 21, 1943, he wrote:

> Everything around here is 'hurry up and wait.' There are all kinds of rumors as to where we're going, but as yet we haven't budged an inch. Some say we'll be headed to Camp Robinson in California or someplace in Oregon. So much for training close to home, huh? Beyond that, we still have no clue if we'll end up fighting Japs or Germans."
>
> Honey, I sure hope you and Sally can come wherever we are for basic. I sure am missing you both.

Harriet laid his letter on the kitchen table. She tried to imagine picking up and moving to some far off place with a baby, but her imagination failed her.

A few days later she finally talked their elderly landlady into watching Sally so she could see Sally at night. Although Harriet loved being at the store, she missed spending time with her baby. It was better than being with her only once a week on Sundays after a thirty-mile drive to her parent's house.

She took a little comfort from the news in Europe. The Germans were evacuating Sicily. Now if they could just get rid of Hitler, the world might begin to be right again.

Chapter 32

Henry didn't write for two days while the train rocked to his unknown destination. When they were sidetracked near Pocatello, Idaho he scribbled a few lines.

Tuesday, August 24, 1943

Dear family,

Our train consisted of thirteen cars until we picked up two cook cars in Lawrence. We went through Nebraska and hit Cheyenne about 6:00 Monday night. Our faces were black as coal from the dirt and cinders thrown back from the train engine. This morning we were in Kemmerer, Wyoming, wherever that is. Now we've stopped somewhere in Idaho.

Hear we're forming a new Division. If we go south to Salt Lake, we'll head for California. If we go north, it'll be Washington or Oregon. I know one thing. When I get to wherever we're going, I'll sure be glad to get off this train.

His next letter came from Camp Adair, Oregon. Harriet settled into the chair at her desk to read it.

Wednesday, August 26, 1943

We went 90 miles south of Portland to Albany, then on to Camp Adair. I'd love to see you both right about now. We're quarantined and confined to the company area for 2 weeks. After that, I'll be able to go into town to look for a place for you and Sally to stay if you'll come out.

We're starting a new Division—the 70th, Bloody-Axe Trailblazers. I'm in the 276 Infantry. Most Fort Scott guys are in the 274th. Don't know a soul here in K Company. There will be about 15,000 men in the Division when we all get here. We'll train for 14 weeks. Don't know how long we'll stay or where we'll go after basic. Looks like it's going to be a dog's life, but I expected that.

According to talk around here, we may be out of this Army before long. Think it's more wishful thinking than true. Everyone forgets we have to whip Japan before this war is over.

I placed a call to you at 5:30. Didn't get through yet. I'll try again tomorrow.

What do you think about coming out here?

Harriet read the letter again. Bloody-Axe Trailblazers. Even the name sent chills down her back. Was this war turning her beloved husband into a killing machine? Would he come back changed from the Henry she knew and loved?

She sat at the desk and drew out the letter she'd begun. She'd finish it now since she had an address to send it to.

As she wrote she was careful to avoid comment on his request to come to Oregon. How could she manage a nine-month-old and drive clear out there? That long a trip must take nearly a week. She might seriously consider it if it were someplace like Nebraska or Oklahoma. But Oregon? That seemed like a world away.

Besides. Who would run the store? What would Uncle Vernon say? Henry didn't even know how long he'd be there. He'd said so himself. This would take a lot more pondering. And right now, Harriet was too tired to give his request any more thought.

As she walked by the post office the next morning, she dropped off the letter.

The next letter she received read:

Well, here it is the 30th of August so you'll probably get this about September 3rd. That date sound familiar? Honey, I know I won't be able to get you anything for our anniversary but I can give you all my love—and that's not rationed! I'll be thinking of you next Friday. That was the same day of the week we were married on, remember? We didn't dream then, that 6 years later we'd be 2,000 miles apart, did we? I only hope this is the last time we'll be away from each other—ever.

Take good care of Sally and give her a big hug and kiss for me. I'd sure like to hold that little bug tonight for about 5 minutes.

The way they act around here the Japs are about to come over the hill after us. The guys who've been here awhile said there are no Japanese people around here since President Roosevelt sent them all to relocation camps farther East. I wonder if they'll do that to the Germans and Italians, too.

Harriet received the letter the day before their anniversary. She sat on the couch to read it over again after she put Sally to bed.

All the pressure and anxiety of the last two months crashed in on her like giant waves. Would there ever be a time when peace reigned again? Would Henry come back? Would their life ever return to normal? Tears flowed until she fell asleep, exhausted.

The first strands of light from early dawn woke her. Immediately, negative thoughts assaulted her. "What if the Japs *do* come over here and attack us?" or "What if Hitler succeeds in his efforts?"

Harriet tiptoed into the bathroom hoping she didn't wake the baby and applied a wet cloth to her swollen eyes. Its coolness cleared her thoughts. All those what ifs had to go. They only borrowed trouble. To worry about things that hadn't happened only pulled her down. She wished Henry were here, but he wasn't.

She'd have to keep her mind occupied with good thoughts. Her grandmother's admonition came to her. "Now Harriet, you can only think one thought at a time and you're in charge of the reins."

Taking a deep breath, she let it out slowly and straightened her shoulders. After all, it could be worse. Henry could be in the South Pacific or somewhere in Europe like her friends' husbands. At least hers was state-side. There was still a chance the war could be over soon.

Sally awoke and called, "Mama!"

Chapter 33

That afternoon Henry's hinted suggestions to come be with him suddenly seemed a possibility. She needed to go to him, even if it *was* clear out in Oregon. This may be the last time they could be together.

By evening, she spread road maps on the kitchen table to calculate the mileage. Somehow, she'd have to get enough ration stamps to cover the gas before she could leave.

Henry's next letter came on their anniversary, September 3rd. He had written it four days earlier on Monday.

> Haven't received any letters yet. Expect it will be 3 or 5 days yet before I hear from you.
>
> The word is our Division should be completely manned by next Sunday night. Haven't heard when or where we'll be sent out. Hopefully, it will be at least 6 months or more.
>
> My buddy, Lloyd wrote he's fighting with Patton, so he must be somewhere in France. Sounds like a pretty rough go over there. I'm sure it's no better in the South Pacific fighting Japs. Sure wish this war would end soon.
>
> Eight more days and we'll be out of quarantine. Be glad when we can go to town. First thing I'll buy is a cap. Mine is filthy and I need it every day. The cold, rainy weather goes right to your bones out here.

A commentator on the radio sounds very optimistic about the war. Doesn't sound like he knows as much about it as he should.

How's business lately? Did you beat last year's figures for the month? You probably aren't getting as much merchandise as you did last year because of the shortages.

Here, the PX is out of lots of items half the time. We do without butter about every other meal.

The 1st Sergeant made it clear last night there would be no passes issued unless you knew the 11 General Orders. All I had to do was brush up on them. I'll give them to him backward if he wants them that way.

As soon as I can get a pass I'll go to town to see what's available for housing. We might be able to share a place with another couple. That would cut the rent cost.

Hope you're planning on coming. It sure is lonesome out here without you and Sally. If you come, bring plenty of money. Hear it's pretty hard to cash checks out here.

Harriet hadn't told Uncle Vernon about her possible move. She knew it would start a firestorm. From Henry's letter, it sounded like he was going to be there for a while. That was good in one way. But on the other hand, she'd be away from the store longer. With more soldiers shipping out all the time, there were fewer men to fill her empty spot. How would she tell Uncle Vernon?

The next day, he came to Fort Scott to check on things. After looking over the books, he seemed pleased, even though they had less merchandise to sell.

As he closed the ledger he said, "You're doing well, Harriet. Keep up the good work."

Well, it was now or never. "Uncle Vernon, Henry wants me to come to Oregon to be with him before he ships out."

His eyebrows shot up. "And?"

"Sally and I are going as soon as Henry can find a place for us."

The veins popped out on Uncle Vernon's neck and his face flushed. "I see. Well, we'll have to get somebody to take your place while you're gone. Any idea how long that will be?"

"Maybe six months. Maybe longer."

Uncle Vernon made no comment as he gathered his briefcase and made a hasty exit.

Had she made the right choice? When she thought of Henry, she knew she had—even if they didn't have a place to stay yet.

That evening she wrote Henry to tell him of her decision—and of Uncle Vernon's reaction.

Word soon got around town Harriet planned to drive to Camp Adair in Oregon. Two local women asked if they could hitch a ride. She was relieved. They could help mind Sally while she drove. Harriet wrote to tell Henry how many miles she figured it was to Oregon. She also asked him how much he thought she should charge the ladies for the ride.

He replied:

> I think you figured about right on the mileage. Ask the ration board for extra gas stamps.
>
> I checked on bus fare here and a one-way ticket is about $50. I imagine $20 from each of them ought to cover it. Just don't come out in the hole. Let them pay all their board and lodgings. Tell them to pack very light. Our old car is getting weaker every day, you know.
>
> You ought to be able to make it out here in 4 or 5 days. Be sure to watch for the cops!
>
> It would be swell if you could bring Sally's crib and mattress.
>
> If I don't find anything before you arrive, we have a guest house here. It's only $.75 a day.

The way they talk, I might be able to stay here as a troop trainer. They call them cadre men. Right now they're so short on cadre that the Lieutenants give the instruction personally.

I have the honor of being the Squad leader (acting Corporal—no pay) of the 1st Squad of the 3rd Platoon. The Staff Sergeant called all acting corps into his room and made us believe we were very highly honored and gave us the duties we're to perform. I don't particularly love the Sergeant but I'm going to try to make something of this. He said most of the present cadre will be moved out before our basic training is over. Surely some of us will be eligible for promotion.

I'm glad Vernon didn't explode on you. I imagine he was expecting that news anyway. I think the bookkeeper would do a fine job running the store. She's a sharp one and always on the ball.

Heard from Oscar. He said David would sure have to go to the Army by October 1st. He said even some of the key men at the airplane plant are being drafted. He said he went up to see Homer in northern California and hardly got to visit with him at all. Said he's working night and day on the rice farm.

Off the record, they're using some wooden guns for training men now. About 30 of us turned in our rifles this evening so another company could use them. We got them back tonight and I had a job cleaning it. I don't like to loan or have anyone even handle my rifle. That's my best friend while I'm in this outfit. Please send me some brass brushes for cleaning rifles. The PX is out of them here. If you can get several, I'll sell the extras.

Within the week, Harriet received another letter written on September 7, 1943.

I put a $5.00 deposit on a furnished room recommended by my Staff Sergeant. It rents for $14 a month. That's a good deal. Most of the single rooms go for $22 a month. If you don't like it, you can get out and find another place when you arrive.

I'll only be able to come in town 2 or 3 nights a week but that's better than nothing.

The officers tell us we're going across when and where they want us, so we might as well be together as long as possible.

Don't be disappointed in what we'll have to live in. There are not many places available. Bring plenty of winter clothes. It's a damp cold out here. Rains about every day.

Could you fold 15 or 20 bucks in your next letter? It's hard to get a money order or a check cashed out here. I will still have $7 or $8 after paying the rent tomorrow but may need more.

Heard through the grapevine tonight that Italy is about to surrender. Hope it's true.

P.S. Disappointment! The room was rented last night. The Sergeant says he's sure he can find another in a day or two. We'll find a place somewhere. A fella by the name of Friedman from Detroit is going with me to look on Sunday.

We have a grand parade with all 15,000 of us on Saturday. We've been spit-shining everything till you can see your face in it.

In the next letter, she heard all about the parade.

What a mob! Never saw so many men together in my life. It took 30 minutes to pass in review, 12 abreast.

Afterward, Friedman and I only had an hour to shop by the time we walked to the bus station and rode into Corvallis. We chose Corvallis over Albany because the Sergeant said there are no whiskey sales there.

You wouldn't believe the prices out here. Wool socks and sunglasses are $.50 a pair. A cap is $2. We stopped to buy two hamburgers and two pops for $.50—outrageous! A pair of wool pants are $12 and poplin shirts are $2.75. T-shirts $1. Remember to bring lots of money.

P.S. Heard from David. He has orders to report September 16th, but he may get deferred until December 1st.

The next Sunday, near the middle of September, he sent Harriet a telegram.

RENTED THREE-ROOM APARTMENT ALBANY START AT ONCE REGISTER GUEST HOUSE WHEN ARRIVE
LOVE=
HENRY

In addition, Henry sent an airmail special delivery letter telling her a little more about the place. He and Friedman rented a three-room basement for $60 a month. They planned on two couples living there. Everything was furnished except the bed linens and Sally's bed. The house was only a short block from the Willamette River and a block from the main part of town.

His letter instructed her:

These are the things you need to bring.

1. Checkbook and plenty of money
2. Bedding
3. Alarm clock
4. Iron
5. Serving utensils
6. Bathroom heater

7. Teakettle

He ended by saying,

> I sure hope you'll like it although it's not what you're used to. I like Albany lots better than Corvallis.

Harriet hoped she did. She scribbled BRASS BRUSHES at the end of her list of things to remember to bring.

She sent him a telegram saying she would start for Oregon on September 24. She and her two riders planned to pack the car the night before.

Henry fired a letter back. He was a little disappointed they weren't coming sooner. He wrote her some last minute instructions:

> Be sure to have everything gone over, especially the battery and tires. Change the oil before you start and change it every 1,000 to 1,200 miles. There's an extra fan belt under the front seat in case you break one. Be sure to watch all the gauges on the way out. If they all remain normal you can't hurt the motor.
>
> Did you get extra ration stamps at the Ration Board? 160 gallons should get you here without any trouble.
>
> I'm counting the days until I can hold you in my arms.
>
> I wonder if David had to report for induction today. I hope not.
>
> P.S. Be sure to bring my fishing items. They're in the trunk. This river looks like it might have possibilities.

Harriet went to the car to see if the fishing equipment was still in the trunk.

She shook her head at Henry's impatience. Didn't he realize all she had to do before she could leave? She still had several things to attend to at the store. That reminded her to call the Woods Transfer and Storage Company to set a date to pick up the furniture and put it in storage. She still had to buy extra diapers and formula—if she could get the milk ration stamps.

Her landlady saw Harriet out front and pulled her car to the curb.

"Just the woman I want to see. I have something for you for your trip."

"Oh? What might that be?"

The woman held a homemade drawstring bag out the car window. "Here. You're going to need this."

"What's this for?"

"Wet diapers."

"Thanks," Harriet called after her. How in the world did those pioneers haul babies clear to Oregon? At least she had a car and a couple of helpers for the journey ahead.

Chapter 34

Early on the 24th of September, 1943, Harriet, Sally, and her two passengers set out in the car. They packed so tightly there wasn't an inch to spare. Harriet was grateful for the extra pair of hands to hold her squirmy ten-month-old.

By noon, they approached Wichita, Kansas. A loud pop woke Sally as Harriet gripped the steering wheel and managed to guide the car to a stop at the side of the road.

"What was that?" the lady in the back said.

Harriet reached for the door handle. "I don't know but I don't like the sound of it." One of her vulcanized tires had disintegrated. The outer rubber lay several yards behind them.

A dilapidated truck pulled in behind hers. An old gentleman stepped out of the cab. "Hey, Missy. Looks like you got a problem there."

She scowled at the ruined tire. "Yes, it does. Do you suppose you could give me a lift into town? I need to see about a new one. We're headed for Oregon."

The old man pushed his hat back and scratched his head. "I'd be glad to give you a ride ma'am, but I doubt you're going to get a new tire—unless you got a passel of them ration stamps."

Harriet did a quick mental check. She didn't have any stamps for tires. Perhaps she could talk someone out of one anyway. She poked her head in the car window. "You all stay here. I'll go in town to try to get another tire."

While the old man drove, she planned what to say to get a tire with no ration stamps. Soon he pulled into the nearest filling station.

When she told the attendant what she needed, he shook his head.

"Lady, even if I had a tire to sell you, I couldn't. This is the deal. No stamps. No tire."

"Do you think someone else might have one?"

"Them things are as scarce as hen's teeth these days. Unless you wanna drive to Oregon with no spare, you better find another way out there. There's a bus leaving at midnight headin' west. Best be on it."

Harriet was not about to leave the car with everything in it. She hired the attendant to change the flat—after they unloaded the trunk to get to the spare.

She told the ladies about the bus. They agreed to take it instead of returning home. She drove them to the bus station, refunded their money, and waved goodbye.

With Sally asleep on the front seat, Harriet headed back to Fort Scott. As she drove, she made plans to put the car in storage and arrange for a train ticket.

The train ticket proved to be almost as scarce as those hen's teeth. It seemed every seat was already taken by troops. The last day of September she finally nabbed tickets for herself and Sally out of Kansas City.

There were hardly any civilians on the train. Most were men in uniform headed who knew where. She plopped into the last available seat which backed up to the bathroom. The train car was so old it was lit with gas lanterns. Before too long they passed through Lawrence, Kansas and picked up more soldiers.

By the time they reached Platte City, Nebraska, she noticed an unpleasant odor. The bottom of her shoes felt sticky. She leaned over and peered at the floor. Urine from careless soldiers leaked under her seat. If only she had included a small bottle of oil of mint in her purse to smear under her nose. But then again, who would have dreamed she would need such for a train ride?

When she complained to the conductor, he merely shrugged and said, "What do you expect lady? We don't have twenty-four-hour maid service on this thing."

Harriet was grateful for the occasional trips to the dining car. One waiter was especially helpful to see to it that Sally's bottle was heated each time she visited.

The next morning Harriet awoke with aching arms and back from holding Sally all night. She changed the baby's soggy diaper and put on a fresh hand-knit wool soaker over the new one. She hoped her skirt would dry soon as she rinsed the wet diaper and soaker in the bathroom lavatory. Wringing it out, she slipped it into the canvas bag the landlady had given her. She smiled as she remembered her mother's remark some months ago about how babies leaked. That was putting it mildly. This was going to be a long trip.

Ten-month-old Sally was not one to sit still. Every chance she got, she shimmied off the seat in an attempt to walk in the aisle, holding onto the nearby seats. Most of the time she fell but got up again. Every uniformed soldier she saw, she reached for calling, "Daddy."

Harriet could tell by the soldiers' faces which men had little ones at home. That one word seemed to cause either a smile of recognition or a quick revulsion.

It seemed at least every hour the conductor made his way down the aisle, very displeased his small passenger had escaped her seat again.

On the third day, Harriet spied a newspaper someone left in a seat across the aisle. The headlines read, "Allies Enter Naples, Italy." She took some comfort in the fact that the Allies would soon be moving up Italy's boot, pushing the Axis powers farther north as they went.

Late on Sunday afternoon the third of October, Harriet's train pulled into Albany, Oregon in a drizzling rain. She was never so glad to see a train station in her life. With fatigued arms, she gathered Sally, the wet diaper bag, and her suitcase and stepped off the train.

Henry spied her from the other end of the platform and let out one of his ear-splitting whistles. Within seconds, he was by her side enfolding the two of them in his embrace.

"You're a sight for sore eyes," he said.

Handing the baby to him she said, "You are too!"

Sally smiled, patted his face, and said, "Daddy!"

Henry ushered them to a borrowed car and headed for their new home.

"Now I know this place is not quite what you're used to, but you can get out and scout around and find something else if this doesn't suit."

At this point, Harriet felt any bed with four walls and a roof would do.

"I have to be back on base by 2100 hours, but we'll have a little time to grab a bite at the local hamburger joint. It's kind of expensive—fifty cents for a burger—but everything here is high. Then we'll go home."

While Harriet fed Sally pieces of her hamburger, she learned their landlord, a local logger, had recently bought the place. Henry and Friedman worked most of their spare time the last two weeks cleaning it and making it suitable.

"Friedman is still waiting to hear from his wife. He's not sure she will come from Detroit. If she doesn't, we can get another couple to move in."

He paused, put his arm around Harriet and whispered in her ear, "I'm so glad to have my family with me again. I've missed you so."

When they arrived at the apartment, Henry opened the door to the walk-out basement. A single bare bulb hung from the ceiling in what Henry called the living room. A gas cook stove sat in one corner. Next to it sat a dishpan on a small table immediately under exposed water pipes. Beside the table sat a very small refrigerator. A toilet and a wash basin stood a few feet away beside a curtain that pulled closed for a partition. The slight odor of mold permeated the room.

Henry turned the taps in the kitchen. "See? We have hot and cold running water. And in here is our bedroom." He neared a closed door as he gestured to another door on the opposite side of the room. "That's the other bedroom." He opened the near door. A dim light filtered from a small, dark room with a tiny table lamp on a cardboard box. More boxes held a cotton mattress off the concrete floor.

Harriet mustered all the strength she had left and smiled. She hoped the smile looked genuine. Inside she wanted to scream and run back to the train station but she was too tired.

"It's nice, honey. Thank you. Where are we going to put Sally?"

He pointed to a rough box made of orange crates on the far side of the bed. A blanket filled the bottom. "Had to put something together quick since you couldn't bring her bed. I hope it's okay."

"It's fine, dear."

Mentally, she began a "To-Do" list. First order of business—find a suitable place to stay, then find a real baby bed. Harriet put Sally down to sleep in her new bed and turned her attention to Henry.

In a couple of hours, Henry had to head back to the base before his pass ran out. He called back to her as he dashed through the rain to the car, "I'll call the people upstairs as soon as I can get another pass."

Harriet closed the door, turned, and leaned against it to look at her new home. A tear rolled down her cheek. Through gritted teeth she whispered, "I hate war, and I hate Hitler!"

Chapter 35

The next morning Harriet wasted no time in finding a newspaper and turned to the FOR RENT column. It was a short one. She circled ads that looked like they might be suitable.

This small town was bursting at the seams with wives coming to be near their husbands. People advertised to rent every attic, basement, and spare room for miles around. As she checked out each ad, either she got there too late, or the place was worse than the arrangement they already had.

Before the week was out, Friedman heard from his wife. She wasn't coming. That left room for another couple.

The next week, Henry arranged for his buddy Bee Wasson and his wife, Marge to join them from Oklahoma City. They had not been able to have children and Marge delighted in Sally. Harriet really enjoyed Marge's company. It made the long lonely days pass faster.

Harriet constantly kept her eye out for a better place. One day in early November while Marge watched Sally, she found a relatively nice apartment to investigate.

When the landlady learned Harriet's husband was an enlisted man and not an officer, she said, "Oh no! I don't rent to enlisted men. They're nothing but trouble."

Harriet threw her sales abilities into high gear assuring the landlady that they were not some lowlifes—that they held an interest in a chain of clothing stores in the Midwest. The lady finally relented. Then Harriet happened to mentioned Sally.

"Who is Sally?"

"Our baby daughter."

With that, the lady pushed her toward the door. "Oh no, lady. I don't allow no children in my apartments. Absolutely not!"

As the door slammed behind her, Harriet's anger boiled. If she had her choice she wouldn't be in this two-bit town with a baby and a husband off base only one night a week. That is, if some soldier didn't anger the commanding officer who confined the whole company to quarters for a couple of weeks at a time.

When she came home, Marge took one look at Harriet and said, "What in the world happened to you?"

"Marge, I'm going to find us someplace decent to live if it kills me—and it might!"

For Thanksgiving, the day after Sally's first birthday, the commander invited wives to join the troops with fancy invitations which even included a printed menu. The spread to end all spreads lay before them—traditional turkey and gravy, pecan and pumpkin pies, and a variety of vegetables. She turned to Henry. "Boy. The commander really pulled out all the stops on this one!"

"Yeah. You wouldn't know there was any rationing looking at all this, for sure."

Harriet sat next to a person who gave her a tip on an above-ground apartment. Early the next day Harriet was at the door, money in hand. She wasn't going to take no for an answer.

When she came back to the basement, Marge looked surprised to see a smile that lit up the whole place.

"Start packing, Marge. We're moving."

"When?"

"Just as soon as we can borrow a car from somebody. Found a place. It's vacant now. I've put money down. It's ours."

The girls wasted no time in moving to the new apartment. It was two rooms on the back of a house. They had to share the kitchen with the owner and the rental couple's bathroom was a make-shift room on a back porch. Harriet laughed. "Well, at least, it's indoors."

Marge made good use of her kitchen privileges to everyone's delight. She was an excellent cook and managed to turn out some delicious meals, in spite of the strict rations. Her chocolate cake, the owner said, was the cat's pajamas. She made it often for him, when she could get enough ration stamps, to keep them in the couple's good graces.

After Thanksgiving when Sally tried to walk unaided, she took a couple of steps and then fell. She'd get up and try again.

Harriet and Marge watched her as they sat at the kitchen table.

"Marge, what do you suppose is wrong with that child?"

"Could be her shoes are too short. Every time you put her shoes on she cries. Why don't you buy her some new ones?"

Harriet shook her head. "I don't have enough ration stamps."

"How many you got?"

Harriet frowned. "I need twenty more for the white ones."

Marge picked up the paper from the table. "Look here. You can get these with the stamps you have. What's wrong with them?"

"They're brown. I don't want my little girl to wear brown shoes. Those are for boys."

Marge's look put Harriet to shame.

"Oh, okay. Let's go to town and buy the brown ones."

That night when Henry came home on a pass, Sally managed a sort-of run to greet him at the door in her new shoes.

Harriet decided she'd have to stop being so picky—at least until the end of the war.

They received a letter that same day from David.

November 28, 1943

Dear Henry and Harriet,

I've joined the Navy rather than going to the Army. I'm for sure called for December 1. I don't know if Lucilee will stay here or go home to live with her folks.

We'll just have to see where I'm stationed after basic training.

I was able to be deferred this fall, but every week we've been expecting the letter. Hopefully, this war will end soon and we can be victorious. It's sure going to take every one of us to do it, though.

Oscar and his family are doing well. Write when you can. Kiss that niece of mine for me. Sorry, we never got up there to see you all.

Love,
David

Henry took the letter and stared out the bedroom window into the drizzling rain for a long time.

Harriet brought him a cup of coffee and sat on the bed beside him. "You okay?"

"I hoped it wouldn't come to this. I sure hate to think of him out there in the South Pacific on a ship—a sittin' duck for the Japs."

"Well, we'll just have to pray that won't happen."

Henry put his arm around Harriet's shoulder and drew her close. "That we will, my dear."

Chapter 36

In November of ’43, Henry became a cadre man to train troops in Oregon for the South Pacific theater. In Europe, the Russians recaptured Kiev in the Ukraine and large British air raids descended on Berlin.

By January 1944 the Allies landed at Anzio, Italy.

The same month, Marge left Oregon to go back to Oklahoma City to care for her ailing mother. Harriet hated to see her friend go, but she knew Marge’s mother needed her.

When Harriet took Sally on a walk one day during a break in the weather, she saw a house with a FOR RENT sign in the yard. She knocked on the door.

“Is this place for rent?”

“Yes. I have a small apartment in the upper floor of my house. My renters just left yesterday. You interested?”

“May I look at it?” Harriet hoped the landlady liked children better than the old bat who refused to rent to her earlier.

The lady led them around the side of the house and up an outside staircase to a second floor. They entered through a makeshift doorway which used to be a window in a gabled roof. The brief afternoon sun flooded through each window onto bright yellow walls in the living room. Beyond was a small kitchen, next to a tiny bathroom. Past the kitchen was a bedroom/sun porch.

“I haven’t had much of a chance to clean it, but they left it in pretty good shape. When were you looking to move in?”

Harriet smiled and sighed. “Immediately.”

That evening, when Henry came home on a twenty-four-hour pass, she threw her arms around his neck. "Sally and I found a new place today. We're moving tomorrow."

This wasn't the way he'd planned to spend his precious pass hours. But then again, he *had* said for her to find a place she felt was suitable.

They spent the evening packing boxes while she told him about the new apartment and what she wanted to do to it. They moved in the next day.

After they had been there a while, Henry observed Harriet and the landlady had become good friends. She even let Harriet borrow her treadle sewing machine to make Sally some new clothes.

A couple of weeks later, Henry managed to borrow a car for the day. They used the few gas ration stamps Harriet had accumulated and took a ride to Corvallis for a change of scenery.

On the way home, Harriet yelled, "Stop!"

He slammed on the brakes and pulled to the side of the road. "What's wrong?"

"There's an iron headboard beside the road back there. Let's take it home."

Henry scowled. "What do we need with an iron headboard?"

"I'm going to slipcover it and make some matching curtains for our bedroom."

Henry knew better than to argue. When his wife made up her mind on something, especially decorating, there was no use putting his two cents in. He backed the car up and lifted the headboard into the trunk.

The next weekend when he was home, they enjoyed their newly decorated bedroom—together. He chuckled. It never hurt to make the little woman happy.

On his next pass, Harriet took him downstairs and showed him the drapes she made the landlady in exchange for the use of her sewing machine.

He watched her as she made some final adjustment to one of the curtains. He hoped he would never have to leave his beautiful wife again.

Surely the Jerrys and Japs would give up soon. For him, today wouldn't be soon enough.

March 15, 1944, a letter came from David.

Dear Henry & Harriet,

Looks like you guys moved again. We're now stationed in Norman, Oklahoma, at the Naval Air Station. I've been assigned to repair airplanes. Pretty good fit, huh?

You're never going to guess who I ran into the other day. Remember Billy Joe, my first roommate from the orphanage? The one that got adopted and then ran away from those folks? He's a Machinist's Mate here on base. Boy, talk about a small world!

Said he bummed around the country for a few years till he could convince the recruiters he was old enough to join the Navy. He looks the same as ever, except he's not so skinny now. He never married. It was sure good to see him again. I've thought about him many times. We're going to have him over for supper next week.

We're doing fine here. Don't know if you've heard from anyone in California lately. Oscar and his wife are having another baby about the middle of August so you'll be an uncle again. He's still working at the airplane factory. Hasn't been reclassified yet. Hoping he won't be. Don't know how Myrtle could get along with three babies to look after by herself.

Homer is still working on that rice farm in northern California.

Well, guess I better close this letter. Write when you can.

Love,

David and Lucilee

Henry's hopes rose during March of 1944. Hitler seemed to be losing his grip. The Soviet troops began an offensive on the Belarus front and the Allies started daylight bombing raids on Berlin and Hamburg, Germany. He was further encouraged in May when the Germans surrendered in the Crimea and retreated from Anzio. How long would it be before the Germans threw in the towel?

In June, 1944, the Allies entered Rome and the next day thousands of Allied troops landed on the northern coast of France on D-Day. Three days later, the Soviets began an assault on the Finnish front. Perhaps Hitler's Third Reich was on the decline.

Like a hornet's nest stirred by a stick, the Nazis retaliated with V-1 buzz bombs over Britain by the middle of June. The Brits' back was against the wall.

Henry didn't discuss it with Harriet, but he knew there was constantly a need for more troops. How long would it be before even the cadre men at his base would be called to fight?

His fears received more confirmation when they got a letter from Harriet's mother with a list of all the local Walker men who had recently been drafted. It seemed as if almost every young man had been sucked into this war machine. Was there anyone his age or younger to grow crops in their area?

After the cadre men of the 70th Division trained three groups of soldiers and shipped them off to southeast Asia, orders came through for Henry and his fellow soldiers to move to Fort Leonard Wood, Missouri. Henry knew this was one step closer to the battlefield. At least he had been able to have his family near him these past nine months. He had no idea how long he would be stationed there but he'd do everything he could to keep them close until he shipped out—whenever that was.

Harriet didn't seem disappointed to leave Oregon. "Be glad to get out of this constant rain—and we'll be closer to home," was her only comment.

The train ride seemed to take forever. By the time they reached Kansas City, he had a better understanding of Harriet's fatigue when she first arrived in Oregon. Sally absolutely refused to sit still except when she napped. While they waited for Harriet's folks to arrive at the train station, they tried to keep up with Sally who walked over every inch of the massive Union Station. After a few hours, Glessner and Pops picked up Harriet and the baby and took them to Walker until Henry could scout out a place in Waynesville, Missouri near Fort Leonard Wood.

His next letter read,

> A couple of guys and I rented a log cabin. We call it 'El Rancho.' Can't wait for you and Sally to see it. Come as soon as you can.

Fortunately, Harriet got some tire ration stamps and bought a spare so she could finally get their car out of storage to drive to Waynesville to be near Henry.

On a hot evening in the last part of July, 1944, he sat to read the paper. "Listen to this. One of Hitler's top officers attempted to assassinate him. The officer placed a bomb under the table at a strategy meeting. No one was killed but some of the officers were injured. Look at this picture in the paper."

She peered at a soldier holding up Hitler's shredded pants. "Too bad the bomb didn't shred more than his pants."

He rolled the paper and slapped it on his knee as he fired a glare at Harriet. "Too bad they didn't kill the old skunk!"

Harriet nodded. "Too bad, indeed."

Hitler may have escaped with his life but by the middle of August he received another stinging defeat. The Allies invaded Southern France and within ten days they liberated Paris.

The couple got word from Henry's brother, Oscar, they had another son, Doyle, born August 19th. Oscar invited them to come to California for a visit. Henry remarked, "We'll have to do that when this blasted war is over."

She smiled and squeezed his hand. "When the war is over. Everything hinges on that phrase, doesn't it?" She whispered a prayer. "Lord, if he has to go fight please bring him home safe and sound."

In early September, 1944, the Allies moved on to the northeast of France and liberated Antwerp and Brussels in Belgium. As Henry heard the report on the evening news, he shot his fist into the air and said, "One more step to victory! Come on, guys. Let's get this over with."

Chapter 37

Unfortunately, Hitler's defeats didn't dampen his determination. He seemed to have an unending supply of soldiers to feed his fiendish fury.

By early October, 1944, the 70th Division received orders to get ready to move out—exactly where they didn't know.

Harriet gathered their few belongings from El Rancho and moved back to Fort Scott. She managed to find a three-room apartment on the second floor of a house near downtown.

Vernon wanted her to come to work immediately, but she'd have to find someone who could keep up with her very busy almost two-year-old.

Glessner volunteered, but Harriet hated to agree to that since her mother was already fifty-four. She placed an ad in the Fort Scott Tribune and hoped she could hire someone quickly.

Henry called the next weekend. He managed to get a three-day pass and arrived on the bus very late on Friday night.

Saturday evening, Harriet said, "How will I know where you are stationed?"

"I've been thinking about that. We're not allowed to write that information in a letter. It's considered classified since it might give the enemy a heads up on where to come after us. I think I've devised a code. If I address the salutation to "Sally" with a dash after, look at the last line of the letter. Take the first letter of each word and put it together. That will tell you where I wrote it from."

Harriet thought about it a while. It did give her some comfort to have a clue where he was—if she could figure it out. She smiled. "Okay. Try it before you ship out. We'll see if it works."

He enfolded her in a comforting hug. She ran her hands across his back and breathed in his scent as she pressed her forehead into his strong neck. She tried to cement this moment in her memory. How long would it be before they would be able to enjoy this intimacy again? Every minute seemed to fly by. Harriet wished she could save these moments in a bottle and pull them out after Henry left in order to savor them.

All too soon he was gone again. Would he ever return?

The next week Harriet received a letter from their former house-mate, Marge, in Oklahoma City.

October 30, 1944

Dear Harriet,

Don't know if you heard, but my mother died last week. God rest her soul. She's finally at peace. With the guys shipping out I decided to apply for a job at a munitions factory near here. They hired me on the spot. At least I can feel like I'm helping the war effort now.

You and Sally come see me when you get a weekend away. It's pretty lonely here without any family. Let me hear what our little doll is doing these days.

Love,
Marge

By the end of October, Harriet gave up trying to find a sitter and took Sally to her parent's home in Walker. Vernon was delighted to see her return to work after over a year away.

Henry's first letter's salutation read, "Sally," with a dash. She looked at the last line to see if she could decipher his code. It read,

Miss Ida should see our utility room inside.

Harriet laughed. Missouri. Of course. He was still in Waynesville, Missouri!

> I think we'll be out of here within 12 days. If you don't hear from me for a little while, figure I'm on a ship somewhere getting seasick.

He included a list of things for her to do to the car to keep it in tip-top shape, and then continued:

> From the sound of your letter, you're blue. Maybe you can arrange to have Sally with you before long. I sorta have that empty feeling too. But I'm going to try to keep busy and not get like I did when I first hit Camp Adair.
>
> The war news sure sounds good. Hope we can whip 'em soon.
>
> I got paid today—$100.38. I'll send it home. Sure don't need it around here. Nothing to do. Nowhere to go. I got my paper with my Technical Sergeant rating on it today.

In her return letter, she let him know her guess on the code.

He was pleased with her detective skills and felt confident she'd be able to decipher his future ones. He wrote:

> Looked in my picture folder today and all my photos stuck together. Please send some more so I can look at my family.
>
> Glad you read the code right. Remember, look for the dash after "Sally."
>
> Bee Wasson came over last night and we went to the PX for a while. Too bad about his mother-in-law.
>
> I'll try to call soon. It takes a really long time to get through. Sergeant Gunn put in one an hour ago. He's still

up there waiting to reach his wife. I'll not call on Sunday. I know you'll be with your folks and that country phone doesn't get the best reception. Besides, I really don't want Central listening to our conversation.

Hope you have some luck finding someone to watch Sally.

Much love and kisses to you both,

Henry

On a Friday night the 17th of November, Harriet received a phone call from him.

"Hey, Hon. It only took fifteen minutes to get through. How lucky can we be? Well, we're still here—hurry up and wait. Just like always."

Hearing his voice filled her with a swirl of emotion. How she wished she could jump through the phone lines into his arms. "Know when you're leaving yet?"

"Your guess is as good as mine. Now they're saying we'll be outta here in about four days. I've got all the equipment and clothing packed for our company. Just waiting for the go order. Have you found someone to care for Sally yet?"

"Yes. I hired a girl today. She's going to start Monday. I'm picking Sally up at Mother's on Sunday."

"That's great! Hope she works out."

"Me too!"

"How are things at the store? Are you getting back in the swing of it?"

"It's kinda like riding a bicycle. Only difference is new merchandise. Are the guys getting nervous about pulling out?"

"Maybe. We've sure had a lot of accidents around here lately."

Harriet hesitated. "What kind of accidents? Have you been hurt?"

"No. I'm fine. Take your worry hat off. Some guy in the 275th dropped a thirty-seven- millimeter dud and put sixteen guys in the hospital. Another fella in the 274th was playing with a grenade and it went off and killed four."

"That's terrible."

"Yeah. Guess some have the jitters real bad. A guy about a half block from us shot at a Lieutenant fifteen times with his carbine. Missed him every time. Next day the shooter blew his brains out. They've been shaking us down for ammunition lately. They must think we're all going to dream up some fireworks."

"Oh Henry, be careful!"

He sighed. "Careful as I can be. Wish I could get a pass. Seems a shame to be so close to home, and yet so far. It's swell to hear your voice."

She blinked back tears. "Love you."

"Love you too, Honey. Kiss our little sweetheart for me."

"I will. Be careful. Let me know when you hear something."

"Will do, Hon."

Two days before Thanksgiving Harriet received a letter written November 20. It had the salutation to her and not Sally.

> I'll just write a letter while I'm riding along. You'll get it after we get to our destination. We've moved but don't know where we're going. Our platoon is pretty lucky. We have a Pullman car made to fit. I'm the car commander. Bee's two cars from me so we get to see each other quite often.
>
> Did you get Sally home with you yet? Glad you're not going to be apart any longer. Hope you and Sally both like the girl you've hired.
>
> I may try to call you some time—if I can get off this train long enough.
>
> Love,
> Henry

Chapter 38

Henry jotted a short note November 24, the day after Thanksgiving to his two-year-old daughter. Harriet noted there was no salutation to Sally—again. If only she could know where he was she might not have such a lonely feeling.

Dear Daughter,

This isn't the way I'd have liked to celebrate your birthday, Sally, but I don't do the choosing. Hope you had a swell birthday. I haven't sent you a present, but I'll try my best before long. Pickens' are pretty scarce at the PX.

Harriet, you've probably received my address card by now. Use that address to send packages. You can send up to 5 pounds in each one. When I get overseas you can send me a carton of cigarettes every week or two if you can get them.

I'm going to try to call tonight. Hope I can get through.

Love,
Henry

Perhaps if he called, she could find out where he was—if some censor wasn't lurking over his shoulder.

Although he tried to call for several hours that night, he didn't get through.

The sitter showed up a half hour late for her first day—a very strict no-no in Harriet's book. Harriet arrived at the store with five minutes to spare.

By mid-morning, the sitter called her. Harriet was busy trying to find a suit to make a large woman look thinner. When she came to the phone, Harriet could hear Sally screaming in the background.

"Miz. Freeman?"

"Yes. What is it?"

"Maybe you better come home. Sally fell off the chest of drawers and cut her head."

"What was she doing up there?"

"I set her up there while I hunted for a diaper."

Harriet dropped the phone and grabbed her coat. As she ran out the front door she said, "I'll be back when I can. Somebody help the lady in the dressing room find a suit."

When she reached the bottom of the stairs to their second-floor apartment she could hear Sally's cries. She took the stairs two at a time.

The sitter held the child out to Harriet at arm's length. Her baby was covered in blood, as well as the sitter and the floor. Harriet resisted the strong urge to throw up. What kind of a nincompoop would set a child on a tall dresser and walk off and leave her?

"I'm so sorry, Miz. Freeman. I don't know how to make her stop."

"Perhaps she wouldn't be crying if she hadn't been left to fall off the dresser in the first place," Harriet said as she grabbed Sally and ran into the bathroom. Wiping the child's face with a wet washrag she choked down more angry words. She pressed the rag against the wound on her child's scalp as Sally continued to scream and tried to push her mother's hand away. When she removed the cloth she gasped at the two-inch gash. "Oh, my Lord! This is going to need stitches."

"You want me to stay here and clean up the mess, Miz. Freeman?"

Laying Sally on the bathroom floor, Harriet reached for the woman's coat, stuffed a bill inside the pocket, and handed it to her.

Struggling to keep an even tone, she said, "I'm sorry. I don't believe your services are needed any longer."

Harriet wrapped a blanket around the wailing child and pushed the sitter ahead of her as she headed for the door.

That afternoon, after the doctor stitched her head, Sally slept on the front seat of the car as Harriet drove to her folk's home. She wondered what she would do next. Surely there was a responsible person to watch her child somewhere—but where?

After supper, Harriet drove home alone. The drone of the motor drowned out her angry sobs as a gentle snow covered the landscape. Loneliness threatened to swallow her whole.

When she ascended the stairs she heard the phone ring. She ran to get it. "Hello?"

"Where were you? I was about to hang up."

The sound of Henry's voice let loose a new wave of tears as she told him of the events of the day.

A week later a letter came for Sally. Harriet opened it. It was a birthday card. A short note flitted to the floor.

Dear Sweetheart,

I'm so sorry the lady didn't work out. I was so in hopes she would. I'm sure something will work out soon.

Found something for Sally. I'll send it in a day or two. This was the only card I could find.

Got a letter from your mom. She said Sally likes the Goldilocks story. Sure appreciate Mom. At least we know she's in good hands there.

We're waiting for a ship to take us somewhere—still don't know where.

War news looks good lately, but each news hound jumps at the chance to outdo the other with more sensational headlines.

If Germany holds out to the last-ditch, the war isn't near over. Hope they'll see the light before long. They're catching everything we can pour on 'em. They're pretty bullheaded if they keep holding out.

Harriet turned her attention to the card. On the front, a much older girl looked at herself in a compact. It read "Happy Birthday, daughter." Inside the verse read:

> Lovingly wishing you everything glad,
> For you're dearer and dearer each birthday you add!

It was signed,

> Happy Birthday, Sally
> Oodles of love,
> Daddy

She curled onto the couch in a tight ball. "Lord, don't let Hitler hold out to the last ditch. Make him throw in the towel—soon. Keep Henry and the others safe so they can come home in one piece."

Harriet couldn't sleep. Every time she drifted off, another round of tears came until exhaustion finally took over.

Winter dawn light streamed in the living room windows and woke Harriet. She unfolded on the couch and stretched as she glanced at her watch. Oh, wow! Just enough time to change clothes before opening the store.

Harriet placed another ad in the *Fort Scott Tribune* for a sitter/housekeeper. The best one to answer the ad was an older lady who assured her that she had watched many children over the years.

The next Sunday, Harriet brought Sally home from her mother's. It felt so good to have her home again. Sally refused to sleep in her own bed and insisted her Mommy lie beside her while she went to sleep.

The next morning the new sitter arrived early. Harriet had plenty of time to introduce her to her charge and outline her duties.

Sally cried when Harriet left. As she drove to work, she decided she would have to put off trimming the windows so she could spend more time with her little girl. Maybe she would even take her to the store and let her learn the retail business from window trimming up.

That evening Harriet came home ready for a warm meal and an evening with her daughter.

Ascending the stairs, Harriet thought it strange she didn't smell anything cooking. When she walked in the apartment she found the lady and Sally on the floor playing pat-a-cake. The dampened laundry still sat in the basket, not ironed. No dinner graced the table.

"Did you cook anything for supper?"

"I'm not much for cooking, Mrs. Freeman."

Harriet picked up a dampened blouse from the laundry basket. "And the ironing?"

"Oh, I never learned to iron. You'll have to send it out." The woman turned her attention back to Sally.

Harriet took a deep, weary breath. If she sent this one packing, Sally would have to go back to her mother. If she instructed the woman what to cook, and how, perhaps they could work this out.

She asked the new hire to come a little early the next morning. After the woman left that evening, Harriet made a rice and bean dish for their supper. She was too tired to make anything fancier.

When the lady arrived the next morning, Harriet showed her the ingredients for macaroni and cheese, complete with the recipe. She showed her how to plug in the iron and demonstrated how to iron an item.

All the while the woman watched and nodded as if she understood every instruction.

Harriet grabbed her hat and coat. "See you all tonight."

That evening, there was no meal. The sprinkled laundry sat soured in the basket.

What had she not understood about the simple instructions? Was she more addlebrained that she looked?

"What did you feed Sally for lunch?"

"She kind of likes bread smeared with lard."

"Is that what you fed her?"

The woman nodded. "Yes ma'am. I never learned to cook. I just eat cans of soup and bread and butter. Works for me."

"And I take it you never learned to iron either."

"Nope."

"Well, this doesn't work for me." Harriet opened her purse and handed her two days' wages. "You needn't come back."

"But—"

"But nothing. I hired you to watch Sally, cook, and iron. You've wasted my time."

Harriet grabbed the woman's coat, went to the door, and opened it.

The woman reached for the coat and mumbled something about, "If that's the way you feel about it." Harriet ushered her out and closed the door behind her.

Very early the next morning, Harriet fumed as she made the sixty-mile round trip to drop Sally at her mother's—again. Would this circus ever end? Would there ever be a time they could have a normal life again? Were there no competent people left in this world?

Harriet reported the struggle to find nanny help to Henry in a short note after she got off work that night.

He replied:

Dear Harriet,

I sure was surprised about the woman not being able to iron or cook. It's not hard to see why she's an old maid. Wonder if she had a trial marriage sometime.

David wrote a long letter. He has a good possibility of making instructor.

Today was payday. About half the fellows are broke, as usual.

Heard from Oscar. He didn't mention his new son. Expect he is pretty busy helping with family duties while he's working overtime repairing some planes. They're converting some old planes over to commercial use for industrial firms.

We went to see Abbott and Costello in "Lost in a Harem" tonight. Quite a crazy picture.

Still don't know when we're shipping out or where we're going.

Bee and I went shopping. Bought Sally some plastic dishes for her birthday. Wanted to get something better but couldn't find anything. For your birthday, I bought some "Evening in Paris" perfume.

Bought your Christmas gift too since I don't know where I'll be by then. It's a gold pin with matching earrings. Bee bought a similar one for Marge. Look for a package soon. Every time he tries to call her, the line's busy. Poor guy."

Chapter 39

Harriet hesitated to put another ad in the paper for a sitter since the others hadn't worked out too well. Two days later a young woman came in the store looking for a job. Harriet didn't have an opening, but the more she talked to the girl, the more confident she felt this one might be the one to care for Sally.

"Do you like children?"

"Oh, yes. I'm the eldest of eight."

Harriet ventured another question. "Can you cook?"

"Yes, ma'am," she said with a smile.

"What about ironing and cleaning?"

"Doesn't everyone?"

"I may have a job for you if you're interested."

Her eyes lit up and a smile graced her face. "What is it?"

"Watching my two-year-old daughter. Interested?"

"Oh, yes. When can I meet her?"

"I can pick her up tonight from my folks. Are you available tomorrow?"

"Yes, ma'am. Give me your address. I'll be at your place bright and early."

Harriet sighed. Surely this one would work out.

She left the store after five and headed for Walker.

"Sure hate to see Sally go. We have such fun together," Glessner said as she helped her daughter carry Sally's things to the car.

"Thanks, Mom. I hate to impose on you."

"No imposition, my dear. I know how much you miss her. Glad you two can be together. Bring her back anytime."

As Harriet carried Sally into the apartment, the phone rang. It was Henry. He was glad to hear Harriet had a new sitter.

"Bee finally got through to Marge last night. He was sure happy to talk to her. My buddy, Joe got through to his wife, too. They must have talked for twenty minutes."

"Wow! Bet that cost him a pretty penny."

"I'm sure. I think it would have been shorter, but she was crying about half the time. Honey, I'm proud of you. You're so brave."

Harriet pushed down the tears. She didn't want him to know the hours she cried over this mess. She finally managed to say, "Well, crying won't make you feel better about being away from home."

"That's my girl."

She breathed deep to steady her voice. "Do you hear any more about shipping out?"

"Well, you know how it is. One rumor chases another. Last I heard, it could be any day now. Not holding my breath, though. I'll just take it as it comes. Worrying about it won't change anything. I'll try to call when I know something. Don't forget our code on the last line of a letter written to Sally with a dash after it. Hope you can figure out where I am by that."

"I will. Love you, Honey."

"Love you too, Sweetheart. Give Sally a kiss and hug for me."

After she got Sally to bed, she sat in the dark living room. Tears came. She could hold them back no longer. Grateful for the call, but grieved over the separation. How long would this war go on? Would Henry come back? Would he be all right? Henry's words echoed in her ears about worry not changing things.

She decided to be grateful for the new nanny and having Sally back with her again. Harriet crept into the bedroom and watched her toddler asleep in the soft light of the moon through the window. Sliding under the warm blanket she drew the baby close and fell asleep.

The sitter, Val, showed up early as promised. Harriet outlined her duties and showed her around the small apartment.

Hearing the voices, Sally awoke. She seemed to like Val, which made Harriet feel a new peace.

That evening, Val had a savory vegetable soup simmering on the stove when Harriet came home. Red and green paper chains adorned the front window. It added a nice Christmas touch to the drab room.

"Where did the decorations come from?"

"You like it?"

Harriet smiled. "Looks very festive."

"Sally and I made it this afternoon after her nap."

Val's father honked his horn outside. She glanced out the window, put on her coat, and said, "See you tomorrow."

Fatigue lifted from Harriet's shoulders as she sat to enjoy the meal. When she went to change clothes after supper, her newly-ironed clothes hung in the closet. Finally! Evidently, this girl was going to work out well.

A couple of nights later, when she was about to fall asleep, Harriet heard the phone ring. It was Henry again.

"We're to board ship early in the morning. I've been trying to get through to you for two days. Circuits are all busy. Guess everyone's trying to make one last call. There's a long line still waiting to use the phones so I'll have to make this short."

"Where are you going?"

"Scuttlebutt is Europe. Don't know where we'll land, though."

"What's the name of the ship?"

"Can't tell you, sweetheart. Love you. Is your lady working out?"

Harriet's mind whirled trying to think of things to ask him. She wanted to stretch the conversation as long as she could. Who knew when she'd be able to hear his reassuring voice again.

"Yes. She's wonderful. Hope she keeps up the good work."

"Great, honey. Gotta run so the other guys can make calls. Give Sally a hug for me. Love you."

"Love you too, honey. Be careful."

"Don't worry. I'm coming back. Write often."

"I will."

The sound of the click rang in her ear. How long before she could speak to him again? How long before he could walk U.S. soil? "Oh God! Keep him safe!"

At first light, she opened one tear-swollen eye. Her gaze fell on Henry's picture on the bedside table. How would she manage with him gone? "Help me Lord. I need Your strength."

She went to the bathroom to soak her eyes with a cool rag before dressing.

The next day, Harriet received the promised packages at the store. She noted the box her jewelry came in was from a shop in Taunton, Massachusetts.

On her lunch break, she stopped by the library and asked the librarian to assist her to discover Henry and Bee must have been at Camp Myles Standish. It was the closest military instillation to Taunton. She smiled. There was more than one way to find out where her husband was, in spite of strict government regulations.

A week before Christmas, Harriet received her first letter from Henry since he left. It was dated Friday, December 8, 1944.

> Somewhere in the Atlantic
> Hi Honey and Little Honey,
>
> We're on a large ship. Can't tell you the name of it but it used to be a luxury line. It's one of the largest the U.S. ever built. Rides nice, but I got seasick yesterday. Had to be up too long, but after I got to lay down I felt better right away. We have to take turns in the bunks because we're carrying twice the men this boat was built for. Been feeling fine today and have been out on deck

most of the time. It was only rough the first couple of days.

We eat two meals a day at 8:30 a.m. and 4 p.m. If I get hungry I go rummaging for a candy bar. Send me some if you can get any. We can get cigarettes for $.50 a carton but they clamp down on us for smoking too much.

You asked me if your letters are censored. So far they haven't been, but all ours are. Guess they don't want anyone giving hints as to where we are. All I know is we're in the middle of a very calm sea.

We don't do anything except sleep or go up on the deck. We're down in the forward hold. It's not bad at all but we have to go so far to get up on deck. It rides a lot better down there than it does higher up.

I got a Christmas card from David.

Hope you have a happy birthday. Maybe next year we can celebrate it together. Can't believe we've been at this war three years, already. Surely that old skunk Hitler will give up soon.

Love,

Henry

P.S. They just told us where we're going. Can't tell you, but maybe I'll get to see my old buddy Lloyd."

Harriet's stomach rolled thinking about Henry on a ship heading for a battle zone. Where was Lloyd when they last heard from him? France? She was grateful for his subtle hint. She'd have to get a map of France. Maybe he could send one of his coded letters soon.

Chapter 40

The day after Christmas, Harriet received a V-mail—short for Victory mail. The soldier could only use the front sheet of 8 ½ x 11 piece of paper for his message. After the censors read and cleared it, the letter was photographed and shrunk to a 4 x 6 piece of photo paper to save space in the mailbags. She squinted at the tiny words. It was dated Sunday, December 17, 1944.

Dear Wifey and daughter,

We're in the same country as Lloyd—can't tell you where. All the streets are narrow paved alleys. There are open latrines on the street.

I haven't been in this nearby town yet. Not too anxious to go. Some of the boys went in yesterday. They said there's plenty of wine, women, song and thievery. Sounds nice doesn't it?

My buddies Bee and Joe are okay. Wish we could call you gals and talk for a while.

The weather isn't much different than Oregon except the wind is really cold. It goes right through you when it comes down over the mountains.

I wrote Lloyd a letter. I talked with the chaplain to help me find him.

How's Sally? Is the new girl still working out?

Hopefully, I'll get some mail from you soon. It's starting to come in now. I'm going to write your next letter air mail to see which is faster. These V-mails are so short. I just get wound up and then I'm out of paper.

After they departed the ship, the 70th Division pitched tents on French soil and waited for a train to take them to the battle front four days before Christmas, 1944.

Bee heard of a spring-stream about a mile from their camp. "Whad'ya say we go down there and do some laundry while we wait?"

Henry said, "Sounds like a good idea. Think I'll take a bar of soap and have a bath."

"In this cold? Are you crazy?"

"No. Just dirty."

"You must be pretty desperate."

"I am. Let's go."

And so they went.

After much cajoling on Henry's part, Bee finally joined Henry in the stream after they finished their laundry duties.

"Lordy, this is cold! I must have been nuts to let you talk me into such a fool idea. I may never get warm again!"

Henry laughed as he climbed out of the water. "I feel a hundred percent better. How about you?"

"You crazy guy. Don't know if I'll ever feel my feet again."

Soon they headed back, clean, rifles over their shoulders, with their arms filled with half-frozen laundry.

Bee said, as he ducked into the tent, "Some guys will do anything for a bath. I think next time I'll stay dirty."

Henry crawled into his sleeping bag and wrote a letter home.

Dear sweetheart and little sweetheart,

Hit the jackpot today. Got my first mail from you. You wrote it December 4.

How are you little sweetheart?

It's getting cold here in the tent so I'll have to get out by the fire. Then I'll get wet again. At night, we're warm in our sleeping bags but the ground sure is hard.

I started growing a mustache. When I get home we're going to build a house with lots of lights around the bathroom mirror. When I shave here I don't even have a mirror.

Two days before Christmas, trains arrived for the G.I.s and they were herded into boxcars like so many cattle.

The day before Christmas Henry wrote:

Ask old Mac Wooden from Walker if he ever heard of 40 & 8s. They used them in WW I when he served over here with Truman. I imagine he'll give you an earful. They're boxcars. You can haul 40 men or 8 horses. We've been in one since yesterday going who knows where. They ride pretty rough.

I've only received one letter from you since I've been here. They'll probably all come at once.

Harriet's flow of letters stopped for several days. She worried. What if he'd been injured? Would the Army let her know if that happened? Surely they would.

Finally, she received two. With shaking hands, she ripped one open.

It was a V-mail dated December 29, 1944. The salutation read, "Dear Sally—". At last a letter with a code in it!

How's my little sweetheart? It's cold where Daddy is. We've been on a train several days. Now we're in tents. We use fire to keep warm. Help Mommy and give her a big kiss from me and tell her to give you a big smooch from me.

So Evelyn liked the zoo?

Love, Daddy

Her heart skipped a beat. She read the last line and deciphered Seltz. Harriet rushed to her new map of France. After much searching she discovered he was in the north-east of France on the Rhine River—at least that's where he was on the 29th of December. She marveled Henry's code slipped past the censors, unnoticed.

Poor Henry! If only he'd taken French in high school like she did, he'd be able to talk with the local people. She guessed his ready smile would have to be his method of communication.

Henry wrote one night:

> Honey, haven't been able to write the last few days for various reasons. I really wanted to, especially Christmas Day. Know you worry because you haven't received many letters. Remember what you promised me—if I don't worry, you don't worry. There are times I won't be able to write. I'll take good care of myself against these Krauts.
>
> We'll be getting a turkey dinner tomorrow. On Christmas we ate hard rations in one of those 40 & 8 boxcars. We're at a new destination.
>
> You're never going to believe this. Lloyd walked in a couple of days ago. I thought from what the chaplain said I'd have to wait quite a while before we could get together. Lloyd has more freedom than I do. As a medic, he's got transportation and I don't. He found me without much trouble. He brought a camera. We took some pictures. If they turn out, I'll send you some. Then you can see my mustache. He brought a couple of buddies with him.
>
> We went to see Bee. He moved. He's got a real set up over there. Even has a bed to sleep in, but today he got

moved back to where I am. Said he sure was gonna miss that bed.

Got a package from your mom. Had a big pecan roll and a can of apricots in it. It's the first mail I've received in quite a spell. I gave each man in the platoon a sample of the nut roll.

We had our first real experience with the Krauts' "eggs" yesterday. Nobody was hurt, though.

Henry decided he better stop there. He didn't want to give Harriet any more fuel to fire her worry. But then, he didn't want her to think they were over here on a European holiday, either.

In truth, they had a pretty rough time of it. He and Bee were almost hit by mortar fire. Had they been a few yards closer to the enemy, they would have been picked up by some G.I. burial detail. When he tried to sleep, the whole scene played out repeatedly in his head. He was unable to stop the terror of the moment, no matter how he tried.

As he put more days past the incident, he gained some perspective he'd not had before. That close call strengthened his resolve to return home whole in body and soul to his precious wife and child.

Chapter 41

Harriet did pretty well as long as she could stay busy at work. In the evenings after Val left, she played with Sally.

Each night it was the same.

"Time for bed, little one. Let's brush your teeth and put on your jammies."

After a race to the bed, Sally kissed Daddy's picture with a big smack and said her prayers including a special prayer for him. Then Mommy tucked her in.

Harriet dreaded the silence that followed. In those quiet moments, Mrs. Willey's prediction that the men would not come home gnawed at her. At times like those she prayed, "Oh God, keep him safe. Bring him home to me—soon."

Many nights she curled on the couch, looked out the window, and wondered if Henry was someplace where he had seen the moon that evening. She longed to feel his strong arms around her—to hear his encouraging words—to see his blue eyes and reassuring smile. Many nights she took out his letters and re-read them deep into the night.

On the way to work one day she passed the photography shop. She went in and made an appointment for her and Sally to have some new pictures taken for Henry. Perhaps that would cheer him like looking at his picture cheered her.

Harriet next heard from Henry in early January.

I got several letters from you and your mom today. Your latest letter was December 19th. That's the best time yet. Your mom's was November 29. A little late, huh?

Harriet had written previously about a fur coat he had urged her to buy. She told him,

Sally likes to snuggle up to it every chance she gets.

He responded,

I'm sure glad you got the fur coat. I want you to enjoy some of the money you're making. I haven't spent 10 francs in the last two weeks. There isn't any chance to spend any money around here.

Sure enjoy hearing about Sally's antics. I'm afraid she'll know my pictures real well, but if I walked in on her I bet she wouldn't know me. Keep talking to her about me and we'll just hope she remembers me when I get home.

According to the *Stars and Stripes*, things don't look too hot. Congress predicts our war with Japan is just starting. I also see where Representative Sheridan from Pennsylvania says there aren't a hundred men who want to come home before this thing is over. I can show him that many in less time than it takes to tell it.

In your mom's letter she said she sure misses having Sally around. She told me when Sally last stayed with her, she put beans down the well so they would grow. Quite the little farmer, huh?

You and your mom's letters were censored. Those guys must read every line of ever letter. Wish I could tell you where we are, but that might get me in a lot of hot water.

The night you mentioned in your last letter you wondered if I could see the moon that night, we were going through Marseilles. I wondered where you were at the same time.

I'm sitting in a foxhole by a fire. It's about 15 degrees. It's trying to snow a little. It's too cold to write more so I'll close for now. Maybe I can write a long one in a few days.

Harriet wished she could give him her fur coat. She shed a few prayerful tears for her husband and the others trapped in the cold. She looked up Marseilles on her map, circled it, and dated it.

One day seemed to melt into another. She didn't know she could be so lonely. Even with Sally with her, the ache of Henry's absence seemed to grow more painful with each day. She thought back to those days before the war when they took their togetherness for granted. What she would give now to have the luxury to spend one night with him again.

In mid-January Henry reported he and his buddy, Bee, had returned from a couple of days' rest at the field hospital.

Harriet's pulse quickened when she read that line.

It's sure tough being out all the time. Looks like we'll never get to be inside.

Got back to duty today and had six letters waiting for me. I'm homesick. I'd sure like to see both of you. I wasn't injured. Feel pretty good now but am still a little jumpy.

Bee got banged around quite a bit. This kind of work is not for fellows as old as we are. I think he'll come out of this OK, though.

I was picked to represent our battalion for Burial Registration. We'll have to collect the dead soldiers and see that they're properly buried and registered. I'll be on this detail for a few days I guess. Won't get any mail until

I get back to the company, but received your letter of January 3 today before my detail left.

It's been miserably cold for quite a while now. Have a cold and am so hoarse I can hardly talk. I'm wearing several layers of clothes. I can hardly wiggle. After you stay out so long you get chilled through, even with the extra layers.

Harriet reread the letter. When would this madness be over? Since when was her husband a mortician? This war certainly required unexpected duty from its inductees. She sighed. At least he wasn't one of the unfortunate heroes being picked up from the battlefield. Harriet said a prayer for Henry and his fellow soldiers.

She wondered if Bee's wife, Marge, knew of his hospital stay. Harriet picked up the phone to call her, but thought better of it. If Marge didn't know, Harriet didn't want to be the one to tell her. From what Henry said, Marge didn't need any encouragement to worry more.

If Henry thought he was cold before, he discovered a new level of freezing as he and his fellow soldiers on the Collection Squad picked up frozen bodies off the battlefield from the Battle of the Bulge. There was not even a foxhole to crawl into to escape the frigid wind and deep snow.

They noted where each body fell and transported the frozen corpses to a litter jeep. It had a wide flat board mounted on its hood to carry the dead soldiers to the Collection Station. There, the person in charge fingerprinted all ten fingers and noted any identifying marks.

Henry and his coworkers then drove the bodies to the Evacuation Squad where their personal effects were listed and placed in a cotton bag with a drawstring. Those bags were returned to the soldier's families back home.

The Collection Squad wrapped the bodies in a blanket, sheet, or mattress cover, secured by horse blanket safety pins. They made sure one of the soldier's dog tags was attached to him before internment and his second tag went into a bottle buried down six inches at the head of his grave. The Burial Squad hammered a stake eighteen inches into the frozen ground at each plot in the area marked off as a cemetery.

When daylight faded, Henry had trouble sleeping. The faces of the soldiers appeared to him, even in his dreams. So many dead. So much grief. Those poor families back home. The fight for freedom carried such a high price.

By the time Henry's duty was complete, his cold had almost developed into pneumonia. When he returned to his platoon, his first stop was the hospital for a brief stay.

In Henry's January 18, 1945 letter he reported they had moved from their last position. They had briefly stopped in Saverne in north-east France.

> Wish I could tell you where we are now, but that would get the censor's tail in a knot. This is a nice town and a lot livelier than where we have been. There's always a big manure pile in front of each house. The cows, chickens, goats and hogs live in part of the house. You can tell a man's standing in the community by the size of his manure pile.

Harriet thought about her early years on the farm. Although she considered it quite primitive with an outhouse and her unheated bedroom in the attic, she couldn't imagine barn animals sharing the same roof! Maybe her early years weren't so bad after all.

He continued:

> I'm back with the company and have a new job. Believe it or not, I'm Supply Sergeant now. Don't know how I'll like it but I expect I'll get along OK. At least I get to be inside some of the time.

Bee and Joe are back at a rest camp. While I was gone on burial detail they went through some rough fighting. They'll be there 3 or 4 days.

It warmed up considerable today. Hope it doesn't start raining like they say it's supposed to.

Got a letter from Lloyd. He said at one time we were within a mile of each other. "Too far to holler," he said. I'll finish this later.

Now it's evening. Worked at my new job today. It's not bad after I catch on to it.

The temperature dropped. It's snowing and blowing. I'll be glad when summer gets here. Then we won't have to wear a thousand pounds of clothes to keep warm.

That evening when Harriet put Sally to bed, they said special prayers for Bee and Joe, as well as Henry. Harriet added a P.S. on to their prayer while Sally kissed her daddy's picture. "And Lord, please send Henry a special encouragement."

Chapter 42

Henry's letter of January 22, 1945 read:

> We're staying with a really nice couple who let me use their fiddle tonight. Only 3 strings work but that's better than none. Can't understand their language. Tonight they gave me some whipped cream and peaches.
>
> Bee and Joe are back from the rest camp. Bee's still shaken up. Might have a nervous breakdown. Don't tell Marge. She's so unstrung. Glad you're brave. Helps to know my girls are steady in the rough times. You sounded blue in your last letter. Don't worry. I'll be home one of these days.
>
> Got two Fort Scott papers today dated Dec. 5 & 6. Fresh news. Right up to the minute!
>
> Marge sent Bee a box of candy. She makes candy as good as she makes chocolate cake. Send anything except cigarettes. They give us more than we can smoke. They're issued the same as rations.
>
> War looks good tonight—especially in the Russian and French 1st Army.
>
> Glad Val is getting along so well with Sally. Hope she stays on. Pay her double if she'll stay.
>
> We get the *Stars and Stripes* Army newspaper about every day and keep up fairly well with the news. We made some news a while back.

Henry decided not to tell her the details of the last month. Their first big battle happened in Wingen, France against two battalions of SS Mountain troops. The G.I.s were outnumbered eight to one. Many of Henry's buddies were captured and held for three days in a Catholic church without food or water. After house to house combat, part of the 70th Division finally took the town. What was left of the enemy army limped away in retreat.

Unfortunately, they regrouped near the Maginot Line. For ten days the troops fought in the open in the worst winter in fifty years. Their drinking water turned to ice in their canteens. Automatic weapons froze with the slightest hint of moisture. In order for Henry to get rations, ammo, and clothing to the troops, he sometimes had to drag it up steep icy trails. He also delivered candles for the guys to use for heat in their dugouts. These deliveries had to be made at night.

One night after they made their last drop, they headed back to base. Their commander was in the lead. They heard a small squeak. Two seconds later he was blown to kingdom come by exploding shrapnel. He'd stepped on a trip wire connected to a land mine they called a Bouncing Betty.

Henry's stomach churned. He was next in command. He signaled everyone down. They crawled on their bellies probing the dirt in front of them with their pocket knives looking for buried explosives.

The woods were alive with Jerrys. As Henry crept along, the words he learned at his mother's knee came to mind. He whispered them as they inched forward.

"The Lord is my shepherd—I shall not want. He makes me lie down in green pastures."

Henry signaled a pause to his fellow troops to listen for the enemy. Hearing nothing, they continued and the words began again—as if someone spoke them to him.

"Yea, though I walk through the valley of the shadow of death, I will fear no evil—for thou art with me."

A strange peace descended on him. He and his buddies continued to move forward. Henry concentrated on the words as each phrase poured into him.

"Thy rod and thy staff they comfort me."

Just before dawn, they made it safely back to base.

He had a new calm about himself—a new knowing his life really was in God's hands. Whatever happened to him was God's will.

Henry closed his letter to Harriet with the simple statement:

> Our 7th Army has been a little active the last day or two.

No need to upset Harriet.

Harriet smiled as she sat at the kitchen table when she read the letter. She remembered the prayer she prayed for encouragement for Henry. He loved to fiddle. Before the war, he'd sit and saw on an old fiddle his grandfather played. Henry could figure out any instrument, given a little time.

After supper, Sally watched as Harriet got out her pen and paper. "Write Daddy," Sally said as she picked up the pencil. "Dear Sally."

Harriet smiled. "No, punkin', we're going to say, 'Dear Daddy.'"

Sally sat on Harriet's lap as she penned a letter to her husband.

Soon, Sally yawned. Kissing the top of her daughter's head, Harriet said, "We need to get you to bed, little one."

It didn't take long for Sally's quick bath and a jump into her jammies. While Harriet made some warm milk, Sally shuffled to the couch in her house slippers and robe. She plopped down with a new book Val bought her.

Harriet turned from the stove to pour a cup for herself and Sally and caught a glance of Sally. A wave of grief washed over her. Henry was missing these precious days which could never be relived because the world had gone mad.

As she sat to write again, she told her hubby each detail of the evening. It would be second-hand, but at least he wouldn't miss it entirely.

Before she folded the letter she remembered a bit of news she kept forgetting to tell him about the Nevada store. Just before Christmas a guy came in with a gun near quitting time and demanded the jewelry in the display case. He made off with $2,500 worth of watches and diamond rings. He was still on the loose.

She slipped the letter into the envelope and turned out the light. The phone rang. Her stomach tightened. Who could be calling at this hour? Had Henry been injured?

It was her mother. "Harriet, we just got the word. Your grandpa Edmiston died tonight. Wanted you to know. I'll call again with details."

Thoughts of her grandfather played in her head through the night. He was the grandparent she liked best. She'd miss his deep bass voice calling to her in his Kentucky drawl, "Har'et, come sit a spell." His interest in her everyday life never ceased to please her. Now, suddenly without warning, he was gone.

In the morning, she put a p.s. on Henry's letter to tell him of Grandfather's passing.

The Edmiston stores and all its branches closed for two days with a notice on the doors:

CLOSED DUE TO THE DEATH OF
JAMES MALCOLM EDMISTON,
FATHER OF
VERNON EDMISTON, PROPRIETOR

Vernon placed a large ad in the paper in memory of his father. A black wreath adorned Grandmother Edmiston's front door.

Val watched Sally while Harriet attended the funeral in Nevada. On the way home, solid ice glazed the roads. By the time she returned home, her daughter was asleep.

The night after the funeral Harriet penned another letter to her husband. As usual, she reported on the sales of the store that week so Henry could feel a connection to something other than the craziness of war.

Sold two men's suits and a fur coat today. Did $573. We showed a loss for the *week from last year because we were closed those two days.*

I saw Pauline Graves in the store today. She's never heard anything from her husband, Fatso, since he got to France with you all last December. She's afraid he's a prisoner of war. Have you heard anything on your end about him?

I'm listening to the 11 o'clock news. It sounds good. Hopefully, this war will be over soon.

Chapter 43

The end of January, Henry and five of his buddies accepted an invitation to supper from the family they were staying with. The Frenchman had butchered a hog. When the Germans occupied their territory, he managed to hide his animals in a remote area. Otherwise, the Germans would have made quick work of his livestock because their supplies were so low.

First, the old man passed a plate of thin-sliced raw fresh pork. None of the G.I.s had ever eaten raw pork before, Henry included. Rather than offend his host, he ate it, hoping it had no worms. The hostess passed a large plate with four different salads and a relish.

Their host opened some of his prize wine and poured each of them a glass. The wife served pork chops and fresh liver. Henry had never tasted better.

For dessert, they had a custard with a delicious fruit sauce. Henry had been away from home for so long he'd forgotten how a real meal tasted.

Like all others, their house, barn, and sheds were under one roof—incinerator, smoke house, and all. As usual, their manure pile stood close to the front door. Henry noted their well was downhill from the manure pile, like so many other farms.

Only one G.I. could speak French and acted as their interpreter. The others communicated with smiles and hand motions.

This couple often baked pies for them and gave them apples, milk, and whipped cream.

In turn, they gave the farmer candy, chocolate bars, and coffee. Whenever they gave the old man cigarettes and cigars, he'd smile and say, "I'm rich!"

When Harriet heard of this kindness she overflowed with gratitude to know God had sent someone to look out for her man.

Harriet's next letter to Henry read:

> *Honey, I walked into the bedroom the other evening to get Sally ready for bed. She was talking to your picture. She said, "Come home, Daddy. I kiss your face." Then she kissed your picture with a big smack. I hope that doesn't make you sad. Oh how I wish you were here so both of us could kiss your face! We miss you so. One day soon you will be with us again.*
>
> *I'm sending you a package with some chocolate bars and some homemade candy. I also included some cheese and crackers. It won't be as good as what the French lady made for you, but when you get home I'll cook you some yummy dinners—without the raw pork.*
>
> *The other night when I got Sally out of the bathtub she ran into the living room and slipped and fell on the hot floor furnace on her bum. Now she has a waffle bottom. She showed Val her "bumpity" first thing when she got here the next morning. Hopefully, it will heal quickly. That kid is about two steps ahead of me all the time.*

Three weeks later, Henry's reply made its way through the censors and back to the States.

> I heard from David. He's permanently stationed at Norman, Oklahoma. He's repairing airplanes. Guess that job at the airplane factory in California helped get his assignment in Norman. Hope he can stay there. Sure is better than being on a battlefield or a ship somewhere.
>
> The Russians are pile-driving now. They're only 92 miles from Berlin. Hopefully, they'll make 'em holler uncle soon.
>
> Bee is better. I think he'll be all right now.
>
> Was sorry to hear about the robbery at the Nevada store. I'll bet that sure hurt the jewelry department figures for the month of December—$2,500 isn't easy to take. You'd think with the man shortage there'd be plenty of jobs—no need to go rob a store. I guess some people just won't work for an honest living. Hope the police catch the guy.
>
> Sorry I haven't written much lately. We're too busy chasing Krauts. Your letters take about two weeks to get here.
>
> I love you telling me about what Sally does. I'm glad she talks to my picture. It lets me dream I am with you at home for the moment. Hope I can barge in the door before very long and have her still remember me.
>
> I'll see you in my dreams. Keep a stiff upper lip, honey. You're doing fine. We'll always be lonesome for each other as long as we're apart, but there's nothing we can do about it. Lovin' you always. Cuddle our little daughter up close and sleep tight.

Through the month of January after the battle to take Wingen, France, the Commanding Officers kept Henry's 70th Division on the move. Henry spent part of his time on the battlefield; the rest as Supply Sergeant.

Some of the German POWs reported they were under "stand or die" orders from Hitler. The G.I.s systematically worked their way through the French border towns toward Saarbrucken, Germany, located on the east side of the Saar River.

His letter of February 4, 1945, read:

> Bee and I and several others were awarded the Combat Infantry Expert Badge for our participation in battle. That means $5.00 more a month.
>
> It quit snowing for a couple of days. It's warming a little, but the thaw brings gummy mud. The melting snow around each foxhole makes a good target for the Jerrys. This is the worst winter they've had in fifty years. How come we're so lucky to be out in it?
>
> The store figures look great. I'd give it all up to be back with my little family.

He continued the letter on February 10, 1945.

> We've moved again. I got to take my first shower today since we got here 7 weeks ago. We're in a large house in town with electric lights. What a thrill to turn on a switch. Foxholes don't have such luxuries.
>
> My supplies are in a room about 18 x 18 with a heating stove and draw shutters for blackouts. Really a palace.
>
> Bee's in the hospital again. He just can't take it, as old and crippled as he is—but still they put him on the line. They put hot towels on his legs and took x-rays. They may operate.
>
> I'll be glad when a man can do whatever he wants again. Lots of our men are in the infirmary.

Sounds like the Russians are really putting the pressure on. Hope they keep going. The sooner this is over the sooner we can go home.

They can say what they want about V-mail but I prefer air mail. I got your last letter in 7 days.

Wish I could tell you where I am, but I don't dare chance it. The censors are really pouring it on.

Harriet hung on every word from the war correspondents in the newspaper and on the radio. From what they said, it sounded like the Allies were winning the war—but when would the end come? Her main focus was on Europe because that's where Henry was. She wished he would try out their little message system again, but if that put him in jeopardy, she'd forgo the knowing.

She seldom put much stock in dreams, but the memory of one wouldn't let go.

In her dream, it was Easter Sunday. The pastor stood to preach with a big grin.

"Instead of a sermon today, we are going to devote our time to praising God for the blessing of Hitler's defeat."

Harriet awoke wondering how she missed the news of this momentous event. When she turned on the radio, she was disappointed to learn it was only a dream. It had seemed so real.

After several days, she wrote Henry, sharing the incident with him.

Do you think God might be telling us that the war will end on Easter Sunday?

Henry commented,

Don't put too much hope into an Easter ending. I hope you're right, but I'm afraid we'll still be going strong until after Easter. Watch our smoke from now on, though. The news we hear over here sounds good.

Chapter 44

After two days in the last place, Henry's outfit was on the move again closer to the Saar River. The U.S. Army Corps arrived with a vengeance. Henry and Joe watched from a hillside.

"Man! I'd sure hate to be down there right now," Joe said. "Glad it's our planes and not theirs."

"You and me both, brother!"

The weather warmed. The rainy season began in northeastern France. Slick mud made the roads as treacherous to vehicles as the ice had been—only dirtier. Foot soldiers slogged in mud past their ankles in addition to dodging heavy enemy fire.

Harriet wrote Henry she learned Fatso was indeed a POW. She also asked Henry what put him and Bee the infirmary the first time.

As he read her questions, he thought about how much to tell her. He didn't want to give her too much information for fear it would fuel her worry. Also he avoided any mention of where they encountered the Krauts for fear the censors would cut it out of his letter.

> Dear Sweetheart,
>
> I can tell you more about it now, although I don't think you'll be too interested in most of it. It was my first time to meet the Krauts and Bee's second. He tangled with them the night before. The fighting was so fierce it

knocked us a little batty. We were evacuated to the clearing station for a couple of days to sorta rest up. We weren't wounded but it was a dirty mess from start to finish. Don't worry about me being in danger all the time. I'm OK.

To get her mind on something else he continued:

My buddy, Joe, is going to Officer's Candidate School in England, but he hasn't left yet. He'll be in training for 18 weeks. Maybe this mess will be over by then. I turned the opportunity down. I'll stay an enlisted man. None of this career Army stuff for me.

Haven't heard from Lloyd for quite a while. No clue where he is.

Bee is assistant jeep driver now. Wish they would send him to the rear echelon.

Tell my little sweetheart, "Keep saying your prayers each night for Daddy. Jesus will answer your prayers, honey. Help Mommy fix the store windows and listen for news of Daddy over the radio. Love you lots."

Do you or your mom have a map that shows Forbach on it?

Got your package with the French harp in it. It's a great morale builder. Thanks a million.

Some of the fellows got to Paris on 3-day passes. Guess I won't be that lucky. I haven't been on any sight-seeing trips other than government-chaperoned ones since I hit this country. I'd like to see some of it without having to fight my way through it.

Harriet wondered if his reference to the town of Forbach was his way of hinting that's where he was. If so, the censors missed it.

His next letter arrived written on the back of the letter she had sent him dated January 28.

February 21, 1945

This is the last straw! Writing on the back of your letters! Since I have a foxhole instead of a nice USO club to write in, this'll have to do. Don't worry when I don't write. The Krauts are keeping us busy. Have to make this short. Just wanted you to know I'm OK. Thinking about you and Sally.

Henry decided not to mention the house to house battles to take Forbach. Snipers popped up around every corner. The G.I.s captured 100 soldiers that day—their highest ever one-day catch. The Americans fought into the evening with a new weapon—huge searchlights to locate their targets.

By the next week, the enemy threw everything they had at the 70th Division. In an attempt to keep the G.I.s on the French side of the Saar River, they fired two-hour barrages with nine to twelve shells a minute at the American troops. In spite of it all, the G.I.s captured 463 German soldiers that month—some were mere boys. Henry knew they must be pretty desperate if they were sending ones this young into battle.

Henry wrote his next letter on February 25, 1945, on a raggedy piece of paper—the only unused one he could find.

Sorry for the letter delay. Haven't had time to write.

Six of us sat in on a family-style dinner tonight. One of the cooks stays in a house with a complete set of china. He found an old lace curtain for a tablecloth and located some potatoes for French fries. We also had spam, baked whole apples, and coffee, at a real table. The front is a half-mile away with shells landing here and there, but we're used to that. We enjoyed it anyway, just because it was something different.

They really have some beautiful homes here. Much different than the ones farther back in France. Of course, the manure pile still is in evidence in a lot of places but the homes are very nice and modern. When the German Army comes through, they tear the whey out of them.

I couldn't believe Sally's pictures you sent me. She's so grown up! She is really cute, and you can tell her so.

The *Stars and Stripes* carried an article recently about our Division when we fought a battle in January farther back in France in Wingen.

When Harriet read that last line she knew her suspicions were correct on Henry's whereabouts. When she looked on the map she realized they were pressing toward the German border. She continued to read:

Got a letter from Bee. He says they're really going to fix his legs this time. He's missing out on a lot of this fighting now. I'm glad. He wasn't up to it.

Don't think a Supply Sergeant ever gets caught up on his work. I don't anyway.

I forgot to mention it, but a friend I met here named Caple was wounded by shrapnel at our first battle in the Lichtenburg Forest. From what I hear, he'll lose most of his hand.

Money sure doesn't mean much over here. Some guys pick up as much as 100,000 marks lying in the street. Not good for anything but wiping on. I haven't spent a franc since I bought a pie from a local woman. If you have a chocolate bar or cigarettes, you can buy most anything here. You can get a good hair cut for a chocolate bar.

A couple of days ago I was classified as Limited Service. With that classification I can't fight on the front line. Yesterday, we passed out clean clothes to the men within 150 yards of the front. I wonder how far back they consider the front line to be?

Harriet sighed in relief when she read that line. Now if Hitler would just admit defeat, all the soldiers could come home and quit this craziness.

Henry's next letter at the end of February came about five days later.

The Germans are in retreat on the other side of the Saar River. Now France is free of the Nazi occupation. The locals are rejoicing.

The war picture looks pretty good, but still not fast enough to suit me. Tell me if you want to hear some of the war happenings.

I've included a clipping. You can see we've been in the headlines. Those Germans are plenty tough, but we've got a fightin' outfit.

My buddy, Joe, left today for that 18-week course to be an officer.

It's rained the last 3 days. It's bad on the men who are out. If a humble little home isn't fully appreciated by every ex-serviceman after this war is over, there's something wrong with him. I want a nice home after this but won't squawk if I live in an old weather-beaten house for a while.

The War Department notified Bee's wife he'd been injured in action. Bet that sent her into a tizzy. Wish they'd be careful about how and what they report. He wasn't injured in action. He only had a scratch on his face. It's his legs that are dealing him fits. If you get a message like that about me, don't believe it!

We hear the Russians are giving the Krauts plenty of trouble. We're stretched out on a wide front. I'll be glad when we can shake hands with the Russians. Maybe then we can have a little peace and quiet.

How's my little Sally gal? Remind her to say her prayers for us each night.

Harriet couldn't agree with Henry more. She prayed for the day when there was no more fight left in the Nazi machine. Then they could have their life back again.

Harriet decided to come home for a quick visit with Sally over lunch in early March. When she got there, Val and Sally were nowhere in sight. Perhaps they went on a walk on this nice spring day. Harriet made a bologna sandwich and ate it quickly. She left a note for Val on the kitchen table to let her know she'd been home for lunch.

When she returned that evening, Val still wasn't there. It didn't appear she had been home during the afternoon. Where could they have gone? Had Sally missed her nap? Had something happened? She searched the kitchen for a note.

She heard voices coming from the stairwell. As she opened the door, she was greeted by Val. A strange man carried Sally asleep on his shoulder.

Harriet frowned. "Where have you been and who is this person?" She reached for Sally. He had alcohol on his breath. The hair stood up on Harriet's neck. Alcohol was something strictly forbidden in her household. When she took Sally in her arms, the child was so tired she barely stirred. Harriet quickly laid her on the bed and closed the door before she came back to the kitchen.

In slightly slurred speech Val answered, "Oh, this is my friend, Mitch. We took a little ride to the country this afternoon."

Harriet grabbed the note off the table and held it in front of Val's face. "You've been gone since before noon when I came home for lunch. Where did you get the idea you could take off? Your job is to stay here and watch Sally—not go for country rides. Have you done this before?"

Val took a step back and looked at the floor. “Only a couple of times. We meant no harm, Mrs. Freeman.”

“No harm? You didn’t even leave me a note! I never gave you permission to have a male friend over here or to go anywhere with one. This will never do.” Harriet fumbled for her purse and quickly calculated the money she owed Val. Handing it to her she said, “I’m sorry, Val. I can’t tolerate this.”

The young man opened his mouth to protest.

“Leave! Now!”

He put his arm around Val and reached for the door.

“And don’t come back.” With shaking hands, Harriet locked the door behind them. Now what would she do? She certainly couldn’t take Sally to work with her. She went to call her mother.

Chapter 45

After Glessner listened to her daughter's tale about Val, she said, "You know we're glad to take her, Harriet."

"Mom, I don't want you to have to keep her again. It's a strain on you. I want her here with me. She's been tossed around enough."

"I understand, honey. I'll check around here and see if I can locate a dependable woman."

"Thanks, Mom." She had no clue who that person might be.

The next day, Central, the telephone operator, called Glessner. "Miz Edmiston, uh, I overheard your conversation last night with Harriet."

Glessner didn't say it, but she knew the operator spent her days listening in on almost every call that came through her living room switchboard. "And?"

"Well, I heard Miz Gant's sister is visiting in town. She might be able to help Harriet. Her name's Leota Hammer. Want me to connect you to their residence?"

Glessner remembered Mrs. Gant's sister when she was introduced at church the previous Sunday. The woman had appeared to be in her fifties. They said Leota had come from Kansas City after sitting with an elderly person who had died. Perhaps that was their answer. "Yes. Why don't you do that? Thanks."

On their regular Sunday afternoon visit to Walker, Harriet and Sally went to meet Miss Hammer at her sister's home. The woman was a short, frail-looking lady with a tight little bun on the back of her head. Round wire glasses framed her eyes. She smelled of Listerine.

"Would you be interested in coming to live with us and sit with Sally while I go to work? You would need to do some cooking and light cleaning. My apartment is small but you could sleep on the couch in the living room."

Miss Hammer frowned. "Oh, dear. I don't know. I've never been in charge of a child before. I usually sit for old people."

Sally slid off her mother's lap and sat at Miss Hammer's feet, looking into her face with a wide grin.

At least Sally liked her. That was a plus.

"I could bring you for visits with your sister on Sunday when I come see my folks."

"That would be very nice. May I have some time to think over your offer?"

Harriet chose her words carefully. She wanted to scream, "What is there to think over? Just say yes and let's get on with it." Instead, she smiled and said, "Of course. How long do you think you'll need?"

Miss Hammer cocked her head. "What about next Sunday? Would that be soon enough?"

With a sinking heart Harriet answered, "Yes. That would be fine." Now she would have to leave Sally with her mother for yet another week—if Miss Hammer decided she could handle the job.

When she arrived home that night she wrote Henry of the latest babysitter developments. Would this circus ever end? She doubted it.

The next Sunday afternoon, Harriet called the Gant residence.

"Have you made a decision yet, Miss Hammer?"

"Yes. I think I'd like to come to work for you. It would be a nice change."

Harriet gave a mental sigh of relief. "Wonderful. Can we pick you up this afternoon?"

"Yes. I think I can be packed by six."

"That's great. See you then." Harriet hung up the phone and let out a war whoop and clapped her hands. "She's coming! We have a sitter!"

When Harriet and Sally pulled up to the Gant home promptly at six, Miss Hammer stepped out the door and adjusted her clip-on sunglasses. With a small bag in one hand she made her way carefully to the car, turned to wave at her sister, and climbed into the back seat with Sally.

"Welcome aboard, Miss Hammer," Harriet said as she pulled away from the curb.

"Oh pshaw. Call me Leota."

All the way home Leota entertained Sally, reciting poetry and telling her about the three bears and Goldilocks.

Harriet breathed a sigh of relief. Hopefully, this little lady wouldn't have any male friends to take them on country rides.

After Leota was settled on the couch in the living room and Sally was in bed, Harriet sat to write Henry about Leota. She also included the news that Pops bought another 400-acre farm a mile east of Walker so he could run more cattle.

With relief, Henry commented in his next letter,

> So glad you were able to find a sitter. Hope Miss Hammer works out for you. Sounds like Sally likes her. That's good. Hope she stays till I can get home. That kid has been handed off too many times already.
>
> Pops is acquiring more real estate now, is he? I guess he can't resist the temptation. Well, if that's what he wants, more power to him. Looks like we're going to have to raise some grandsons to help him take care of it though.

When Harriet read that line she cringed. From his comment, he still wanted to have more children. Perhaps after the war he would be content to be home again and forget about increasing their family. At least she hoped so.

Henry's next letter was written from a nice house on the French side of the French/German border. It had lights and running water. He guessed they would soon to be on the move farther into enemy territory—one step closer to going home.

I'm now a Staff Sergeant as of March 17th. The rank doesn't mean much to me. Since I've been here that stuff has lost its glitter.

He didn't write Harriet where they were going so he wouldn't get in trouble with the censors, but they were preparing to cross the Saar River into Saarbrucken, Germany.

When Henry caught the first glimpse of the crossing he could hardly believe his eyes. On the German side of the Saar sat three rows of barriers all along the river. He learned the first barriers were called Dragon's Teeth. They were three-foot high barricades set every three feet to stop the G.I.s trucks and tanks. The next, a heavy snarl of barbed wire. Beyond that lay curved rails set upward to make it impossible for any vehicle to move forward. This was going to be a monumental task.

On their first attempt on the 15th of March under heavy German fire, the G.I.s were driven back repeatedly.

Three days later American aircraft strafed troop trains headed east, deeper into Germany. Because of heavy fire, the G.I.s doubted the Germans were pulling out.

Two days later the first of the 70th Division launched an attack across the river in small boats. They crawled up the bank toward the Dragon's Teeth. Where was the enemy fire? Were the Germans waiting until they got in point-blank range? After several quiet minutes the troops realized the enemy had evacuated. Many unfortunate G.I.s discovered the well-salted areas of land mines. Some, were booby-trapped to explode when anyone tried to remove them.

The Altbruck (Old Bridge) built four hundred years earlier, was the major crossing of the Saar for tanks, trucks, and jeeps. The Germans had only blown the middle of the bridge. The 70th Engineers quickly went to work repairing the damage. When they entered the city they set up a command post in a university building and discovered 150 pounds of TNT on a time-device before it went off.

A day later, the G.I.s captured the German in charge of the bridge demolition. He said they'd intended to blow the entire bridge with a 600-pound charge but they only succeeded in blowing the middle. Their wires to each end of the bridge had been severed to the detonator by heavy G.I. artillery fire.

When Henry heard this news, he thanked God for His mercy and timing. If the Germans had succeeded in blowing up the entire bridge, it would have delayed their advance into Germany for weeks.

The center of Saarbrucken, the Queen of the Saar Valley, lay in complete rubble.

March 20th ended with the 70th Division on German soil. Henry wondered how much longer it would be before they could shake the hands of those Russians soldiers he so desired to see. Easter Sunday, April 1, wasn't so far away. He wondered if Harriet's dream might come true after all.

Henry made a find in one of the German houses that pleased him greatly and wrote Harriet about it.

> I got a violin. The Germans vacated the last town we were in. They left everything—canned fruit, musical instruments—everything. Really enjoyed playing it. This one has all four strings. I still have the French harp you sent me. Have to work it over once in a while to get the dirt out, but it still plays pretty good.
>
> Here, German civilians don't welcome us so warmly. They need to stay out of our way. We're ordered not to fraternize with them. Doesn't bother me any. If they had any sense 10 years ago we wouldn't be in this war. They'll have to take the consequences.
>
> Most all the towns here in Germany are evacuated. They aren't flattened like in France.
>
> A lot of things would make nice souvenirs but I'm not going to bother. It's a lot of red tape to send anything home.

The last couple of days we've had it easy since we pushed them toward the trap. We're pretty far back from the front.

In Forbach I saw the counter-attack from a ringside seat about a half mile away in a castle. All hell broke loose. Our company caught the prisoners on the rebound. There were plenty of 'em.

I'm sure glad Pauline finally heard from Fatso. I've felt all along he was a prisoner of war. Hope he makes it through to the end of this mess. The Jerrys sure take their sweet time letting you know about prisoners. Of course, we do too.

Chapter 46

Val saw Harriet in the store soon after Leota came to watch Sally. In an attempt to avoid her, Harriet headed down another aisle.

"Mrs. Freeman, can we talk?"

Val was the last person she wanted to talk to.

"Did you find anyone to watch Sally? I'm so sorry about what happened. Is there a chance I could watch her again?"

"No, I'm sorry, Val. I have someone else."

With slumped shoulders, the girl nodded and walked away.

Harriet felt sorry for her, but perhaps this would be an important lesson for her in future employments. She took a long breath. Things were going well with Leota, even though the woman had little experience with small children. Hopefully, the good times would continue.

In Harriet's letter that night to Henry she reported the encounter with Val.

When Henry read that letter anger rose within him. He fired a response dated March 24, 1945.

> So Val wants to come back? She should have thought a little further ahead when she took her joy rides. It would have made things a lot simpler for everyone.
>
> We just got settled. We got word we'll move out in the morning for parts unknown. I knew it was too good to

be true to sit 50 miles behind the lines. I may not get to write for a few days, so don't worry.

I was about to hunt for my buddy, Lloyd, when this move blew up. We confiscated a half ton panel truck and 2 motorcycles. We take anything we need from the Germans for as long as we want it. I'm so thankful this war is over here and not in the States. I'd hate to turn my car over to the Krauts."

After their move Henry sat to write in their new quarters, even though he felt exhausted from hauling the ordinance, clothing, and supplies closer to the front lines for the umpteenth time.

I hear the Saar Valley is the richest in the world. It sure looks it. I saw scenery today that'd put Colorado in the shade. When we make our millions we'll travel to Europe with our daughter and son. I know you'll enjoy it. The German people here are more friendly that the ones farther back. About half of them speak English, too. Some have sons who moved to America. Some of those boys are U.S. soldiers fighting the Japs.

We moved 45-miles today. We're still a way back from the front lines. Our guys are really pushing the Krauts now.

I tried playing an accordion tonight. Got so I could pick out a tune or two. The accordions over here have buttons instead of keys.

I'm one of about 5 old men left in this outfit now. The younger guys call us 'Pops.' To me, Pops is a guy your dad's age.

We've had it pretty nice lately living in homes. We kick the Germans out and move in. We hand them our clothes to wash and thank them when they're done. They do a good job, too. This town was very lucky. Not one house was damaged.

Your prediction of an Easter Armistice looks pretty good, according to tonight's *Stars and Stripes*. Sure hope it's over soon.

Keep your chin up, sweetheart. It can't last forever. The Krauts are whipped now but they don't know how to end it.

Harriet re-read the letter and bristled at the line about touring Europe with a son. How could he be so sure a second child would be a boy? Even if a son could be a sure thing, she was not about to go through another birth again—even if Henry thought it a necessary addition.

Uncle Vernon came in the store on Good Friday the end of March. "Harriet, meet me in the stock room. I want to talk."

Had she done something wrong? It wasn't time for March's sales figures yet. She finished writing a sales slip for her customer and headed to the back to talk with Uncle Vernon.

"What's on your mind?" Harriet perched on a large box filled with new merchandise.

"I'm purchasing a clothing store in Ottawa. It's offered at a good price, and I need you to go there to manage it."

"Ottawa, Kansas?" Was he serious? What made him think she would pick up and move clear up there? That was at least an hour and a half, maybe two, north of Fort Scott—even farther from Walker. What if Leota didn't want to go? That would mean a new sitter. Sally and Leota got along so well. More new people. A new church. "I—I'm not sure I want to do that."

Waving her off he said, "Oh, you'll do fine. You always do. Besides, you're the only one I can trust to do the inventory right. You've done well here. Take a couple of days off to go find a place to live. I'll meet you there next week to introduce you to the previous owner and the employees. Then you can show the help how to do a proper inventory before I sign the final papers and give him a check."

"But—"

As Vernon headed for the door he said, "We don't have much time. He's in poor health. See you Monday."

"But what about Easter?"

He kept walking, ignoring her final comment.

She muttered as she shook her head, "That Vernon. How is he so sure I can find a place in three days—or that I'll even go?"

Harriet went home for lunch so she could ask Leota if she'd be willing to move to Ottawa. If she wasn't, Harriet decided she wouldn't go. She wasn't willing to find another sitter. Besides, Sally had already been tossed around like a spare basketball. Vernon would just have to find someone else.

When she pulled in front of the house, she smiled. A feeling of pride rose up within her. Vernon had chosen her over some man. Still, she'd leave the decision to Leota's response.

When asked, Leota said, "Hmmm. I've never lived in Ottawa. Never even been there. Guess it's as good a place as any. Would you still be going to Walker every Sunday?"

"Probably not. That would take gas ration stamps I don't have. Guess we'll have to cancel this Sunday's visit over there, too. I have to go to Ottawa this afternoon to find us a place to live—if there is one."

Harriet threw a couple of things into a bag and bid goodbye to Sally and Leota. "I'll be back as soon as I can. Not sure how long this'll take." She was on the road by two.

When she arrived in Ottawa around four, Harriet drove past the store. It was nice looking in the heart of downtown on Main Street. The town didn't look a lot different from Fort Scott. She could see she'd have to do some rearranging of the window displays. They had way too much merchandise to showcase the better pieces.

"Okay, Lord. Now where do I go from here?" She drove up and down each street close to downtown. If she could walk to work it would save on gas. She hadn't seen one house for rent yet.

When she got to 5th Street she turned right. Just across the railroad tracks that ran parallel to Main, she spotted a FOR RENT sign in the front yard of a little bungalow. She took down the number and went to locate a pay phone. She found one at the drugstore.

"Do you have a house for rent on 5th street?"

A pleasant-sounding female voice said, "Why, yes. I do. Are you interested?"

"Very. Could you show it to me this afternoon? I'm moving here soon and need a place right away."

"Very well. I'll meet you there directly."

When the lady arrived she shook Harriet's hand. "Hello, dear. I'm Mrs. Kingsley. And you are?"

"Harriet Freeman. From Fort Scott."

"Come inside and take a look, my dear. I still have one room to paint before it's ready." She rubbed her shoulder. "Just not as young as I used to be."

Harriet looked the house over and said she'd take it. She offered to paint the kitchen if the lady would take some off the first month's rent.

With the deal sealed, Harriet headed back to Fort Scott that evening so she could start packing on Saturday. That way they could still go to Easter services and make a last trip to Walker on Sunday afternoon.

Back in Fort Scott that evening she dashed off a note to Henry about their move and their new address. She also began to jot notes on a "To Do" list. This quick move required some tall planning.

Chapter 47

Easter Day dawned with no word of the war ending, contrary to Harriet's vivid dream. Each time she recalled it she remembered the euphoria she felt before she was fully awake.

They moved to Ottawa the next week.

Leota settled into a small attic room whose closed staircase and doorway sat at the edge of the dining room which Harriet made into her bedroom. Sally slept with her mother.

Harriet spent long hours at the store during the transition.

One night Harriet lay in bed and reflected on her good fortune to have found Leota before this move. What if Val had been her babysitter when Vernon said, "Move!"

Then she prayed the war would end soon. Russia had cut Vienna in half. How long could Hitler hang on?

Henry didn't want Easter to pass without a letter to Harriet. She so depended on his regular letters so he wrote one before turning in.

April 1, 1945

We spent today in our usual mode—moving. It seems we always move at 8:00 on a Sunday morning or a holiday. On Christ's birthday we were on that 40 & 8 boxcar and on His Resurrection Day we're headed farther past the Saar River.

We've cut off Germany's supply of gas and oil. They don't have enough to run their trucks while they retreat.

Tons of their equipment is stacked along the highway. Our planes have knocked out convoy after convoy. The Krauts loaded their vehicles on flat cars. Then our planes knocked out the trains.

They've been whipped and ready to quit for quite a while now. If only someone higher up would say the word. Every POW I've seen (and I've seen plenty) has a big smile on his face. He knows he'll get rations and protection because his fighting days are over.

Last I heard, we're slicing Germany to ribbons. If I never get any other satisfaction out of this whole war, I want to see Hitler and his tribe of murderers dealt with like they've dished it out to others.

This younger generation just out of high school doesn't know French. Only German and English. It's easy to figure out why. Hitler ordered English taught in all the schools so they'd be able to get the Americans in line when he conquered the U.S.

Most German people are fine citizens. They want peace. They hate Hitler.

The Mess Sergeant and I get together every night. I play the accordion and he plays the French harp. I lost the one you sent me, but they're several floating around here.

Got a letter from David. He has the mumps. Hope he can stay in Norman until this whole thing is over. We'll have to whip the Japs as soon as we get through scrubbing this place.

Your prediction was nearly right about the Krauts quitting by Easter. They're pretty well dispersed. When one of the guys asked a young POW why we haven't seen any German planes for the last month, he retorted, "That's because they've gone to bomb the U.S." What a propaganda machine they're running!

Got to see Bee the other day. He is now a locator for misaddressed letters. Gets to work inside all the time. Glad for him. He deserves it.

Sure thankful Sally is with you now.

I finally managed to get a 3-day pass to go see Lloyd. When I got there I found out he left that morning on a 4-day pass to Paris. Can't believe I missed him.

Oh well, I got to see some of this place without a gun in my hand. Worms, Mannheim, and Mainz are flattened. Heidelberg is practically untouched. I thumbed a ride part of the way. Traveled close to 225 miles. Doubt I'll get to see Paris now.

When I got back I had a package from you with candy and cookies. Shared them with the other guys. I really liked the pictures of you and Sally. She looks so grown up!

Henry's letter of April 13, 1945, read:

We heard of Roosevelt's death late last night. It hit everyone pretty hard. I hope Truman can continue where he left off. All the boys over here sorta looked up to Roosevelt as a leader to pull them out of this mess as soon as possible.

How does Miss Hammer like Ottawa? Hope she doesn't quit. She sounds like a good choice.

Wow! That Vernon is quite a businessman! Hope the store is going well. Are you able to get much merchandise?

Some of the guys went to Paris. According to them, it's quite a town.

Henry kept the accordion close at hand in the supply room so at odd times he could practice. It wasn't long before he could pick out tunes like, "Among My Souvenirs," "Let Me call You Sweetheart," "Darling Nellie Grey," and "I'll Take You Home Again, Kathleen."

After he mastered those, he began work on "Star Dust," which he and Harriet considered their special song. While he played, he remembered those good times before the war when that tune came on the radio. He'd catch Harriet's eye, take her in his arms, and enjoy an intimate slow dance around the living room. Oh, to be back there again!

The fellows laughed at him when they saw him play the accordion because he played the chord buttons with his right hand and the note buttons with his left. To Henry, it seemed perfectly natural.

A couple of days later Henry jotted notes to Harriet between G.I. requests for supplies and accordion practice.

> Tonight the *Stars and Stripes* sound really optimistic. They say the war's about over. I'll believe it when I see it. They say Japan's willing to call it quits. If she knows what's good for her, she will. Wouldn't it be wonderful if the war would end?
>
> We've been behind the rear echelon for two weeks now. We're over 200 meters from the front. Doesn't look like we'll be going closer which suits me to a T. It still seems like a dream after all the hell we went through taking Forbach and Oeting and all the other narrow escapes before that. An armistice would seem like a dream come true! You get so used to warfare that when you get out of it, it seems like you're born free again.
>
> Last night we got a power plant unit. Another fellow and I put it to work for us. Battalion got it from the Krauts. It'll light up a whole town. We get to keep it wherever we go. It's a pleasure to have a nice bright light and radio after using candles most of the time.
>
> We're about to change locations soon—about as far as where you are from Kansas City.
>
> Please send cigarettes.

Chapter 48

Rationing made merchandise extremely hard to get for the store. In order to supplement the meager shipments, Harriet made regular trips to the garment district of Kansas City. Every week or so, she boarded the train mid-morning in Ottawa and arrived downtown by noon. After a couple of hours pulling things off the rack at buying houses like Nelly Don and Gay Gibson, she boarded the train to be home by five. Her purchases arrived at the store the next day.

Every time they received a shipment of nylon hose, word spread like wildfire. Women stood in line down the block and around the corner to buy this rare commodity.

When Uncle Vernon saw the monthly profits he remarked, "Harriet, this is great! I knew you could do it."

She smiled. She knew the nearby Sunflower munitions plant didn't hurt business any. Those women had money to spend for the first time in their lives. And she got to do what she loved best—shop for them.

Leota and Sally settled into a workable routine of household chores in the morning and a walk to the nearby park in the afternoon following a nap. To help Leota occupy Sally, Harriet built a small sandbox beside one corner of the house. It worked for a little while, but Sally didn't like to sit still for long.

One day Harriet received a breathless call at the store from Leota.

"Mrs. Freeman, I can't find Sally anywhere! She was in the sand pile one minute, and the next she was gone!"

Harriet's heart drummed in her ears. Her throat tightened. "I'll be right home." As she ran the three blocks, all manner of fears assaulted her. Was Leota too old to watch such an active child? Had someone stolen her from the sandbox? Should she have called the police before she left the store? "Oh dear God! Help!"

After they searched the house, top to bottom, Harriet thought to check the garage. There she found her child, asleep in the back seat. Harriet grabbed her by the feet and pulled her out. "Oh, Sally, don't *ever* do that again!"

Sally seemed a little confused over all the commotion. Didn't she often sleep in the back seat of the car? The only difference, today they weren't riding anywhere.

Henry's April 19th letter was full of good news about the war.

> We heard the Russians captured Goebbels and Goering in Berlin. In light of Goebbels propaganda, and Goering's headship of the Gestapo, I think the Russians will know what to do with them. Patton has crossed the Czechoslovakian border. If only we could keep up with him the war would be over before long.
>
> I'm busy getting supplies out to the boys. They're in 6 different places, several miles apart. It's quite a way to the supply base which doesn't help much.
>
> We saw Frankfurt. We bombed that place flat. Not a building left standing. It's the largest town we've seen yet.
>
> I wish you could see the mansion eight of us are in now. There's an inlaid piano here I'd love to send to your mother. We can take our pick of easy chairs. There are 10 rooms downstairs, 2 toilets, 1 bathroom with a shower and tub, electric heat, 2 sun porches, an electric range, and beautiful built-in cabinets. Sure beats a fox-hole.
>
> There's a bunch of bedrooms upstairs. The full basement has 6 or 8 rooms. I noticed 10 large crates of excellent china that has never been unpacked.
>
> In the piano room is a large 5 ½ foot tall pendulum clock with a deep rich strike.

This place is one of 6 we're occupying. We have a refrigerator but it doesn't work. We even have hot water.

People are farming everywhere with the crudest of implements. They work about an acre of land with a pair of cows, then milk them at night. Ask Pop if he would like to be a farmer over here and keep his cows in his house!

Very few men are working. There are just old men and women who would do well to walk a mile, plus a few young women, and boys and girls.

Lloyd was really disappointed when he got back from Paris and found I had been there to see him.

I spent half of last night doing paperwork. I wonder what they'd do if they ever ran out of paper?

We fired up the furnace last night. Steam heat! Wow. We have municipal electricity now and have the radio on most of the time. We hear some broadcasts from the States. The boys go crazy when they hear good old American music. It's great after 4 months of nothing but a steady diet of 88s' shells going off.

Even though the war news sounded good, Henry could hardly wait until this craziness ended. He had received a letter from Harriet telling him about discussions she and Sally had recently.

He responded:

April 24, 1945

Dear little sweetheart,

I'm so glad when I get your letters and cards. Be a good little girl. Keep watching for those trains and ships. Daddy will be on one, one of these days, and will come home to see you and Mommy. Say your prayers with Mommy every night so you will have sweet dreams.

I love you heaps and heaps.

Daddy

He then added a P.S. to Harriet.

How in the world does she know I'll be coming home on a ship and a train? I hope I can be with her before she gets too much older. Keep your letters coming. That's what I thrive on.

I can play a few more tunes on the accordion. I can't bring the violin home. A fellow got three accordions yesterday. Gave me one. Wish I could bring it home.

What do Pop and Vernon think of the new president? The boys over here seem to be 100% behind Truman so far.

Pop could probably get a better truck if he were over here. We see a lot that aren't running—only because they have no gas. Same with the planes and motorcycles.

Near the end of April, Henry looked up as his buddy Bee hobbled into the supply room. "What's wrong with you? You look like you've seen a ghost. Are you sick?"

Bee threw photos on Henry's desk. "I might be if I look at those pictures again. You won't believe what Hitler has done to these poor people."

Henry's gaze fell on pictures of stacks of dead bodies thrown in an endless pile like so much cord wood. Bodies reduced to nothing but skin and bones. Others were living, half-naked skeletons, peering through high fences herded in like so many cattle in a slaughter house.

"Where is this? Where did you get these?"

Bee sunk into a nearby chair. "It's the Bergen-Belsen concentration camp. The Brits liberated it a few days ago. One of the guys brought these to the COs office. I hear General Eisenhower ordered the pictures taken as evidence."

"My God!" If Henry had any doubts about their reason for being there, they melted as he stared into the eyes of these poor creatures. He looked up from his desk. "How could . . . ?"

With a slow, sad, shake of his head, Bee raised his hand to silence Henry." I asked the same question. What kind of animal could do this?"

The two sat quiet for a long while. Finally, Bee stood and gathered the pictures with reverence and left without a word.

The next day the *Stars and Stripes* carried the full story of the liberation. After he read every word Henry picked up a pen to write Harriet.

> I've seen pictures of the concentration camp at Bergen-Belsen. I've seen a lot of death, agony, and suffering but I've *never* seen or heard of anything like this before. How any human being could do this to another is beyond my conception.
>
> At least on the battle front, a soldier has a way to defend himself—but these poor creatures were fenced in so tight they couldn't all lay down at once--then they were starved until they were nothing but skin and bones. The SS troops beat, crippled, and maimed them. They locked them in a building and set fire to it. Sometimes they buried them alive. It's really beyond human comprehension. *No* men or women on earth deserve what they received!
>
> I've thought about how Hitler should be punished if and when they do catch him. There's no way to make him suffer the way he has caused 10, 20, or 30 million people to live—maybe more than that. There's only one satisfaction I'll ever have. He'll have to answer to the One who is much greater than he is. His SS troops won't be able to crash the pearly gates for him.
>
> This camp in Belsen isn't the only one we've found, nor will it be the last. There'll be a lot of people tried for treason. Most will have to pay for it in blood—theirs, for a change.
>
> I honestly can't look a man in the eye here between the ages of 16 and 60 without wondering where and when he threw lead at us.
>
> Guess you have heard by now the SS troopers shot at their own German soldiers retreating from the Berlin battle. Those retreating troops turned the table on them

and wiped out the SS troopers. The SS knows if they lose the war, their life isn't worth a plug nickel.

Harriet read Henry's latest letter in the stockroom on May 1 as she ate a mayonnaise sandwich. So those whispered rumors about concentration camps were really true! She could hardly believe anyone could be so evil.

She hoped the Allies could continue their rapid sweep and finish the Axis Powers soon. She tuned in the little radio she'd brought from home. The broadcaster painted a rosy picture.

"The Allies are charging through Italy. Berlin lies in ruin."

Harriet breathed a deep sigh. "Today wouldn't be too soon to see victory."

As she reached to switch off the radio, there was a news bulletin. "It has been reported and confirmed that Adolph Hitler along with his companion, Eva Braun, committed suicide last night in his bunker in Berlin."

She stood, stunned. Could this really be true?

Reports throughout the day confirmed the fact. Finally, the old devil was dead. Thank God!

Chapter 49

On April 30, 1945, Henry sat to write Harriet, but instead, the first lines of a poem came to him. He wrote down the words and more followed. Within a few minutes, his scribble covered three pages. He made a copy for her.

Dear Harriet,

I was inspired after hearing of Hitler's death. I'll include a copy to you. Going to send it to our Division newspaper the *Trailblazer* and to the *Stars and Stripes.*

POEM BY S/Sgt. H. S. FREEMAN
Co "K", 276th Inf.

Trouble in Hell

Here's to you, Old devil, who runs all HELL,
you have a new customer—we wish you well.

The news spread fast: "ADOLPH IS DEAD!"
you now have your "Stooge," so make up his bed!

Now here's a little tip, in case you don't know,
About this man Adolph, who used to run the show:

He'll tell you He is God! And he'll lie like hell,
he will keep you fascinated for quite a spell.

Make yourself comfortable, for he's a long-winded goat,
he'll tell you of purges, of which he likes to gloat—

of thousands of people who were in his way,
how he starved or killed them and let them lay.

This man has no conscience, (which you probably knew.)
Eighty million people (except maybe a few,)

Heiled this Pied Piper who bled the Deutschland—
upon hearing his name, they'd hoist up their hands!

He grabbed up the reins in Nineteen thirty-three.
He caused more commotion than You'll ever again see.

He raped his neighboring countries, with the help of his spies,
And held off his aggressors with murderous lies.

He gathered up women from place to place,
and bred them to his gangsters, to make his "Super-race"!

Some failed to look "Nordic," so he shipped them back
to work as slaves for the help that he lacked.

You used to know some "corkers," to torture a man,

but Adolph devised some new ones—beat them if you can!

We've tried to forget them but think we better tell,
so you can try them on Hitler, down deep in hell!

Pulling a man apart, tied to two tanks, is a neat little trick—
you look pale, Old Devil, but don't get sick—

We'll tell you about hot salt water, used through a hose,
or of red hot wires, poked up your nose!

Cutting a man's fingers has its effects,
or removal of the breasts of the opposite sex.

Try cutting half-way through his wrists and let them swing,
or peel off narrow strips of skin—he'll probably sing!

Yes, Old Devil, your "Stooge" worked well and poisoned lots of minds,
but a few of us here didn't like his kind.

So we went after Adolph, though the going seemed slow,
we teamed up with GOD—a fellow Hitler didn't know!

So now we turn him over to you, Old Devil, to do as you see fit.
Whatever "Reward" you wish to pay him, we don't mind a bit.

We may have a few troubles around here yet for a spell,
But our troubles are no troubles, compared to the ones you now have in Hell!

His letter to Harriet continued.

Guess the old buzzard who took Hitler's place has a twist in his brain too. Says he's going to carry on where Hitler left off except Hitler didn't leave much to carry on with. I never dreamed it would last as long as it has.

Just heard Italy's thrown in the towel. Everything may come to a head soon.

There's a rumor that a few men out of the regiment will get to go home on a 45-day furlough. They'll probably be knocked out of a chance to go home to stay. I'm pretty sure our outfit is earmarked for the Army of Occupation.

On the 5th of May he wrote:

How does the war situation look to you now? We may have them where we want them. The 10 o'clock news last night said the Netherlands and Denmark gave up.

Sounds like the war in the Pacific is progressing, but we still have a lot of fighting to do there yet. Guess we'll have to keep a tight belt at home so we can feed Europe now. Gas will probably be one of the big items that'll be in short supply. I hear we're going to have to buy our own cigarettes soon. Send me a carton occasionally.

Chapter 50

Harriet arrived at the store early to finish some paperwork Tuesday morning, May 8, 1945. She couldn't believe Hitler had already been dead over a week. How long would these stubborn Germans hold on?

By eight, she unlocked the door. Within a few minutes, Main Street became clogged with honking horns, and people waving American flags.

Harriet rushed out. She asked a passerby, "What's happened?"

"Haven't you heard? President Truman announced Germany's surrender."

Another screamed, "The war's over in Europe! It's really over!"

Was this true? Was she dreaming? Harriet ran in to listen to the radio. The commentator confirmed the news. She bowed her head and wept. "Oh, praise God!" The words she had longed to hear for so long rang in her ears. Henry could come home at last! They could be together again. The weight of the past three and a half years lifted off her shoulders like a heavy lead blanket.

The phone rang. It was Uncle Vernon. "Did you hear the news?"

"Yes! Isn't it wonderful?"

"Put a sign on the door that says, 'Closed for the Day!' Go out and celebrate! Nobody will be interested in buying clothes today anyway."

Was he serious? Was this really Uncle Vernon or someone playing a joke? "Are you closing Nevada?"

"Of course! I'm closing all the stores. It's a red-letter day."

Harriet dismissed the employees and followed his orders before he called to change his mind. She made her way through the streets filled with revelers who shouted and hugged one another.

When she got home, Leota met her at the door. "What in the world is going on? Why are all those people honking?"

With overwhelming joy, Harriet folded the little lady in a giant bear hug. "It's over, Leota! It's over! The war is over in Germany!"

Sally giggled and clapped her hands when she saw her mother acting so silly.

Harriet danced with Sally through the house. "Your daddy can come home! This is so wonderful!"

Sally pointed to Henry's picture beside the bed in the dining room. "Daddy! Daddy! Is he going to the train?"

"Oh, not yet, little one. But he *will* come home to us one day soon."

She wriggled out of her mother's arms, grabbed his picture and kissed it. "Daddy! Get on the train."

The phone rang. It was her sister-in-law from Nevada.

"Let's meet in Kansas City to celebrate!"

"What'll we do there?"

"I don't know. Let's go join the celebration. I'm so glad it's over!"

"Meet you under the big clock in Union Station."

Before Harriet could answer, the phone went dead.

Harriet left Sally with Leota and took the next train to the city. When she arrived she joined the throngs making their way through the station. It seemed as if everyone had the same idea. Elbowing toward the huge clock suspended from the ceiling, she wondered how she'd ever find her sister-in-law in all these people.

She heard a faint, "Harriet! Harriet! I'm over here!"

They hugged and found their way to the nearest door where they were carried along with the throng toward downtown. The city looked like everyone had gone mad. People kissed strangers. Some waved flags. Those in office buildings threw confetti out the windows. Others danced with one another in giddy glee. People spilled out of bars, mugs in hand. All traffic stopped. The streets filled with people. It seemed the whole world had come to celebrate.

Through the crowd mania, Harriet yelled, "This must be what it's like in Times Square on New Year's."

"Only better!"

As evening fell, the two exhausted women made their way back to the train station. Before boarding, Harriet stopped at the public restroom. She caught a glance of herself in the mirror and laughed aloud. Her hat was on backwards and her suit had beer spilled on it. She'd lost one of her earrings. Had it been any other day, she would have been upset—but not today. Today was V-E Day—Victory in Europe Day!

In President Truman's announcement about the war, he cautioned it wasn't over—it was only half won. Surely now, Japan would give up their aggression. Then everyone could enjoy peace again.

On the seventh of May Henry penned this letter to commemorate the occasion.

> On this gala day I have to write to tell you all the news even though you've already heard it by now.
>
> At 2:15 this afternoon we heard Norway surrendered and 26 minutes later we heard ALL of Germany had surrendered unconditionally! We dragged out some champagne we'd saved for the occasion and toasted everyone to an early trip home.
>
> I wonder how people acted there. We didn't do much the rest of the day. I guess when things look blackest, it may be the time for the clouds to roll away!
>
> Now getting home is the major objective. It would be the height of disappointment if a fellow had to go from here to fight the Yellow Rats out in the Pacific and China. I really believe my age and having dependents at home is going to have a lot of weight in the matter, but don't build your hopes too high.
>
> My Commanding Officer really got stewed tonight. He said, "Hank, let me shake your hand. I hope you get to go home soon to that beautiful wife and that little Sally girl. I'm young yet. The other guys and I will take care of the Japs. You old fellows get ready to go home. I hope it's soon."
>
> Honey I hope I don't have to write many more letters before I can tell you in person, I LOVE YOU! Happy Mother's Day!

When she read Henry's letter, one line took her breath away. What if Henry had to go to the South Pacific and fight the Japs? That would be the last straw—the height of injustice. She sank into a chair. Tears flowed.

"Oh Lord! Let him come home to stay. Please find a way to end this awful war, the world over, once and for all, in Jesus' name. Amen."

Henry's next letter said:

> The Germans didn't hear about the Armistice until the day after we did. A lot of them are celebrating and having parades. I'll bet they're as anxious to get this thing finished as we are. In the last war, all the Doughboy had to worry about was the Army of Occupation. Now, we have to sweat out the Pacific theater also. Wish I was over 42. Then I'd know for sure I didn't have to go to the South Pacific.
>
> How did they celebrate in Ottawa?
>
> I hope my cigarettes get here soon. I'm clear out. We haven't gotten as many as we did when we were in combat. They haven't put any out for sale yet.
>
> Blackout restrictions lifted today. Oh, and we're moving again.
>
> In your mom's letter she said the ration board turned Pop down again for a truck. Hope he gets one before long.

Chapter 51

Each day Harriet looked for a letter with word of Henry's discharge. His letter of May 11, 1945, severely dampened her optimism.

Rumor has it our next move will be to Frankfurt. No one really knows for sure. Hope to see you in the next year, anyway!

We have to have 96 points in order to come home right away. I'll probably stay here with the Occupational Army. I only have 44 points—22 for being in for 22 months; 5 for the months overseas; 12 for Sally and 5 for my battle star. Wish they counted the 36 months I was in the Army from before. Then I'd have 80. I wonder how many of my Fort Scott buddies have enough points to go home.

Guess I shouldn't complain. The boys in the Pacific would be glad to change places with me right now. Some guys said they thought the war in Japan would be over within 6 months. I think it's wishful thinking. Hope they're right.

Do you remember Gordon, that guy I trained while I was in Oregon? They sent him to Southeast Asia. Got a letter from him the other day. He said, "When we can't get the Japs out of their caves on Okinawa, we just dynamite the entrance shut and forget them." Sounds like pretty fierce fighting there. If they can take that island, we'll have an airbase to hit Japan.

Also got a letter from Stringer—the guy who lost most of his hand. He had to go for a physical to see if he was fit for overseas duty in Japan! Don't tell me they're that short of men!

I haven't seen any of these atrocity camps over here and I don't want to. They're a lot worse than you imagine from reading the paper.

You asked if I think about the store. I do now that I'm not dodging 88s, 24 hours a day. I wouldn't know how to act if I went into a store. I haven't been in one since we left Camp Myles Standish before we shipped out last December.

My poem appeared in our daily Regimental bulletin. It may be in the *Trailblazer* before long.

Honey, if I'm part of the Occupational Army and they let wives come, would you be interested in moving over here?

I'm always thinking of you and Sally. I hope and pray for the day when I'll be with you again. When you get down in the dumps, think of the time we'll be together again. I LOVE YOU, I WILL ALWAYS LOVE YOU. (I have lots of love left.)

Reading Henry's letter, she pondered moving to Germany. After being alone, it didn't seem such a far-fetched idea as Oregon had seemed. She'd rather not, but if that's what it took to be with him again, she'd go. Surely, he wouldn't have to fight in Japan.

His next letter of May 20 had a lot to say about Japan.

They say they'll send the cream of the crop to the Pacific. I wish those Japs would use a little common sense—but that's too much to expect! If they called the whole thing off now they'd spare thousands of men.

They say they've got ten million men to sacrifice in this war effort. If that's all they think of their people we need to get rid of all of 'em to make the world safe for humanity.

Finally got to go to church today—Pentecost Sunday.

Vernon wrote with the figures from the stores. Looks good. He tickles me, though. Never says anything about anything but the stores. Guess that's his whole life.

Now that the war is over here I can tell you where we are. The day before Mother's Day on May 13, we came to Berg Nassau from Neudstadt. We're in a beautiful old hotel. Our day room is about 80 x 80 that leads to a terrace. We eat outdoors at tables overlooking the river. A lot of the boys have rooms with a lavatory. It's real nice, and there's no hotel bill!

When I ran up to Battalion at Diez for supplies I found Bee there. I got 4 packs of cigarettes from him. They're worth their weight in gold now. No more government issue like in combat.

Headquarters is 25 miles from us over hairpin mountain roads.

No one can get a pass, and there's no entertainment. We're forbidden to talk to civilians so we put together a G.I. show by ourselves, for ourselves last night. Had 9 different acts. I was first. I played the accordion with a fellow at the piano, then I played a violin, next a French harp. For my last part I played the piano while a fellow held the French harp for me. The whole show lasted about 2 hours. Afterward the cooks served rolls and coffee.

I may not be in the Army of Occupation now. We've been transferred to the 7th Army. Hope we get to go through the States on our way East if I have to go. It'll take a year to get our boys over there to start on the Japs. Even the guys with 85 points and higher haven't been discharged yet—1,300,000 men in 85 Divisions is a lot of men to move!

Enjoyed your clippings from the *Kansas City Star* about Truman. Really played him up, didn't they?

I have a bunch of boils on my rear and now they're on my upper legs. If they don't ease off, I'm going to have to see the doc. They won't heal after the core comes out.

Henry's next letter the end of May sounded encouraging.

Looks like our guys are advancing in Okinawa. When that's secure they'll be about 350 miles from Japan. That's a strategic island—a good toe-hold, for sure. One more step in this long road.

Sounds like you all had quite a time in Kansas City on V-E Day. Ever find your earring?

Harriet's frustration grew. She wasn't sure that long path Henry spoke of in his last letter really did have an end. What if he had to go Japan? Those Kamikaze pilots seemed even crazier than the Germans. The uncertainty of it all kept her awake, even when she fell into bed exhausted. First, "Come to Germany," then, "I'm headed for Japan." Their life was a tug-of-war with no winner at either end.

Her irritation increased when Sally, now two-and-a-half, asked almost every day, "Daddy coming today?"

Amidst the uncertainty there was one bright spot. Sally no longer cried every time Harriet left for work. Sally and Leota had formed a comfortable bond, and they seemed to look forward to their frequent walks in the park. Although Leota had little experience with small children, she let Sally help stir cookie dough or assist with household chores.

Sally told her grandmother one day she was "Leota's little helper."

Glessner responded, "And you're my apple-dumplin'."

"Um hum. And I'm Daddy's feet-heart."

Harriet chimed in, "You're my little doll."

Soon it became Sally's mantra whenever she met someone.

"I'm Daddy's feet-heart, Mommy's little doll, Leota's little helper, and Grandma's apple-dumplin'."

One night when Harriet couldn't sleep, something her grandmother often said came to mind.

"Just remember, Harriet, all things come to those who wait."

She pondered that truth. Surely they had waited. Hopefully, long enough. This war couldn't last forever. She decided to be grateful Henry was alive and in relative safety. He wasn't in a German prisoner-of-war camp like Fatso. He wrote often. He wanted to be with them as much as they wanted to be with him. She was employed at a job she loved while he was away. She had a good, dependable sitter to watch Sally.

Soon she fell into a restful slumber—the first in weeks.

Chapter 52

Henry's letter of May 31 read:

We got our ETO (European Theater of Operations) ribbons today. Gives me 5 more points. That makes 49. We may get another ribbon, but it still won't give me enough to get out anytime soon.

We got to go to a Red Cross movie in Wiesbaden yesterday and saw "The Merry Monahans." It was really good. Wanted to buy you something, but nothing was open. Most large buildings are destroyed.

They're starting the Paris excursions again. Maybe I'll get to go before too long.

New rumor. All men under 32 with less than 60 points will be transferred to the Pacific in 6 weeks or less. If that's true, this almost 35-year-old will get a break.

Sure want to get home soon to hear that little parrot talk you tell me so much about. I expect I'll be surprised when I see her.

His June 5th letter raised Harriet's worry level.

My boils got so bad doc sent me to the hospital today in Katzenelbogen. Get penicillin shots every 3 hours, 24 hours a day. These places turned into big sores that won't heal. They're all over my tail-end, thighs, and right leg.

We took the super highway (autobahn) from Diez to Katzenelbogen. The hospital looks like it might have been a large school.

The next day he continued the letter:

Been here 24 hours now. My rear end feels like a sieve. Boils are healing somewhat.

They feed good here. Hotcakes for breakfast, beef, peas, gravy and potatoes for dinner. For supper, we had French fried potatoes, corn, and beans. They've cut our rations 10%. We don't have as much as we did before but we get along.

Henry held the letter till the third day and wrote:

Still in the hospital. Legs healing up. This penicillin is really OK.

Been reading a lot. I see the V.D. rate has increased dramatically. Very few over here were left disease-free by the Germans. The fellas who don't observe the no-fraternization order will bring a whole lot of sickness home to their unsuspecting families.

They say this is a Christian war. Doesn't look that way, does it? Many men will have to overcome selfishness and self-pity before we call ourselves leaders in Christianity.

The May *Reader's Digest* and the April *Coronet* have articles about starting your own business. I've thought for a long time about starting a Chevrolet agency. I figure it will take at least $10,000 to open one. Veterans are entitled to a government loan. I'd hate to borrow over 25% to get started.

I figure an $800 car sale will gross around $200. The service department will make money too. During the last year, one of Fort Scott's dealerships sold almost a car a day. We could sell more than that, if we could get the cars.

I like the clothing business, but I'd prefer the car business. If they'd only turn me loose from the Army I could do a lot of things.

Tell me what you think.

Harriet thought about his car dealership idea for several days. How would their life change if Henry no longer worked at the store? Would Uncle Vernon boot them both if Henry quit? If Henry pulled their interest out of the store, would that end their family ties with this clothing tycoon?

She wasn't of a mind to become a car dealerships accountant in place of her position at the clothing store. That would be unbearable drudgery in her estimation. She'd have to think about his idea some more before she answered.

Henry's hospital stay ended after six days on June 10th.

He read a clipping she sent him about a Congressman May's proposal to allow all servicemen over thirty-five to be discharged. Unfortunately, the bill failed to pass, much to Henry's disappointment.

About his transfer to the 7th Army he reasoned:

At least in the 7th Army I'll have a better chance of staying here. If I go to the States on a furlough, I'll probably be sent to fight Japs. Sure don't want to do that. I've had a belly full of fighting.

In the fatigue of waiting for Henry to come home, Harriet confessed her patience was wearing thin. She said it seemed harder every day to bully her way through—that she wasn't sure he was ever coming out of the Army. In protest, she wrote letters to her congressmen complaining the soldiers were not being sent home.

Henry responded:

> I'm so grateful for your faithfulness. It keeps me from throwing my life to the four winds. I have something to live for.
>
> When you get down in the dumps, just count it another day nearer the time we'll be together again. Then we can reap our reward for being diligent.
>
> You might do like your mother does—face the situation as it arises and hope for the best. In the end, it generally turns out OK.
>
> Today we were officially activated into the 7th Army. The Colonel told us we were in class 4. That means we'll be split up and sent to other outfits. We have trained for everything but jungle warfare. It's been scheduled four times but they canceled it each time.
>
> Remember, no more down in the dumps from now on. Eventually, this *will* end and we 'll be together again.
>
> Love you, Honey.

Summer was in full swing. With longer daylight, Harriet and Sally usually took an evening walk to the park to give Leota a rest after supper.

When she put Sally to bed each night the child's question never varied. "When will Daddy come home?"

"One day soon, precious one."

One night after a long pause, Sally said, "Okay. Let's say prayers. Then I can get candy. Then you can blow me out."

Harriet pondered her statement. "Blow you out?"

Sally nodded. "Grandma always blows me out."

"Oh. All right. Whuuf. Did that do it?"

With a grin and a nod Sally grabbed her teddy and closed her eyes.

Although Harriet didn't understand, she decided to call her mother. Never mind the expense. She had to find out about this.

"Mom, Sally said you blow her out at bedtime. What's that all about?"

Glessner laughed. "That's how I get her to be quiet and go to sleep, I tell her I'm blowing her out as I blow out the lantern by her bed. Works every time."

"Great idea! I'll have to use it."

"Better get a coal oil lamp first."

"I'll bring one of yours home next time I'm there."

Her mother chuckled. "Now that we have electricity, I use them a lot less. Think I can spare one."

Before going to bed, Harriet jotted her husband his daily letter and included the events of the evening. She added:

> *Luggage sales are strong. Several women plan to meet their husbands in New York when they return. How I wish you were on one of those boats soon. Shall I plan to meet you there?*

When Henry read that letter, he had a good laugh. He hoped one day soon to hold his little chatterbox on his lap and never let her go.

> Sally sure has an imagination, wanting you to blow her out! She is more right than she realizes, though. She's the light of our hearts. God bless her.
>
> Don't plan on meeting me in New York. I'll be there just as long as it takes to get on a train. I read where the hotel rooms in New York are all taken up. Still the women flock there to see their husbands.
>
> Went to see Bee the other day and found out Marge was laid off at the munitions plant in Oklahoma City.

The engineers finally got a bridge across the river here. We had to cross on a ferry before. It's the only crossing this side of Diez. The Krauts never missed a beat in blowing up every bridge, no matter how important it was. The masterpieces they blew up makes me sick. The damage in bridges alone would run into the billions.

Behind us is a castle with a high tower built in 1124! We paid a penny to walk to the top of it. We could see across the river to Nassau and for miles in every direction.

Some of the boys went hunting this morning. They got a wild bear and a deer.

Latest rumor: We may move to Bavaria or Austria. Those darn stories fly around here like a swarm of gnats—and have as much weight as thin air. Another says us older guys are going to be left here for the Army of Occupation. One thing about this place—there's no shortage of those dad-blamed rumors.

I went fishing at the river for about 15 minutes today. Didn't catch anything.

The Mess Sergeant got me a 20-pound basket of strawberries for 1 mark. That's about a dime in our money. Some difference in prices here and at home, huh?

The place on my leg got worse. Doc wanted to send me back to the hospital. I talked him out of it. Can't understand why it won't heal. It's on top of the bone halfway between my knee and ankle. Have to check in with him again this afternoon.

I'm watching these poor farmers make hay across the river. They mow it with scythes. Three fellows follow behind and fork the hay all over the field. After it's cured about a half-day, they fork it up in windrows, bring in a dilapidated wagon, and the whole family loads it. Some of those women throw fork loads of hay on a tall load that'd put big men to shame. When they're done, there isn't a straw left on the ground. An acre is a big field for them.

We've only sent one group of guys home from our outfit so far.

They issued us swimming trunks the other day, but we can't swim in the river until the medics pronounce the water fit to swim in. We've been here a little over a month. Wonder how long it takes to test the water?

The locals carry a little box with them. When they see a used cigarette butt on the ground they collect it in their box to smoke later.

P.S. Saw the doc this afternoon. He says I have to go back to the hospital.

Chapter 53

Oh how Harriet wished he was home! She'd bind a piece of beef-steak to Henry's sores. That would fix him, for sure. Penicillin might work, but her remedy undoubtedly would work better.

Rumors ran rampant about when the men would return, but very few had actually come home. Each wife, sweetheart, or mother longed for that blessed news with every letter. Some soldiers received orders for the South Pacific which sent shivers down Harriet's back. How much longer would those crazy Japs hold out?

The nearby munitions plant was still going full force, which kept Uncle Vernon happy each time he called for weekly figures at the store.

Harriet's back door neighbor spotted Harriet and Sally in the sand box one Sunday afternoon. She knew little of this neighbor except her husband served somewhere far away in the Army.

The neighbor came to the fence and peered in at them. "Haven't seen you around much. Do you just work all the time?"

Harriet smiled. "Guess you could say that."

The neighbor leaned on the fence with her elbows. "Someone said you might be just the one we need for a fourth for our bridge group. Meets every Thursday night at my place."

"I think I'll pass. Thanks anyway."

"Oh come on. Just because our husband's aren't here doesn't mean we can't have a little fun. You can't work all the time."

What about "no" did this neighbor not understand? Harriet didn't want to be rude, but maybe that was the only way she could get rid of her. She stood Sally up and dusted the sand from her clothes.

"It's only one night a week. Of course if you stayed home in the daytime we could play on Monday and Wednesday afternoons, too."

The thought of wasting all that time at a bridge table made Harriet's irritation level rise even further. She picked Sally up and headed for the back door as she called over her shoulder. "I'd rather spend what precious time I have at home with my child, not dallying over a deck of cards."

Evidently, the neighbor got the message—she seldom spoke when their paths crossed after that. It didn't hurt Harriet's feelings in the least. Family was more important than making that lady happy.

On June 23, Henry wrote from the hospital again.

> Can't get those places to heal without penicillin. Yesterday they sent me to a field hospital. It's in Montabaur, up north of Diez.
>
> The doc just came in and said these aren't boils. They're some kind of bug bites. There are several cases around. I suspected that when I was in the hospital before. When I got back, I sprayed my bed and blankets with DDT. It didn't do much good, I guess.
>
> Getting penicillin every 3 hours again. Not going to be in such a hurry to leave this time—don't want to have to come back.
>
> I sure feel sorry for those guys in POW camps without any medical care. If they had anything like this, they'd have gone crazy. When these places finally heal up, they leave an ugly scar.
>
> Our company planned another show last night. Sure sorry I missed it.
>
> The latest article in the *Stars and Stripes* says there will be no lowering of age limits for the older guys to go home.
>
> Also read in the *S & S* that some Senator from Indiana said he has it on good authority that Japan is seeking peace terms. With Okinawa under our thumb, maybe they're seeing the light. Hope that Senator knows

what he's talking about. If we could reduce the Japanese Air Force, we could whip 'em. Those Kamikaze pilots must be nuts. I can't figure where the Japs get all their oil.

I read where they're going to start making new cars back home again. Buy one if they'll sell you one at any price.

Harriet paused. Why should they spend money on a new car? This one ran fine—if they could only get some decent tires. It seemed every time she wanted to go any distance, another one blew. Even with the war over in Europe, tires were still a precious commodity. One day—one day this war would be over and they would be able to buy four new tires. As long as those wheels turned on the car they had, they didn't need a new one. She continued to read.

I hear G.I.s who get to England can call the States now. $12 for 3 minutes. If I ever got to England, I'd sure take advantage of that. It'd be worth every penny.

This morning I had the privilege of a mirror to shave. I've got gray hairs and my hairline is receding. Guess I'm getting old. Don't worry. I still have a few young ideas!

Harriet would love to hear Henry's voice again—even if it cost a week's salary. But then, if he called, she'd probably not be able to stand the wait until he could come home. At least with his letters she could read them over and over, not like a voice heard and then gone.

She chuckled at his last line. She was glad he still had some young ideas. She did too.

After a week in the hospital, Henry was discharged with only one unhealed bite on his leg. Harriet breathed a sigh of relief to hear he was out. Now if the Japs would only give in. Hopefully, that wasn't wishful thinking.

In celebration of the 4th of July, the store closed that Tuesday. Harriet took Sally to the Kansas City Zoo. They rode the early morning train out of Ottawa and took a taxi from Union Station.

While Sally took delight in the different animals, Harriet noticed there were still very few men about. When would they ever be allowed to come home?

By late afternoon, they boarded the train again for Ottawa.

As the train rocked along the tracks, Harriet held her sleeping child on her lap. She mused how much more pleasant this train ride was than the one they endured twenty-one months before on their way to Oregon. How their life had been turned up-side-down these past three and a half years! It had been a long time since she allowed herself to dream of a future. Of one day when warring voices would be silenced and peace would again reign.

She smiled as she remembered V-E Day. The day everyone seemed to be one happy family, even though they were total strangers. What unity. Would it ever return?

Shortly after Henry returned from his second stay in the hospital, he learned from the Commanding Officer that within a short time ninety-five percent of their Division would ship out to the States—for redeployment to Japan.

The weight of that news nearly took his breath. How would he tell Harriet? She had such high hopes for his soon return. They were Japan bound, except a select few. He was sure with his luck he wouldn't be one of those left behind. He couldn't bring himself to write her any of this latest news.

As if to underline the edict, he got orders to ready 1,700 soldiers to be shipped out. He had to make sure they had all their necessary equipment and clothing for their next assignment in Japan. How could these battle-weary soldiers face another enemy halfway around the world?

Later that week Henry's buddy, Bee, came to see him from headquarters.

"Did ya hear the latest?"

"Afraid to ask. What now?"

"Your CO misunderstood. Instead of ninety-five percent of the Division *definitely* shipping out, he should have told you that they *could* ship ninety-five percent to fight the Japs."

"You sure?"

Bee nodded. "Heard it from the head guy himself."

Henry breathed a deep sigh of relief. "Maybe your bad legs and my Limited Service rating will keep us out of those next battles."

"One can only hope, my friend."

Just after July 4th they were on the move again to an area near Wetzlar on the Lahn River.

On July 8 he wrote from their new location.

> We've been in some pretty fancy places but this one tops them all. We're in Rodheim. It's a private home with 10 acres around it. Our supply room is a 35-foot square with 15-foot ceilings. There's a grand piano with beautiful inlay, a huge brass chandelier in the center, and a massive fireplace. The sun room off one end is a 20-foot square with huge windows, floor to ceiling. Everything is trimmed in brass with walnut woodwork. The kitchen looks like it belongs in a hotel, it's so big. I don't know how many bedrooms are upstairs, but each one has running water with at least one lavatory. There are also several bathrooms.

Harriet pondered the irony of this situation. Through the winter Henry had frozen in foxholes and now in the good weather he had the finest accommodations, complete with a grand piano and chandeliers. She'd love to see the place first hand.

He added in a later letter in July:

> We found out the grand piano cost $5,000. The owners squawked because we piled our supplies on it.

She shook her head at his last statement. She was sure Henry must have gotten an earful from the owner. Even on his best day Henry was never overly careful around delicate things like furniture or clothing. How horrible it must be for the Germans to see enemy soldiers move into their homes and kick them out of their own property.

> We shipped out a bunch of men the other day. They'll be home by the 24th of July. As soon as their furloughs are over, they'll proceed to Ft. Ord, California, as replacements for the Pacific.
>
> If I can stay in this Division I won't be home before the first of 1946, according to the *Stars and Stripes.*
>
> I got a new CO. We'll have to inventory everything I'm responsible for, which will screw up the weekend. This is the second officer change this week.
>
> Read an article in the *Stars and Stripes* that said they wouldn't ship men over 35 to the Pacific unless all the others had been shipped first. Since I'll be 35 this month, I hope they have enough!
>
> Another article in the *Stars and Stripes* gives us a second battle star.
>
> The boys insisted I sit in on a friendly poker game last night. I finally consented. Walked away with $69.00 for the evening's entertainment. Guess they won't pester me to sit in again anytime soon.

Chuckling, she wondered if she could sic Henry on her back door neighbor. He could sit in on a friendly bridge game involving money and rake in a few bucks when he got home.

Chapter 54

Harriet's letter to Henry of July 15, 1945, read:

We've had nothing but rain here the past couple of weeks. It hasn't hurt business any. It's doubled from last year. The Marais des Cygnes River flooded and water is everywhere.

When Sally and I were out in the car the other day we had to drive through some water over the road. Sally cried because I wouldn't let her get out and play in it. She kept crying even when we got home. Our kid sure is head-strong.

I've decided if it ever stops raining I'll sign her up for swimming lessons at the city pool. I doubt she'll have much fear of the water.

My folks came up the weekend after the 4th. I was surprised Pops trusted the hired hand to look after the cattle and milk the cow. He must have wanted to see Sally awfully bad.

I've been thinking about your idea to have a car dealership. If that's what you'd like to do after the war, it's fine with me. I want you to do what you feel is best. We'll just have to deal with Vernon when the time comes. I know he'll not like it, but you deserve to do what you want.

We had another blow-out. I haven't been able to get a tire. Will these rations will ever end? I've not seen any new cars for sale around here. Maybe it was a rumor about making new cars again.

Sally told me the other night she doesn't want to sleep with me anymore. She wants to sleep in the little spare bed in the attic with Leota. Says she's a "big girl" now.

I've been thinking of sending her to play school. What do you think? There's one down the street from us.

Henry continued to face the constant stress of new COs and little down time. His letter of Saturday, July 21 read:

I'm one of the 11 original members of this company. When passes are issued to Belgium, Paris, Rivera, or England, everyone gets to go except me and my co-worker Andy. Some of the men who came to the company since our combat activities have been to a rest camp, or one of those cities 2 or 3 times.

I asked the 1st Sergeant some time ago for a pass. He promised me the next one to Paris. Two passes to

Paris have been issued since then. From now on, I'm going to be heard.

Beginning at 4:30 this morning, every house in the American sector will be searched before Monday morning. There's a lot of black market activity around involving government belongings. Guess the searches uncovered everything from soap to truck tires. I didn't have to go because I've been working on papers to transfer 24 men out.

A few days later on his birthday, July 24th, his mood had brightened somewhat.

Well, my ire the other day did some good after all. My co-worker, Andy, is leaving on a pass tomorrow morning to Marseilles. He sure is a hard worker. All I have to do is mention something and before I know it, he has the situation in hand. He's been with the Division ever since it was activated and did the same job all the time. Who knows, maybe I'll get a pass one day.

What do you want to do after I get out of the Army? Where do you want to live? Do you want to build a new home right away? How many extra bedrooms do you want? I've picked up a few ideas from houses over here. I figure it will cost at least $12,000—maybe more. I want an electric eye to open and close the garage door. The sunroom we have here has double walls of plate glass. It keeps the heat in and the cold out. I want plenty of light to shave by in the bathroom. I've felt my whiskers off too many times over here.

For your part of the house—I want you to have a most modern kitchen. I want you to have one of those infra-red cookers that take only seconds to cook a chicken or turkey. We'll have an electric stove and even an electric dishwasher. How does that sound?

Planned a holiday today but, as usual, things didn't turn out that way. I did go swimming in the morning. Then in the afternoon, I took some pictures with the locals. I helped them harvest. They sure have a hard row to hoe over here.

I think play school would be good for Sally. She needs to be with other kids.

Got your package with the candy and carton of cigarettes. I was out so they'll come in handy. During the last cigarette shortage, they were selling for $2 a pack. I think I'd quit before I'd pay that price.

Harriet was amused at her husband's wild ideas about their future house. Imagine. A device to open and close a garage door and another to cook a chicken in seconds! She wondered if he had read about all this stuff or he just planned on inventing it when he got home. At least he had time to dream those crazy dreams instead of picking up bodies or freezing in foxholes. She'd have to give house plans some thought.

On July 26, 1945 Henry's letter commented on Japan again.

I heard on the radio today that Truman, Churchill, and Chiang Kai-shek issued terms for surrender to Japan. From what the cook heard, Japan wants a conditional surrender. Doubt the Allies will go for that.

I heard the Allies promised the Japs "prompt and utter destruction" if they didn't negotiate a peace. Sounds like a lot more fighting from us to make good on that promised destruction. Maybe they'll give up soon—unconditionally. Then we can come home.

I picked up a souvenir from a fellow today. It's a 3rd class Honor Cross from Hitler to a mother for having over 4 children. The 2nd class ones are for 6-9 children. 1st class is for having over 9.

The Lieutenant we have now thinks he qualifies for a $50,000 a year executive job. In my estimation he couldn't make a profit from a popcorn stand. This guy's been with us since we left the States. Wish he'd get sent elsewhere. The Staff Sergeant under him does all the work. In the Lieutenant's eyes, if anything is wrong, it's your fault—it couldn't be his. Any time we look for him, he's driving all over the country taking pictures, enjoying a scotch and soda at the officer's club, or trying to make arrangements for some frauleins for the night. And yes—he writes his wife almost every day.

I see Truman says rather than sending the service men's wives over here, he wants to send the soldiers home on furlough. It'd suit me if he would just send us home PERIOD!

Lloyd wrote that everyone but him and two others have been shipped out of his outfit. Hope he doesn't have to go to the Pacific. He's been over here so long he's got over 100 points now!

Harriet enrolled Sally in the play school down the street the first day of August. She held tightly to her mother's hand as they entered the play room in Mrs. Ward's home.

"Oh look, Sally. They're playing Jack-jumped-over-the-candle-stick—just like in the book Leota reads to you."

Sally wrapped her free hand around her mother's arm like an octopus.

"Let's sit and watch for a while," Harriet said, hoping her daughter's death-grip would ease a bit.

Although Sally sat as asked, the grip on her mother's arm never loosened.

After an hour it was time for lunch. Mrs. Ward said, "I think maybe Sally needs a little more time. Let's try again in a couple of months when she's nearer three."

Had Harriet's absence caused Sally to be slow to adjust to other children? She'd write Henry her concerns if the next school day failed.

Leota prepared to bathe Sally the next day. She said, "I'll do it myself," as she pushed Leota toward the bathroom door.

When Harriet came home that evening Sally announced, "I took my bath by myself."

Her mother looked behind her ears. "I can see that. Perhaps we need to get a place you missed."

In an effort to get Sally ready for another attempt at play school, Harriet bought her a little art kit complete with crayons and plastic scissors.

Sally grabbed a crayon and went in search of a piece of paper immediately. Perhaps this was the very push she needed.

The next day Leota busied herself in the kitchen. Sally decided to try out the scissors—on her bangs.

Snip. Snip. Soon she had only a few sprigs sprouting from her scalp where her bangs had been.

Now Harriet wasn't so sure scissors were a good idea.

This child had a great fascination with the car. If she found a key, she'd sit sideways on the stairs, insert the key into a small knothole on the side of the staircase, and pretend to drive.

One day, Sally slipped out to the garage, sat behind the wheel with her bottom on the edge of the seat, and pushed on the clutch pedal. The car rolled out the open garage door and blocked the alley. Leota found her a few minutes later, still in the car. Leota didn't drive so she called Harriet at the store to come home to pull the car back into the garage.

When Harriet responded to Leota's call, she wondered what her daughter would think of next. She hoped Henry would drop the idea of another child. This one proved to keep at least two people busy, full time.

Chapter 55

As the days turned into weeks, then months, anxiety grew.

August 4, 1945

We've shipped 250,000 men home in the 3 months since V-E Day. Some Senator says we have 5 million too many men in the Army now. We have about 1,000 men in our Battalion stationed around here within a 10-mile radius. Half the Company (50 men) could carry on the work we're doing and have men to spare. The ships to carry us home are busy delivering men to the Pacific.

I don't know why they don't get Britain, France, and Russia to go after the Japs.

I hear Jack Benny is coming. I'd like to go see him just so I could say I saw him in Oregon and here also. Maybe I'll get to go.

On August 6, 1945, the U.S. dropped the first atomic bomb on Hiroshima.

Henry commented on August 8.

We heard about the new bomb they turned loose on Japan on the 6th. I guess this world won't be worth living in if they let just any country have access to it. I can't imagine the damage that one bomb created. I don't see how Japan can hold out for very long if they drop more of them. Hope she sees the light—quick!

When Harriet first heard of the bomb the U.S. dropped on Hiroshima she could hardly believe the reports of devastation.

Eleven days earlier the U.S., Britain, and China delivered a document called the Potsdam Declaration to the Japanese government announcing the terms of Japan's surrender, which they ignored. The document stated if they refused to surrender, Japan would face "prompt and utter destruction." Harriet guessed those officials knew what they were talking about. "Utter destruction" described that bomb perfectly.

She received a handful of letters the same day from Henry and sat to read each one in order so she could get his impression of the unfolding events.

August 9, 1945, after the U.S. dropped the second atomic bomb on Nagasaki, Henry wrote:

Just after I finished your letter yesterday the news came over the radio that Russia had declared war against Japan. With that news, and the new bomb, maybe it won't be too long now. I still can't imagine its destructive power. If the Japs had an ounce of gray matter they'd see the handwriting on the wall pretty fast.

I read the article in *Readers Digest* about the Americans meeting up with the Russians North of Berlin. Bet they remember that for some time.

After reading the news in the *Stars and Stripes* tonight I can't help but feel this thing is about to wind up. I read the bomb destroyed 4 square miles and they couldn't tell men from women. It also said it was impossible to count the dead because they all disintegrated in the intense heat. I'd think the Emperor would be impressed. I hope they don't have to use very many more, even though they're our enemies. It's too severe a weapon to use against any human being.

Henry's Saturday, August 11th letter read:

It looks like it's about all over but the shouting! We heard Japan was willing to surrender *unconditionally* if they could keep their Emperor.

According to the latest news broadcasts, we're going to accept the deal—as long as the Emperor takes orders from us. It seems sorta funny we would let him stay in. He's about the same as Hitler. If you look at it from the Jap's point of view, their Emperor is their God. They'll follow him in peace or war. With me, it makes no difference just as long as we tell that Emperor what to do. ALL I WANT IS TO GET HOME!

Do you remember when we were in Oregon talking to Bee's dad? He said he worked at some strange place in Washington State where no one knew what it was going to be? Said some of the walls were real thick. I'll bet that was one of those atomic bomb plants. I noticed in the paper that our government had one of those plants at Richland, Washington. They sure kept everything a secret about those bombs, didn't they?

Goose bumps ran over Harriet's body when she realized they had been so close to the construction of such a destructive bomb. Surely after all this horrible destruction the Emperor would holler uncle soon.

His Sunday, August 12 letter read:

Since this war is over (which I hope it is) they may decide to ship this Division home as a unit and then disband, instead of breaking up over here. In that case, I may be classed "Essential to the Organization" and might get to go home with the high-pointers. All the old men have left the Companies and Battalion, except me and my coworker Andy.

Several of our guys got to leave last night. We stayed up till 1:00 to see them off. Some of them came into the Division when I did. I really feel lost without them.

Japan hasn't surrendered yet. I guess the Allies are pushing harder than ever. The Russians are really driving hard through Manchuria. It may take another atomic bomb or two to put the clincher on the deal. It's a shame to have to murder thousands of them just to prove they're whipped.

We have a 2nd Lieutenant for a CO now—the only officer left in the company.

Today's paper said they don't expect Japan to commit herself before Monday. I'm going to listen close to the radio tomorrow.

Keep hoping and praying. Maybe this mess will be over soon.

Henry didn't write on Monday because he listened to every radio bulletin for news about Japan's surrender.

On Tuesday, August 14, he wrote:

I couldn't get in the mood to write last night. Now I'm glad I didn't. Just heard the 8 o'clock news. Looks like it won't be long now until we hear what we've been waiting for. All the bulletins were unofficial, but one said Japan would accept our terms. Maybe we'll hear the official announcement of Japan's surrender in a few hours. I'll stick close to the radio so I won't miss anything.

My CO told me yesterday to get all property ready to turn in because it wouldn't be long until we'd disband. There's a rumor that the Mess Sergeant and I are going to be the last to go.

Honey, when I get home I want you and Sally to declare at least a 30-day holiday. I've missed out on a lot since I've been over here. We'll make up for it when I get back.

Some of the boys are running a regular red-light district in their billets. Some girls even come clear from Nassau. These guys think they're having a good time, but they're only undermining their character and cheating their wives. I'd sure hate to come back to you and Sally after carrying on like some of these hot shots that claim to be some of our best husbands. I want to get out of the Army so bad, not just because I am so homesick for you and Sally. I want to get away from some of the worst vice you can imagine.

I'll write you a "V-J" letter tomorrow!

Harriet stopped reading and thanked God her man was faithful. Surely, they wouldn't have to wait much longer. She hoped Sally would remember her daddy when he got home. It would crush him if she didn't.

The next day, August 15, 1945, Henry wrote:

According to the radio, Japan has accepted our terms of unconditional surrender. Now we need to sign it.

We got the official word today. We're to disband where we are now. They say there'll be no 70th Division in another 2 or 3 weeks. The 1st Sergeant, Mail Clerk, Mess Sergeant, and myself will be the last ones to leave.

August 14 was like any other day in Ottawa, Kansas, until the news of Japan's unconditional surrender hit the streets.

If Harriet thought people acted crazy on V-E Day three months before, it was nothing compared to Victory in Japan Day. Not only were the streets filled with honking cars, people seemed to come out of the woodwork. Everyone looked for another person to hug. People lit fireworks. Some fired their shotguns into the air. Others blew trumpets and sang songs. One old fellow played his big bass drum as he marched down Main. It was as if the whole world had gone crazy.

"It's over! The war's over!" everyone shouted.

Harriet's joy knew no bounds. She didn't know if she should laugh or cry—so she did both. She headed for the phone to call Uncle Vernon. It rang as she reached for it.

"Close the store! By God, close it tomorrow too! Go celebrate this great day. This is the best news ever!"

Before she could respond, Uncle Vernon hung up.

She turned and watched the pandemonium among the clerks. "Listen everyone," she shouted. "The boss says, 'Take today and tomorrow off!' Don't come back till Friday. Go celebrate with your family and friends."

Before she left she quickly lettered a sign on poster board which read, "CLOSED UNTIL AUGUST 16th", and taped it inside the store's front door before she locked it. She shoved her way through the jostling crowd down Main.

Bursting in the door at home, she nearly scared Leota to death. "It's over! It's over! The war's over!" Harriet grabbed Sally and gave her a long hug as she let a flood of grateful tears flow.

Sally saw her mother's tears and looked as if she might cry, too. "Oh, honey. It's all right. Don't cry. This is a happy day. Now Daddy can come home to stay!"

Leota grabbed the hem of her apron and dabbed her eyes. "I wondered if we would ever live to see this day. Hallelujah!"

"Let's celebrate. Leota, you thaw the beef roast we've been saving. I'll use the last of the sugar and make a banana pie for supper."

Over three and a half years of war had finally ended. Harriet didn't know how long it would be before Henry could come home, but she knew one thing for sure—he wouldn't have to fight anyone, anymore.

That night, when she said prayers with Sally, she was filled with gratitude and anticipation of the day their family could finally be together once again.

Chapter 56

Henry's terse letter of August 17, contained only a few lines.

> Well, the war's officially over and we're stuck in Germany. A report came over the phone tonight that we only have to stay here twenty more weeks! Is this nightmare ever going to end? Maybe President Truman will change the requirement that we have to be in the Army till 6 months after the war ends.
>
> Twenty men were to leave at 8:30 in the morning. That's been canceled at the last minute. With the end of the war in Japan, it'll put us way behind in getting home according to all the rumors going around. At least we'll be better off than last winter with a roof over our heads and no Jerrys shooting at us.

Harriet received that letter and another one on the same day. What was the point of keeping the guys there for another five months? Who dreamed up that requirement, anyway? Hadn't they endured enough? Government! Is this the thanks the people of this nation received? She ripped open the next letter.

> Now we've learned this Division won't be busted up as they said before. There's only one hitch. They're allowed to take back only 800 men with less than 85

points. So don't set your hopes too high. I wasn't going to mention it to you but I talked to a fellow who swore up and down he saw the order in black and white. Maybe I can be home by Christmas after all.

More startling news. I got a pass for Brussels. Leaving tomorrow. Be gone for a week. If the pass had been to Paris, I'd have turned it down because it sometimes takes guys 3 weeks to finally get back from there because of poor transportation.

As I'm writing this, I got an order for my co-worker, Andy, and me to be at Regiment Headquarters at 1:30 tomorrow to meet with the Regiment Supply Officer. I'm going to cancel my pass. It might be some solid news about our going home. Wouldn't want to miss the boat!

Harriet laid the two letters side by side. How in the world did the Army function, anyway? They changed their mind more than a flighty woman in a dressing room.

Henry's next letter reported on the meeting at Regiment. She wondered if she should believe even a word of what the next report would be. Whatever they told him, she wouldn't put any stock in it—she'd just wait till she saw him at the train station.

Sunday, August 19, 1945

When Andy and I went to the meeting at Regiment today they told us to get everything ready to turn in. We'll be on the move to the States before too long! I didn't tell him, but I'm all ready and my reports are in order.

If they don't transfer me to another outfit to be their Supply Sergeant, and *if* they'll let me go even with my low points, I'll be leaving with the rest of the Division.

We have to turn in automatic rifles tomorrow and our wrist watches and machine guns the next day. I'll sure miss a watch. Wish I had sent for mine. I thought we'd be able to take our government issued ones to the States with us.

Our former CO came by to see us tonight. He was supposed to leave a week ago, but they had too many officers with that group, so they drew names out of a hat. He had to stay behind. I felt sorry for him. His wife had a baby about a week ago. He did get to hear from her, though. They have a baby boy.

This letter gave her little comfort. Now his homecoming would still be in the hands of an Army official who could flip a coin to keep her husband in Germany. Even this Commanding Officer didn't enjoy the special privilege of going home to see his wife and new baby. What chance did her lowly Staff Sergeant have?

Monday, August 20, 1945

We just heard on the radio that the 70th Division is slated to leave for the States around the middle of September. My Commanding Officer told me tonight that my co-worker, Andy, the Mess Sergeant, one cook, and myself were among the few that he declared as essential so we'll get to leave with the Division. The transfer list hasn't come out yet so I won't be sure of leaving until it gets here. We'll be in the staging area for 9 days and then pull out for HOME!

We've turned in all of our equipment except Ordnance. We were the only Company that has turned in everything we were supposed to.

One of the men in "M" Company turned up with Typhus yesterday so the whole Battalion got out the DDT and began dusting. I went through everything I had and put it all over myself, including my hair. I don't want anything like that to catch up with me at this late stage in the game! We were vaccinated for it though, on the 4th of July.

Typhus! That was something new to worry about. Would he come home whole? She sat back in her chair and closed her eyes. He did say he'd been vaccinated. That was some comfort. She took a deep breath and prayed. All her worry wouldn't help get him home sooner or in better health. She'd have to leave all this in God's hands. Again, she felt that peace. Her heart was no longer in her throat.

"Thank You, Lord. I trust You to get him home, safe and sound, at the right time."

August 24, 1945

The shipping list came out today. My co-worker, Andy, wasn't on it. They transferred him to another outfit. The let-down is almost more than he can take. He's older than me. Hope they don't transfer me to some other outfit after we get to the port!

The Mess Sergeant and I are the only low-pointers now that will go with the Division in this Company. We're scheduled to arrive at the assembly area the 17th of September. Don't know when we'll sail.

All we have here now is a bunch of weapons to turn in—rifles, carbines, BARs, and pistols. Then we'll only have kitchen equipment to turn in. We'll leave here with a bugle (with no one to toot it) and our flag.

Poor Andy! These men are like so many marionettes—objects on strings being pulled here and there for no obvious reason. Harriet's body grew tense. Would Henry be the next to be pulled off the list to go home? Closing her eyes, her recent prayer came to mind. She'd choose to trust God for her husband's soon return. She refused the urge to worry—then continued to read.

The fellow who took my place on the pass to Brussels looked for something for you and Sally. He thought you smoked and got you a wooden shoe ashtray. He also got a small wooden ship. I'll send these to you. I wanted something real nice for our anniversary but he didn't find anything. I'll make up for our anniversary when I get back.

According to my buddy, Brussels is in pretty bad shape. One girl came up to him and asked him to come to her room for the night. He said she looked about 18 and very attractive. He asked her how long she'd been in the business. She said about 3 months. Said it was the only way she could eat. One meal cost about 120 francs. A dress cost 1000 francs (about $23.00). Wages pay about 80 francs a day. He gave her some money but didn't go to her room. Such a sad situation.

That poor girl! Things are tight here, but nothing like in Brussels—or all of Europe, for that matter. Lord, help those people. Meet their needs. Restore order. End this awful time.

Sunday, August 26, 1945

One of my buddies just got back from the Riviera on a pass. He brought me a box of perfume for you. I'll ship it tomorrow for your anniversary present. I hope I can be with you soon to tell you how it smells.

Saw Bee today. He said General Herrin decided 800 low-point men was too many and cut it to 400. That's why Andy and some of the others didn't get to go. We go to Camp St. Louis at Rheims September 11th and get on the boat about the 18th. If my luck holds out, I'll make it. Keep your fingers crossed!

I got a letter from Lloyd. He got transferred to the 275 Infantry so he's going home with this Division. We'll be on the boat together.

The paper tonight said MacArthur will discharge all men 35 and over who had in over 2 years' service. Looks like I'll be discharged by the time I get home. Sounds good to me!

Discharge! What a wonderful word to read in his letter. Now, if the government would keep their word, this family could be rid of the Army forever.

With each letter that came, Harriet grew more anxious to see Henry. With every spare moment she cleaned and re-cleaned the house. She made Sally a new dress to meet her daddy at the train and picked out an especially nice suit for herself at the store. Now when Sally asked when Daddy was coming home, her mother could say, "Soon" with a new emphasis.

It didn't seem possible they would observe their eighth wedding anniversary apart—again. But this year held a promise for a lot brighter outlook than the past two years had been.

Tuesday, September 4, 1945, he wrote from Rodheim, Germany:

This is the last letter I'll write you from Germany. Tomorrow the last mail goes out. We'll leave here Friday, September 7th. I made a formal application to the CO for a discharge under the new age limit tonight. When we hit the States I can go with the rest of the men to the separation center to get discharged.

When we get on that boat I'm going to heave a sigh of relief you can hear over there in the States.

When Harriet read the first line she felt all giddy inside. "Last letter from Germany!" She read that line over again. How she had longed to read those words. All their hopes, dreams, and prayers—finally coming to pass. And a discharge to boot. Thank God! Oh thank God!

When she read the next letter she realized they had moved from Rodheim, Germany to Camp St. Louis in Rheims.

Henry's letter of Wednesday, September 26, 1945, was written from camp Phillip Morris, Le Havre, France. They were really on the move. How long would it take them to come home?

When she received the next letter she let out a war hoop. Now she had a date to mark on the calendar.

Guess we'll shove off for England tomorrow for sure. As far as I know we'll be in the States about the 10th of October. Allow about 5 more days for me to get home. I'll try my best to let you know when I get there.

Saturday, September 29, 1945, he wrote:

This will probably be the last I'll write because I doubt if you'll get this before we get to New York. We set sail on the Queen Mary on Thursday the 4th of October. I figure I'll be in Leavenworth around the 15th. I am definitely going to a separation center. Oh, to be free of this Army!

I applied for a pass to go to London but all I got was a 12-hour one, so I gave it to another fellow. Twelve hours isn't enough for that place. I'll write my own pass when I get home and stay as long as I like!

We'll be 2 to a bed on the Queen.

England is a beautiful country, but there's no place like home.

I ran into Bee a little while ago. I guess all of the 70th Division will be on the same boat.

See you soon.

Chapter 57

When the Queen Mary pulled into the New York harbor on October 9, 1945, 15,000 crowded onto the deck. When the Statue of Liberty came into view, a great roar went up from the crowd. Home—at last!

Soon, everyone headed below deck to gather their things so they could disembark and claim their foot lockers as they were unloaded by the longshoremen.

The soldier's waiting ticked into hours. All unloading from the ship stopped. Henry noticed a heated discussion among the dock workers. He and Bee pressed closer to see if they could determine the delay.

Some of the longshoremen turned and stalked off as they hurled disparaging remarks.

"What's the trouble here?" Henry asked one of the workers.

"By our union rules, these loads are too heavy. We're walkin'."

Henry caught a glance of Bee out of the corner of his eye. He stood with clenched fists, ready to throw some punches. Although Henry felt like he'd like to unloose a few jabs himself, he grabbed Bee's arm. "Come on. Let's find a place to cool down for a while."

"But—"

"Never mind. We've made it this far. I'm done fighting. We'll wait for these guys to work this out."

That afternoon in Ottawa, the telegraph boy handed Harriet an envelope. With a worried look, he said, "Shall I wait for a reply, ma'am?"

Harriet saw his hesitation. She figured he had delivered too many telegrams over the past four years to waiting wives and mothers, and sweethearts containing bad news.

Harriet tore open the envelope and read the few lines quickly.

ARRIVED SAFELY EXPECT TO SEE YOU SOON DON'T ATTEMPT TO CONTACT OR WRITE ME HERE
LOVE HENRY

"No. No reply," she said with a smile. "He'll be home soon."

The boy breathed a sigh of relief, returned to his bicycle, and gave a little wave as he headed down the street.

Harriet took a deep breath. He was finally on American soil. Praise God!

It took until the next day before the powers-that-be lessened the load weight limits so the longshore union men would come back to work.

The afternoon of Wednesday, October 10, Henry and Bee boarded their troop train with several hundred other soldiers. Finally, they were on the last leg of the journey they had begun twenty-seven months before.

On the way west, Henry ran into his old partner, Lloyd seated in the last car of their train. "Lloyd! Is that you?"

He glanced up from his newspaper. "Henry, old buddy! I looked for you on the ship but couldn't find anyone who knew you."

"Guess we missed each other there just like in Germany. Course, with 15,000 on one ship, guess it's pretty easy to miss seeing a few folks. Can't believe we ended up on the same train. You going back to Walker?"

"No. I think Betty and I will settle in Kansas City—if I can find work. She's grown kind of partial to city life. With dad gone there's nothing to draw us back to Walker."

"You?"

"Don't know. I think Harriet likes Fort Scott better than Ottawa. We may move back there. Look us up when you're down our way."

"Will do."

As the train made its way to the west, Henry encountered more Fort Scott men who began their war journey at Fort Leavenworth, but had served in other Companies of the 70th Division.

When he inquired about Fatso, one of the guys told him, "I heard he made it out alive. Think he'll be coming home a little later."

Henry was relieved. How wrong Mrs. Willie's prediction was when she said they'd not be coming home. By God's grace, *all* thirteen would be home safe.

When they reached Fort Leavenworth, the guys stood in line to receive their discharge papers and the first of three $100.00 payments of their muster-out pay. Henry received an additional $6.40 allowance for the train ticket home.

Henry bid Bee and Lloyd farewell and headed for the train station as the moonlight filtered through the falling leaves.

He stepped up to the ticket window. "When is the next train for Ottawa, Kansas?"

"There's one tonight. Leaves in about an hour, young fella."

"Give me a ticket. I'm headed home! I'll be there before she could drive here."

The minutes seemed to crawl by before his train arrived. He was the first to board. How he'd dreamed of this moment—and now it was finally here. As the train rocked along the tracks, he thought over the last four years. How their lives had been altered in both good and bad ways. Now it was time for his family to get on with their lives—to make up for lost time.

He chuckled to himself as he realized he was sitting on the edge of his seat, as if he could push the train faster toward Ottawa and his waiting wife and child.

Harriet got Sally to bed in the attic bedroom an hour before Leota turned in for the night.

As Harriet brushed her teeth she counted the days. According to his last letter, tomorrow should be the earliest she could receive a call from Henry—if he had managed to get a seat on the train. It had been a year since she felt his loving embrace. A little giggle escaped her lips. Tomorrow he might be home!

The scenario played in her head as she crawled into bed. She and Sally would meet him at the station in Fort Leavenworth. She'd wear the perfume he'd sent her for their eighth anniversary. Her new suit hung in the closet, pressed and ready beside Sally's new dress.

The phone rang. She jumped.

"Hello?"

"Hi sweetheart. Want to come to the train station to get me?"

"Oh, Henry! It's really you! I'll have to get dressed first. Then it'll take me a couple of hours to get there."

She dropped the phone on its cradle and ran for the closet. She'd leave Sally asleep.

The phone rang again.

"Hello?"

"You hung up before I could tell you I'm not in Leavenworth. I'm here in Ottawa. At the train station."

Harriet sank into the nearby chair. "You—you're *here*? Oh sweetheart! I'll be right there!"

She threw on the first thing she found in the closet. No time for suits or perfume. She scribbled a note to Leota and stuck it on the inside of the door leading to the attic bedroom and quietly closed it. The note read, "HE'S HOME. PLEASE KNOCK BEFORE ENTERING."

At the station, her knees went weak as she caught sight of Henry in his uniform standing on the platform in the dim light. How she had dreamed of this moment. He ran toward her and enveloped her in his arms—those arms she'd hungered to feel for a year.

He drew her tight for a lingering kiss. Their waiting had finally ended. Henry was home at last!

The next morning, Sally awoke as the first few beams of light streamed in the attic window. She descended the stairs and opened the door into the make-shift bedroom in the dining room.

Who was that strange man in her mother's bed? She stood next to her mother, then poked her.

Mother opened one eye. She pulled Sally into bed. "Guess what. Daddy came home last night!"

Sally eyed her father and scrunched up her nose. "Daddy?"

Henry awoke and rolled over. "Little sweetheart!" He held out his arms to her.

She hesitated. Her gaze went from his face to his picture next to the bed and back. "Daddy!" Sally leapt for him and planted her hands on his cheeks. "I kiss your face.

All the Freeman boys and their families joined Harriet's family the Christmas of 1945. As Henry sat for their Christmas feast, he placed Sally on his lap.

"You want to tell the family what I taught you since I've been home?"

In a timid voice, Sally began, "The Lord's my shepherd . . . I shall not want."

She paused and Henry prompted her, "He makes me . . ."

"lie down in green pastures . . ."

As she continued the rest of the Psalm with his occasional prompting, Henry's heart felt as if it would burst. These past two months back on U.S. soil had been heaven on earth.

His gaze rested on David. He remembered the promise he gave him over twelve years earlier. "We'll always be family, no matter what, little brother." Although severely tested, that promise had come to pass, in spite of the odds.

Epilogue

Over the course of their lifetime, Henry Freeman and his brother-in-law, joined in a partnership as owner/operators of an Oldsmobile dealership, a local motel, and an asphalt paving business, in Fort Scott, Kansas.

He and Harriet had no more children.

In 1983, Henry died one month short of forty years after his July 13, 1943 bus trip to Fort Leavenworth for his second hitch in the United States Army.

Harriet served as the buyer of women's and children's clothing for the chain of Edmiston stores until she retired. She outlived Henry by twenty years.

Henry's brother, David and his wife Lucilee, had two children after the war. David became the Vice-President and sat on the Board of Directors of a national insurance company based in Fort Scott. He sang for many weddings and funerals, in and around the surrounding area. He also hosted a hymn-sing five mornings a week on the local radio station for over 45 years.

Oscar served as Crew Chief at Edwards Air Force Base in California for the X-15, the first plane to break the sound barrier. It still holds the world record for the fastest manned, powered aircraft at 4,520 miles per hour.

Homer lived out his life as a rice farmer in Lincoln, California.

Discussion Questions

1. If you found yourself in young Henry's circumstance, what would you do?

2. Which character do you feel changed the most in the story?

3. What parallels did you see between then and now?

4. What did you learn about life from 1933 to 1945 that is different from now?

5. As you read the book, did you glean some new wisdom or a fresh perspective on anything?

6. Describe a time in your life when it appeared everything was going wrong but turned out better than expected?

7. What are some family stories you might like to pass on to your children or grandchildren?

Acknowledgements

Thank you to my critique partners in Homer's Orphans, Heart of America Christian Writers Network, and Monday Writers Group. Also thanks to readers John, Melinda, and Connie.

I wish to thank Fred and Gary who helped me understand WW II jargon and practices.

Warren Ludwig took my dad's picture and turned out a striking cover.

A special thanks to those in the Kansas City Writers Group who have coached, prodded, and poked me for twenty years to help me become the best writer I can be.

Most of all I thank my wonderful family who put up with me while my head was in book land and dinner was late or laundry lagged behind.

About the Author

Sally Jadlow, an award-winning author, is a native of Kansas where she has spent most of her life. She is the wife of one, mother of four, and grandmother of fourteen. Sally grew up in a family of storytellers.

When not writing or teaching writing, she serves as a chaplain to corporations in the greater Kansas City area. She is available for speaking engagements.

Hard Times in the Heartland took 1st Place at the Oklahoma Writers Federation Conference in 2016. Sally has written for *Focus on the Family, Thriving Family*, *Live*, *Mid-America Poetry Review*, *Kansas City Voices, Guideposts* and many anthologies as well as devotions for Christian Broadcasting Network online editions.

Her website is: SallyJadlow.com

Sally's Amazon Author page is http://amzn.to/2bBX2P1

Facebook: http://facebook.com/SallyJadlowAuthor

She maintains three blogs:

HardTimesintheHeartland.wordpress.com

FamilyFavoritesfromtheHeartland.wordpress.com

Godslittlemiraclebook.wordpress.com

Other works by Sally Jadlow available in paperback and e-reader:

The Late Sooner

The first of a trilogy. Sanford Deering, staked a claim in the Oklahoma Territory in the first land run of 1889. The novel is based on Sanford's one-line-a-day diary in early Oklahoma.

The Late Sooner's Daughter

The second trilogy book. Nora Deering, Sanford's daughter, accompanies her family back to Missouri. How will she find true love in this new place and overcome her hidden fear?

Hard Times in the Heartland

The final trilogy book. Henry, eldest of Nora's six sons, is faced with headship of the clan at twenty-three when his mother dies in 1933. How will he care for his youngest brother, David, age eleven, and keep their family together?

God's Little Miracle Book I, II, III

Each book contains twenty-seven true stories of God's intervention in the lives of every-day people.

Daily Walk with Jesus

Co-authored with Ardythe Kolb, this book contains 365 daily devotionals complete with a scripture of the day and a prayer for a great way to start your day.

Looking Deeper-A 366 Day Devotional

Inspiring scripture devotional digging deep into the words' original meanings. There is room for the reader to jot notes.

Family Favorites from the Heartland

Over 100 delicious recipes to please the palate, tested on family members and friends for over fifty-five years. Simple, easy-to-follow instructions. A great gift for a new bride or an experienced cook looking for fresh ideas.